Change in the
Context of
Group Therapy

Change in the Context of Group Therapy

Mary W. Nicholas, M.Ed., M.S.W.

BRUNNER/MAZEL, *Publishers* • New York

Library of Congress Cataloging in Publication Data

Nicholas, Mary W., 1945–
  Change in the context of group therapy.

  Includes index.
  1. Group psychotherapy. 2. Change (Psychology)
I. Title. [DNLM: 1. Psychotherapy, Group. WM 430
N598c]
RC488.N53   1984   616.89′152   84-1718
ISBN 0-87630-358-0

Published by
BRUNNER/MAZEL, INC.
19 Union Square West
New York, New York 10003

MANUFACTURED IN THE UNITED STATES OF AMERICA

Dedicated:

. . . with affection to my husband Gene Eliasoph, a wonderful group therapist, partner and friend—and an inspiration to me in many ways.

. . . with my fondest best wishes to the Joans, the Terrences, the Ericas, and the Jasons.

. . . with appreciation to both "CTs" (co-therapists), Jim Collins and Jack Novick.

Contents

Introduction

As I drive to the office on a Monday afternoon, I am running through pictures in my mind of the nearly 40 people whom I will see in groups this week, hearing snatches of dialogue from sessions the week before. I focus in on the group I will lead that night.

This group has been through a difficult period of transition recently. Three months ago we accepted three new members out of seven, which made it for all practical purposes a whole new group. Two of the new members, Margaret and Sam, have been difficult to integrate into the group. Margaret acts caring toward others, but also absorbs a lot of group time and energy in negative ways. She gets into masochistic situations with men in her life and solicits group advice which she never follows. She then becomes panicked that the group will become furious at her for not doing as they suggest, and kick her out. In this respect, Margaret is trying to replicate her situation with her cruel and disturbed family of origin who actually did expel her for marrying her now ex-husband. She is still very emotionally tied to them even though she has not seen them in years. She half-consciously sets the group up to get frustrated with her, and then projects that she is a burden to us and that we want to get rid of her. At the same time, a healthier part of her is building a constructive role for the group in her life as a good substitute family. This part of her realizes that the group "family" is not like her family was—that we will not withdraw our emotional support if she makes personal decisions we disagree with.

The wedding of Sam's daughter is finally over, so we no longer have to listen to him obsess about who is going to pick up his parents in the limousine. The group has been very patient with Sam, listening sympathetically to his anxieties about the wedding and endless stories about every little slight perpetrated against him by his embittered mother and father. The proud occasion of his daughter's marriage has led Sam, with the group's help, to question the prominent place in his life he still gives to sour people like his parents, when he could be putting his energies into potentially much more satisfying relationships with friends, other family, and the group. Since the wedding Sam has rambled less in the sessions; for the first time, he seems interested in the other members.

A couple of weeks ago I felt like this group was closing in on me like a large heavy blanket. All eyes were focused on me with every word spoken. No one addressed anyone else. Words were hanging in the air like basketballs suspended. This heavy dull atmosphere had characterized the previous several sessions. I realized it was time for me to shake things up. What was missing in the group was *contact*, so I decided to contact someone myself. I chose Lynn because I was feeling very warmly toward her. I told her I missed hearing from her in the group lately and shared my positive feelings about her, which she, surprised and pleased, reciprocated. The temperature rose in the room. Lynn and I had been talking about 90 seconds before Frank, his sibling rivalry with Lynn ignited, barged into the conversation, complaining about being cut off by Lynn when he had been talking about his trouble with dating. When I pointed out that *I* had started the conversation, not Lynn, and suggested he was jealous of Lynn's intimate interaction with me, Frank became angry at me.

I then said to the whole group that I could understand why Frank might well be jealous, since the group clearly considered me to be the only person worth talking to! Frank, hotly denying that he was jealous, said the group was boring—that "people were bringing in laundry lists of outside problems" and were not dealing with relationships in the room. Margaret said she hadn't wanted to come to group that night and then shared a dream she had had about the group. In the dream members had brought in newspaper articles which they were reading aloud in the session. Everybody laughed, agreeing that was just what it had felt like in the group the past few weeks! Jackie, who had been talking about herself earlier in the session, took the group's dissatisfaction with itself personally and pouted in the corner for the rest of the evening. All the other members, however, became much more alert and spontaneous, and laughingly began catching themselves and each other in the dependent statements and questions they were making to me. By the end of the session they had stopped trying to please me and were confronting each other readily; and since then, the group has been lively, honest, and productive.

The next session, which was last week, was terrific — lively, intense and productive — and I sense the momentum will continue this week. Jackie was all cheered up. Lynn and Frank both addressed important issues with their siblings, which had emerged from their negative transferences to one another as brother and sister over the past few weeks. This sparked Jackie, Margaret, Sam, and Dan to talk in more depth about their mothers, all of whom are critical, irrational, and sadistic. With this collection of mothers I can expect negative transferences to develop toward me. Up until now, however, the group has not been cohesive or trusting enough to withstand the anxiety of seeing me as other than "the perfect mother."

I reflect, as I frequently do, on how and in what ways these clients are changing, together and individually. As the group goes through its periods of stagnation (resistance) and rejuvenation, so do each of the members. In this last mini-crisis, Sam began to face his self-centeredness, Margaret her manipulativeness, Frank his hostility. It seems that, as the group ploughs through troughs and peaks, each person, while hanging on for the ride, unconsciously unfolds or emerges as distinct from the others. The restrictive and negative scripts, messages and beliefs with which clients are encumbered as they enter therapy become underlined in their interaction with one another. These are negative "frames of reference," the modes of thinking which interfere with effective personal and interpersonal functioning, and which are the target for change in group psychotherapy, as this book will demonstrate.

WHAT IS GROUP THERAPY?

Group psychotherapy is a special type of psychotherapy in which a number of people meet to help each other with the expert assistance of the therapist. The aim is to resolve emotional difficulties and work toward personal growth. The therapist selects people who are likely to benefit from this type of therapy and have a useful effect on others in the group. . . . The participants share personal feelings, ideas and difficulties with each other and the resulting interaction often makes them aware of their patterns of behavior, especially because others can see things it is difficult to see in oneself. In the group, one is likely to feel less isolated and alone because others may offer moral support, on the one hand, or objective criticism and useful alternatives on the other (*A Consumer's Guide to Group Therapy*, pamphlet published by The American Group Psychotherapy Association).

The therapy group provides clients with the opportunity to experience and learn about interpersonal relationships and affective interaction within a social context. It is a forum through which the individual client can be heard and understood by others; receive feedback on his ways of being and acting with people; express feelings that have been stifled; and reexperience, analyze and work through troublesome interpersonal conflicts of the past.

Group therapy is a treatment option for anyone who wishes to develop his emotional freedom and interpersonal skills, regardless of psychiatric diagnosis or level of social sophistication. Limitations on who can or cannot participate or benefit from group therapy are a matter of opinion based on individual differences in the clinical orientation and style among group therapists.

Outpatient therapy groups, whether held in clinics or private practice, generally meet once or twice a week for 1½ hours per meeting. Inpatient groups are usually held more frequently. There is no agenda for the meetings; clients' feelings, reactions, opinions, difficulties, successes, and life situations are the topic of discussion. Participants do not take turns talking; they speak as much or as little as they wish, and it is acceptable to interrupt. Clients are encouraged to speak freely about whatever is of concern to them, to share not only their problems but also their feelings toward and observations about others in the group, including the leaders.

The role of the members in a therapy group is to be collaborators in the therapeutic process of the group. They provide feedback and modeling for one another as well as nonjudgmental listening and support. The role of the therapist is ostensibly non-directive, in that the therapist does not usually plan activities or dictate the subject to be discussed; however, the general tone of the group over time is strongly influenced by the leader(s). The therapist contributes his clinical observations of the defensive patterns in the behavior and expressions of individual clients and the group as a whole. The therapist as leader plays many other roles as well, including monitor, referee, encourager, nurturer, instigator, teacher, and group member.

REVIVING A DYING ART

Despite its enormous therapeutic potential, group therapy does not seem to have expanded very much in the past few years. In fact, in some quarters, such as New Haven, there is less group therapy practiced now than there was ten years ago. While most psychotherapists and professional training institutions agree that there is great value in group therapy, there are few clinicians showing the commitment and skill to practice or to teach it in the graduate schools. It is worrisome that such a useful modality as group therapy may be becoming a dying art. I have some thoughts as to why this might be occurring.

First, there has been very little written about group therapy compared to many other treatment methods. Yalom's "bible" of group therapy, entitled *The Theory and Practice of Group Psychotherapy* stands out as the only group therapy book that most therapists are acquainted with. The paucity of research in the field and lack of instructive books and articles goes along with the sparse opportunities for training in group therapy. All of this contributes to the situation today in which therapists generally are grossly uninformed about the therapeutic possibilities of group, not to mention how to lead groups effectively themselves. All too frequently groups are used in clinics and hospitals as "dumping grounds" for clients that clinicians have deemed to be too socially inept, unintelligent, or disturbed to participate properly in individual therapy. Many therapists, seeing only the supportive function of the group and not the other resources, take all the richness out of the group by selecting clients of the same age, gender, or problem, and putting them together in groups, and/or developing a task-oriented and time-limited format. There is nothing wrong with homogeneous groups, but they compete for their membership with similar self-help groups in the community which charge no fee and are held in more convenient and informal locations than the office or clinic. I do time-limited, task-oriented groups, and believe they are very useful for clients under certain circumstances (mine are for clients dealing with weight control); but they are simply a different breed of animal than the "official" kind of group therapy discussed by Yalom and in this book.

Because of inadequate training opportunities and supervision for group therapists and the limited view of what group therapy can do for people therapeutically, relatively few therapy groups succeed in providing high-quality treatment for members. Many groups, enthusiastically begun, quickly lose members and come to a dismal end because the leader has made basic mistakes in putting the group together; misunderstood or discounted group and individual resistances; or failed to make the group interesting enough for the members to want to stay. After such an unsuccessful group experience, the clients and even the therapist(s) are likely to complain that they "tried group therapy and *it* didn't work."

The dearth of group therapy being practiced may reflect a clinging to the medical-model views of psychiatry, where the value of peer support and insight is considered inferior to the contribution of the "doctor." Such a frame of reference leads a clinician to consider group a waste of time for all patients save those incapable of changing anyway. Why would clients want to share their therapy time with other patients, who may be as "sick" as they are, if they could have private time to absorb the wisdom of the physician?

What seems to have been getting lost in many quarters of the psychotherapy field is a sense of *the healing power of the group*, the essential ingredient of successful group therapy. This book attempts to bring to light the ways my therapy groups benefit my clients and help them change. Particularly I wish to emphasize ways in which I have been able to harness the curative power of the group through the use of my own energy and spontaneity as well as my clinical skills and knowledge about groups.

Against a background of a relative paucity of therapy groups, my thriving group practice stands out. I offer here a brief description. In doing so I do not wish to imply that the observations and suggestions made subsequently in the book apply only to my kind of group, for such is not the case. My points about group therapy are relevant to its practice in any setting, including inpatient, and will be helpful to experienced and inexperienced therapists from liberal and conservative persuasions.

MY PRACTICE

My group practice consists of five ongoing (not time-limited) therapy groups, each meeting weekly for 1½ hour sessions. Two of these are co-led. The basic purposes, population and style of the co-led groups are more or less the same as those which I lead alone. My group practice is part of my general private psychotherapy practice, which includes individual, couples, and family therapy. A person referred to me for psychotherapy is likely at some point to be in more than one of these modalities, either concurrently or sequentially. My practice is affiliated with that of three other clinicians, two of whom are my co-therapists, Jim Collins and Jack Novick; the third is Gene Eliasoph, my husband and a leading figure nationally in the field of psychodrama and group therapy. We all work in the same building in downtown New Haven, and enjoy the many benefits of a supportive and intellectually stimulating colleagial relationship.

My caseload is primarily white and middle-class, ranging in age from twenties to sixties, with the highest concentration between 20 and 40. Clients have generally been self-referred to me or to one of my colleagues on the advice of other clients or clinicians, sometimes for group specifically, but usually for psychotherapy in general. They usually present complaints of depression or anxiety attendant to specific relationship difficulties with spouses, partners, parents or children, and/or to traumas related to separation, divorce, or bereavement. The majority have not been psychotic or severely suicidal. About 20% have at some time in their life had one brief hospitalization for acute depression or anxiety, and about half are taking or at some time have taken psychotrophic medication.

While the precipitating factors leading the individuals to treatment are often fairly specific, most clients referred to me need and expect relatively in-depth psychotherapy. Clients who would benefit by something more specific and or time-limited, such as a phobia cure, particular job attainment skills, help with specific marital or child management difficulties, or short-term, concentrated psychodynamically-oriented therapy, are treated in individual or family contexts, which are more conducive to brief treatment than are my ongoing therapy groups. My group clients are in treatment to deal with deep-seated characterological difficulties which have surfaced due to some change in life situation or acute stress. These problems in attitude, disturbances in self-concept, and poor interactional skills have taken their toll in the clients' relationships and have kept them from accomplishing, or in some cases even formulating, their life goals.

Because of the broad scope of our objective in group treatment, most group members who become deeply involved in the process stay two or three years, often longer. As in any other form of therapy, the presenting symptoms often dissipate in the first year of treatment, at which point childhood difficulties — situations of abuse, neglect and trauma, which have formed the foundation of the characterological problems — begin to come to light. Painful conflicts and feelings then need to be faced and worked through.

Characterological change, as will be discussed throughout this book, involves full scale changes in frames of reference. The overall goal thereof is to find the authentic individual buried under years' worth of successful attempts to hide from self and others. Almost half of my clients are children of alcoholics. These clients must work through the layers of confusion, anger, and disappointment generated by their lifelong attempt to adapt to the alcoholic parent, before they can discover and accept their genuine selves. Other clients also must reckon with the false fronts they have cultivated in their efforts to please unpleaseable people — to survive the threat of withdrawal of love or of violence from loved ones in the past. Group therapy helps clients develop the sense of internal security and the cognitive tools to discriminate between what is real and what is false in themselves and in their environment. It helps them develop new frames of reference — new options for relationships, roles, and ways of seeing and experiencing the world. Such a process takes time, but is always well worth it.

THERAPEUTIC ORIENTATION AND MAJOR INFLUENCES

Given the lack of training opportunities mentioned earlier, one might wonder how I came to learn group therapy in such depth. Like many group therapists, I emerged from the ranks of the once-idealistic schoolteachers who became "burnt out." The transition from teacher to group therapist is a natural one. Like group therapists, teachers are accustomed to speaking in front of groups; they try to facilitate interaction among group members, validate the ideas and contributions of each person, recognize and use subgroups creatively, and manage and utilize conflict constructively for maximum learning. From my own elementary school teaching experience I amassed valuable information about developmental stages. Being involved with parents and community taught me about family and social systems. I also accumulated knowledge about learning styles and cognitive functioning.

Long before I stopped teaching I discovered and participated in every kind of group workshop, class, or activity I could find, which in those days (late sixties and early seventies) meant encounter, sensitivity training groups, and humanistic education classes, as well as therapy experiences. Ironically, I found that most of what I hoped to achieve in the classroom with respect to creating a non-authoritarian learning environment was happening much more often in the groups I was attending than in the schools where I was teaching. In groups, in contrast to classrooms, the humanness of members and leaders was recognized and treasured, and affective learning and individual differences were highly valued. In groups people laughed, cried, and made noise while they learned, while in most classrooms they sat stoney-faced and took notes. People in groups almost seemed to get "smarter"; at the very least their language brightened and became richer as their spontaneity increased. Similar phenomena occurred in the creative "open" classrooms I attempted to construct, but I felt I was bucking the tide of "traditional" education, which at that time was endeavoring to keep the children's desks in rows and their minds on drills rather than creative learning. The most exciting and enriching learning programs I developed were usually viewed with suspicion, if not greeted with outright hostility by school administrations.

By the time I left teaching to obtain a masters in social work, I had already been leading groups of one kind or another for ten years and had begun doing individual and family counseling under the auspices of my husband's private practice for five years. Particularly useful aspects of social work training were two intensive clinical internships—one in a community mental health center and another in a comprehensive in- and outpatient psychiatric facility specializing in the treatment of persons with organic brain damage. Also beneficial was the opportunity to study ego psychology and modern psychoanalytic theory and practice.

As important as my formal training, if not more so in my career as a group therapist, is the extension training I obtained on my own in a variety of group modalities — psychodrama, Transactional Analysis, and Gestalt; several week-long intensives and semester courses in group process; four years of training in Neuro-Linguistic Programming and Ericksonian hypnotherapy; and countless workshops in creative therapy modalities such as psychosynthesis, art and music therapy, dreamwork, bioenergetics, and so on. Also useful has been an active personal involvement in Alanon, the support group for relatives and friends of alcoholics.

Every therapist has his or her own set of assumptions, beliefs, and values, which, along with her personal history and training, make up her frame of reference as a clinician. If I had to distill and encapsulate the many and various elements of "me" as a therapist, I would entitle myself a *humanistic* therapist, or at least one who aspires to be so. The Association of Humanistic Psychology, of which I am a member, espouses the following tenets:

- non-authoritarian and non-elitist approaches in teaching and learning;
- development of human potential as opposed to "cure" as the goal of psychotherapy;
- the inclusion of the spiritual realm in psychotherapy;
- psychotherapy *of* and *in* the community as opposed to strictly in institutions;
- group over dyadic contexts of treatment when possible, due to the inherently more democratic structure of groups;
- stressing of nonverbal as well as verbal methods;
- stressing of experiential learning over insight;
- favoring natural remedies over chemical;
- favoring holistic approaches involving mind, body, spirit, and environmental resources in treatment;
- emphasis on the here-and-now as opposed to historical factors in treatment;
- broader interpretation of the role of the therapist to include properties of "healer" as well those of the "doctor" in the medical model.

Much could be written about each of these tenets of the humanistic approach, many of which are as strongly espoused by group therapists of the psychoanalytic and existential schools as they are by those calling themselves "humanistic." However, some emphasis on my strongest beliefs about the role of group therapist are pertinent here. I see the group therapist as playing the role not of "expert" or of a "neutral" vehicle for the projections of members (the psychoanalytic model), but that of *guide*. As such, she is not confined to clinical objectivity, and is not afraid to care. She is also a *model* for the principles of mental and physical health and self-help she is teaching. The humanistic group therapist demands total authenticity of herself and her clients in their relationships with one another. She often makes her personal feelings, vulnerabilities and struggles known, confronts the client head on when necessary, and clearly displays feelings of empathy, anger, affection, and surprise in genuine and spontaneous ways. In the humanistic mode the group therapist as guide shares the psychological and emotional journey of each and every group participant.

As a social worker who has worked in communities, courts, and schools, as well as mental health settings, I am naturally oriented toward a systems approach in treatment. One of my favorite group theorists is J.L. Moreno, who may have been the first real community mental health practitioner and who anticipated the systems viewpoint in psychotherapy. Only slightly younger than Freud, Vienna born, and migratory to the United States in 1925, Moreno was the inventor of a powerful action-oriented group method called psychodrama and a way of doing therapy with families and other groups called "socioanalysis." Moreno carried therapy literally into the streets, conducting open group therapy sessions in a variety of settings throughout the world. Moreno said that "a truly therapeutic method cannot have less a goal than the totality of mankind" (Moreno, 1953, p. 3).

A central concept of Moreno's was his "social atom" theory (Moreno, 1971). Moreno noticed, as had other group analysts, that each group member brings a group "of his own" in his head to each session. The relevant people in each member's life, arranged in some constellation in his head ("his social atom"), come into play in the group interaction. This phenomenon accounts for the interpersonal transferences that inevitably unfold in group therapy. Moreno, however, also believed that the interaction of the group reciprocally affected the real people in the lives (the social atoms) of participants. Here Moreno points toward the work of subsequent family therapy theorists, who subscribe to the notion that change in any part of the system activates further changes throughout the system. It is particularly close to the later theories of Murray Bowen in his "family-therapy-with-one-person approach" (1978). One of my main interests and concerns as a group therapist is to make therapeutic use of this rippling effect, so that families and friends of group clients can benefit from the group along with the members themselves. In social work this is called the "ecological systems" approach, one which considers each client to be in a dynamic relationship with his environment on many fronts and which plans treatment interventions so as to benefit the client in as many of these areas of his life as possible (Siporin, 1975).

As well as a humanist with a systems orientation, I think of myself as an existentialist group therapist. In the manner of existentialists Rollo May (1969; May, Angel, and Ellenberger, 1958), Carl Whitaker (1982; Whitaker and Malone, 1981), Fritz Perls (1969), Clark Moustakas (1972), and Ernest Becker (1975), I try to address in therapy some of the basic human dilemmas that have to do with the "meaning of life"—anxiety, despair, freedom, responsibility, fear of death, autonomy, and authenticity—issues which cross all cultural and educational lines. Hugh Mullan (Mullan and Rosenbaum, 1978), Irving Yalom (1980), and Carl Rogers (1980) were pioneers in integrating existential psychotherapy into an ongoing therapy group format.

Last, but certainly not least, in the list of the underpinnings of my frame of reference as a group therapist, I want to emphasize my dedication to the basic tenets of psychoanalysis and my continued discovery of the way developmental conflicts of individuals are replicated through the transferences in group therapy. The importance I give to psychoanalytic principles in my group work are reflected in several sections of this book, such as the ones on "Change Through the Microcosm," "The Corrective Emotional Experience" (both in Chapter II), and "Contact Operations" (Chapter IV), all of which deal in different ways with the phenomena of regression, fixation, and repetition compulsion, as they are exhibited and addressed therapeutically in group. The theory and practice of Wolf (1963, 1974; Wolf and Schwartz, 1962), Schiedlinger (1980, 1982), Foulkes (1948, 1957) and other psychoanalytic group therapists are important influences on my work.

All these important influences notwithstanding, it is clearly Yalom (1975) and George Bach in his pre-encounter group days (1954) upon whom I have always relied most heavily. In addition to countless invaluable techniques, Yalom's and Bach's books offer guidelines on how to implement an eclectic approach in group therapy. Eclecticism is essential in my orientation as a therapist, particularly in group therapy. I am always learning new techniques and ideas and integrating them into my work. After all, nothing is really *not* relevant to group therapy, whether it be art, poetry, mind-body methods, AA philosophy, or the latest in assertiveness training techniques. Each year, with all I've learned, I marvel how I got by before, not knowing what I do now! So I continue to read, work, think, and rethink what I am doing as a therapist and a leader, knowing that the process of training in this field is one of continually enlarging my repertoire of frames of reference, theories, and techniques.

Change in the
Context of
Group Therapy

CHAPTER I

Changing Lenses
and Frames

We humans are endowed with brains that make flexible thinking possible. Nonetheless, we persist in limiting our learning and understanding by narrowing rather than expanding our focus. This book will illustrate how people learn to shift their attention and expand their perspective in ways that promote learning and growth in themselves and others. It will emphasize the role of other people in the individual's processes of "framing experience." It will show how people, when equipped with a variety of lenses through which to know the world, can generate new frames of reference, which help them encompass and use more of their internal and external resources.

The therapy group has been chosen as a model for understanding the magic of spontaneous change and change over time — through human interaction. I will open up my own group therapy practice for the reader with anecdotes and client reports and try to give a view of therapeutic change in progress, while conveying the aliveness, intensity, and humor that characterize my groups.

THE CONTEXT OF GROUP THERAPY

Most of us are highly dependent on the words and other communications of people around us to charge the batteries of our thinking and feeling. A group of any kind provides stimulation, forcing us to at least consider new ways of viewing or expressing what we know and wonder. Each time we are a part of a group, whether it be family, social, task, academic or therapeu-

3

tic, we are affected in some way, on conscious and unconscious levels. Each group experience creates shifts of minute and major dimensions within us and in our relationships with others.

In group therapy we are offered the lenses of other people through which to view the world. In electron microscopy, the material under the slide is changed by the focusing action of the microscope. Similarly, in group, the processes of observation and change are fused inextricably. As group members, even when we are the therapists, we are part of the system we are investigating. The very act of learning about others changes us and them simultaneously.

In group therapy, individual learning and change take place in an interpersonal context. Particular opportunities and mechanisms for interpersonal learning are afforded by the therapy group which cannot be duplicated in individual therapy. Participation in a therapy group can engender the development of more effective, flexible, and creative modes of thinking and feeling on the part of the individual. These new tools assist the client in his relationships with people as they teach him to cope with his problems. A good therapy group can produce individual change and growth that goes beyond the level of "normal" adjustment and leads to greater life satisfaction, increased spontaneity, productiveness, connectedness with self and others, and even improved physical health.

The therapy group, like all other organizations and living things, is a system. As such, it maintains itself and evolves according to the principles of boundary functioning. Information flow within the system and back and forth through the boundaries between the system and its environment is the process that determines the rate and quality of the system's survival and growth.

The human organization that the therapy group most resembles is the family. The family and the therapy group share a common purpose, which is to foster the growth and development of the individual member through the sharing of human resources such as support, stimulation and feedback. The family and the therapy group are both structured so as to provide benefits for members over time, although the therapy group's time is telescoped compared to the life of a family. Both organizations have at least one, often two, leaders or parents, whose functions as gatekeepers, nurturers, facilitators, structurers, and organizers are vital to the preservation of the boundaries of the system and to the healthy maturation of each individual within it.

As the group is comparable to the family, so is group therapy similar to family therapy. Most good group therapists are good family therapists and vice versa. Family and group therapists both attend to the function and the structure of communication as much or more than to the content. In both kinds of therapy, symptoms and acting-out on the part of individual members are seen, not only in the context of the particular client's problems or psychopathology, but also as communications to other members of the system and the therapist. Such messages have specific meaning in the context of the system as a whole and are responded to consciously or unconsciously as such by other members in the system. In group and family therapy every interaction is viewed by the therapist in terms of its significance for the individuals involved and for the system as a whole.

All good therapists try to figure out the hidden rules and patterns that are governing communication as it is going on. They are alert to the way language is used, including syntax and metaphor, and to nonverbal cues. Unlike the individual therapist, however, group and family therapists do not have the luxury of watching and responding to one person at a time. Group and family therapists must be expert jugglers when it comes to communication. Not only must they constantly take in large quantities of information and make meaning of it, but they must simultaneously be very present in the room — responding verbally and nonverbally to several individuals while also performing a number of different roles in the system as a whole.

A major difference between group and family therapy is their respective relationships to time. Family therapy is necessarily brief therapy — or tries to be. Given that families are in pain and/or are falling apart when they enter therapy, immediate and drastic measures are appropriate. Matters of economy and convenience also dictate that family therapy be as short as possible. A therapy group, by contrast, is not falling apart when it starts, although the individuals entering it may experience themselves that way. Therapy group members, compared to other psychotherapy clients, are not in too much of a hurry to get out of treatment. Most members become absorbed in and fascinated by the process, as they take and give feedback, learn new roles, experiment with new behaviors, and become involved with the other members.

Good family therapy involves the setting of specific goals, which, when achieved, spell the success of the therapy. In group therapy specific goals and the resolution of crises are important, but are only part of the larger kaleidoscopic picture of group therapy. In group, dreams, personalities, allegiances, beliefs, lifestyles, values, even body types are constantly shifting. People are learning "the big things," like how to grow up, fight, love, grieve, and play. Some of these lessons take time. The sense of community that binds the group over time is one of its primary healing agents. This can make "slower" even better than "faster" for the group therapy client in the process of change.

Recently, there has been a proliferation of self-help groups which bring people who have the same problem together in their own communities to help one another. The following are just some of the kinds of self-help groups available.

1) groups for substance abusers and compulsive gamblers (Alcoholics Anonymous, Overeaters Anonymous, Gamblers Anonymous);
2) groups for families and friends of substance abusers and compulsive gamblers (Alanon, Gamanon);
3) groups for victims of abuse (rape, beating, incest);
4) support groups for victims of disease or injury (cancer, herpes, paraplegic, blind, etc.);
5) groups for people in a particular life stage or transition (separation and divorce, adolescence, menopause).

Members of self-help groups, like therapy group members, report feeling validated and relieved that they are not alone in their difficulties. In both kinds of groups, participants receive the warmth and caring of others, as well as helpful and specific advice on their immediate problems, something that a therapist might be unwilling or unable to give. In both self-help and therapy groups the emphasis is on the client's taking responsibility for making changes on his own behalf, with the help of the group, rather than relying on so-called "experts." For many people in crisis, self-help groups are sufficient therapy; when they have resolved the issue at hand satisfactorily, they leave the group. For others whose personal problems may be more severe and/or diffuse, who wish a more in-depth exploration of issues, or who desire to make more thoroughgoing changes in their lives and personalities, a therapy group is more appropriate.

In therapy groups, participants receive much the same kind of assistance from one another that they do in self-help groups, but their goals for themselves extend way beyond the simple receiving of support or information. When a client enters a therapy group, he is generally experiencing some sort of dissatisfaction with himself or his life. He feels deficient in coping with life and other people. He hopes the group will help him, not just with one particular problem, but with the process of becoming a better person, according to his own definitions, dreams, and aspirations.

While the client is not considered to be "sick," he is nonetheless attending group therapy to, in some sense, be "healed." For this reason the therapy group, unlike a self-help group, employs a leader who is also a therapist, in hopes that he or she can help the group maximize its therapeutic potential.

The ongoing therapy group is apt to be longer in duration and have a more stable membership over time than self-help groups. Because self-help groups, like any other group, are subject to the vicissitudes of group dynamics, tensions and rivalries are inevitable. When they occur, a self-help group, not having the leadership or expertise within the group to understand and sort through the problems, will usually founder and lose members. In a therapy group, such strife is considered "grist for the mill." A competent group therapist can help the group cope with its internal stresses in such a way that clients learn about themselves in the process, and the group is able to stay intact as well.

We have suggested that the therapy group is a potent context for change. We will now explain some modern theories of *change* and their application to the behavioral sciences. We will then define the concept of *frame of reference* and explain its relevance in psychotherapy. Finally, we will discuss the phenomena of *paradox* and *metaphor*, and how they provoke changes in frames of reference. These sections will draw on the work and writings of Gregory Bateson, Paul Watzlawick, Milton Erickson, Jay Haley, Richard Bandler and John Grinder, and Stephen and Carol Lankton.

CHANGE

The process of change follows relatively consistent patterns, whether it occurs in the biological, physical, chemical, psychological, animal or human realms. From the cellular to the cosmic level, change occurs by means of parts exchanging information matter or energy; and by grouping, splitting and regrouping.

All models of personality, psychotherapy, and group psychology subscribe to some kind of "parts model" in explaining how change occurs. They all presuppose that the individual or group is not one entity but a conglomerate of subdivisions. Each model conceives of and names the "parts" somewhat differently. For example, psychoanalytic theory describes the individual psyche as a cluster of three structures—id, ego, and superego—whose constant struggles determine our choices and behavior throughout our existence. Transactional analysis, a popular offshoot of psychoanalysis, adopts a similar model—of Parent, Adult, and Child (Berne, 1961), while Psychosynthesis, an elaborate psychotherapy developed by Assagioli, takes a more idiomatic approach, dividing people up into "sub-personalities" with interesting names like the "Judge" and the "Heckler" (Assagioli, 1965).

While individual personality theorists see change as occurring through the rearrangement and redistribution of energy among parts and forces of the "self" system, systems theorists, drawing on the work of cybernetics and general systems theory, think change has more to do with shifts in the balance of power; alliances, allocation of resources, transfer of information, and other phenomena occurring on a larger system level. Family therapists seek to find the crucial variables in the system, which, if changed, would have the greatest impact on the family as a whole and, thereby, each individual in it.

Group therapy is concerned with change on both the micro (individual) and macro (group) levels. It attends to and works with: 1) all parts of the individual; 2) the relationships among individuals and subgroups within the group; 3) the relationship of the individual to the people in his various social systems outside the group; 4) the group as a whole. (Some group therapists, namely those who practice what is called "psychoanalysis in the group" [Alexander Wolf, 1963], Transactional Analysts, and Gestalt therapists, do not consider group dynamics relevant to psychotherapy; however, the work of Foulkes [1957], Bion [1959], Durkin [1964], Whitaker and Lieberman [1964] among others, as well as my own experience, has amply demonstrated for me that there is, in fact, a therapeutic benefit for all members each time a group undergoes a transformation into a higher level of complexity and functioning. (For that reason, I consider group dynamics to be of the utmost importance in group therapy.)

The following ideas about change are relevant to an understanding of what happens in group therapy.

Change Is Never Not Happening/ Change Is How You Look at It

In any system where there is an interaction of parts or subsystems, there is a circular or dynamic flow of energy within the system, causing the parts to influence each other and to exchange information. Each part changes by virtue of its interaction with the next part. As a result of these interchanges, sometimes the larger system is altered and sometimes it is not.

Much activity may be going on within a system that is invisible to the naked eye. A plant, when fully grown, and given adequate sun, soil, water, and temperature, is undergoing thousands of changes every minute; yet, the plant as a whole remains the same in size, texture, color, and function. Since few of the plant's internal processes are noticeable, we are somewhat oblivious to them, unless there is a noticeable change in the appearance of the plant, such as when the plant is beginning to wither. If we are away or not paying attention, we miss the grosser changes as well as the subtle ones. For us, the plant really only changes if *we see* a change. So, we wonder, is a change that we see somehow more relevant than one we do not see? This brings up the old "if the tree falls in a forest where no one hears it" argument. Change for human beings has to do with *shifts in attention* more than with *actual changes,* which are always happening, whether or not we notice them.

If we are paying attention to something, we then have the capacity at any time to *shift our perspective*. For example, we can look at the plant from close up or far away, as well as from above, below, or next to it. We could also look at it through binoculars or look at pieces of it through a microscope and, in doing so, see distinctions that we had not noticed before. In a similar way, change occurs for people in therapy when they obtain a new outlook or a new perspective on a problem or a situation.

Another way we can change our experience of the plant is to move it to a different environment. This is called *changing the context*. If we move the plant to a different (and equally nourishing) environment, it will still be in a constant state of change on the cellular and subsystem level. What we would notice, however, would have nothing to do with this. We would perceive the entire *Gestalt* (gross image) of the plant differently. Put next to a larger plant it would look small; next to a dull one it would look more brightly colored. In the wider spectrum of a forest it may look tiny, while placed with smaller plants it might look rather large.

An effective way to change a system is to place that whole system in a different context. Essentially, that is what we do in psychotherapy when we put the client, who is himself a system, into a larger system, a therapy group. The minute he enters the group he is different — or at least *appears* different to himself and others. We also do the same thing with the group member's problems and ideas. Put in a new context, his issues and difficulties are altered somewhat. The group experience forces the individual to pay attention to different things, adopt new perspectives, and recontextualize problems. These, in time, become ingrained skills for coping and creativity.

Change Begets More Change

The 1977 the Nobel prize-winning chemist Prigogine contributed valuable theories on change to the field of science, and these ideas have been adapted to the realm of human behavior (Ferguson, 1980; Prigogine and Glandsdorff, 1979). Prigogine explained the "irreversible processes" in nature — the movement toward higher and higher orders of life (Ferguson, 1980, p. 165). He said that the greater the complexity of the system, the more potential it has for creating change. As the system develops more complexity, it calibrates itself so as to become even more sensitive to internal and external changes.

It is unstable, has fluctuations or "perturbations," as Prigogine calls them. As these fluctuations increase, they are amplified by the system's many connections, and thus drive the system — whether chemical compound or individual(s) — into a new, altered state, *more ordered and co-*

herent than before. This new state has still greater complexity and hence, even more potential for creating change (Rogers, 1980, p. 131).

The *transformation* from one state to another occurs in what seems to be a spontaneous manner. "It is a sudden shift, a non-linear event, in which many factors act on one another at once" (Rogers, 1980, p. 131). Significant changes for the psychotherapy client likewise occur in a totally non-linear manner. They are like explosions without (necessarily) the noise. Instances of transformation in therapy create thought patterns that are more coherent, complex, and refined. New thinking patterns promote new awarenesses and a host of new responses to the environment. Much of this book will be devoted to describing the "transformations" occurring in group clients in the context of group therapy.

Next we will examine what it is that actually changes for the client when transformations occur—his *frames of reference.*

FRAMES OF REFERENCE

Gregory Bateson (d. 1980), anthropologist, scientist, communication theorist, student of change, described human beings' process of creating mental and psychological constructs:

> Psychological frames are related to what we have called premises. The picture frame tells the viewer that he is not to use the same sort of thinking in interpreting the wallpaper outside of the frame. Or, in terms of the analogy from set theory, the messages enclosed in the imaginary line are defined as members of a class by virtue of their sharing common premises of mutual relevance (Bateson, 1972, p. 187).

Sociologist Erving Goffman, in his book *Frame Analysis,* extends the definition of frames of reference to the social level, assuming that "definitions of a situation are built in accordance with principles of organization which govern events—at least social ones—and our subjective involvement in them" (1974, p. 11). "Frame analysis" refers to "the examination . . . of the *organization of experience*" (Goffman, 1974, p. 11, emphasis added).

It has been suggested by Bateson (1972), Milton Erickson (1980), Paul Watzlawick (1974; Watzlawick, Beavin, and Jackson, 1967), Jay Haley (1963), and others that the cognitive change involved in successful psychotherapy is not limited to change in thinking about the presenting problem, but involves significant shifts in the individual's frames of reference. Watzlawick suggests that most problems brought to the psychotherapist seem inexplicable to the client because his "range of observation is not wide enough to include the context in which the phenomenon occurs" (Watzlawick et al., 1967, pp. 20–21). Somehow, in the course of therapy the person's frame of reference must be expanded to realize "the relationships between an event and the matrix in which it takes place, between an organism and its environment" (Watzlawick et al., 1967, p. 21).

Jean Houston says that "any single lensing is the enemy, restricting our freedom of choice, distorting both percept and concept" (1982, p. 37). In successful therapy, the client not only obtains *new* frames of reference, but learns to *switch* frames flexibly and quickly. He becomes, in every sense, more "open-minded."

Why is a change of frame of reference more profound than a change in behavior or emotional reaction? The change in frame of reference is one of process rather than content and involves changes in perspective, beliefs, premises, and priorities. Logicians will agree that changing the premise of one's thinking is a more thoroughgoing change than coming up with new thoughts to fit into the same set of assumptions. It is obvious, then, that a change in frame of reference will tend to have wider implications than would a change in behavior. For example, let us say a person believes that "mankind is evil" and operates accordingly by protecting himself. If, somehow, he changes that belief to "*some* people are evil," not only will his behavior change toward the ones perceived as good, but he will have to begin distinguishing the evil persons from the good ones. The new frame of reference dictates that not all persons are the same; it demands a process of discrimination which is new and could be adaptive for the individual in many contexts. A change on the frame of reference level is what Grinder and Bandler (1976) call "generative change" in that it creates a rippling of changes in the functioning of the individual, which in turn affects others in his environment.

Regardless of their training or theoretical persuasion, effective therapists knowingly or unknowingly operate to change clients' frames. Traditional psychotherapy methods seek to engender new frames of reference, although forms such as psychoanalysis presuppose the process to be much lengthier than do some modern practitioners of brief therapy, who confront invalid frames of reference and introduce new ones early in the treatment. Milton Erickson (1980) skillfully created "new mental frameworks" for clients, into which the behavioral changes induced in the hypnotherapy would fit. Bandler and Grinder's (1975, 1979) communication techniques address problems and create changes on the level of clients' "presuppositions." Albert Ellis, founder of Rational Emotive Therapy, assuming that thinking creates feeling, trains clients to challenge and rework their own outmoded beliefs (Ellis and Harper, 1976).

Frame of reference changes are not limited to the purely psychological realm. Hard evidence is being brought to the fore to support the idea that there are demonstrable physiological correlates to many of the changes we have always assumed could only be measured subjectively. Neuroscientist Marian Diamond, at an October 1982 conference in Philadelphia on "The Healing Brain," presented her research with rats, which points strongly to the possibility that the quality of social contact and community may affect the size of the visual cortex of the brain. Fantastic new neurological technology, Positon Emission Tomography, presents color-coded images of electrical activity and potential throughout the brain and has shown scientists that different mind states, and perhaps different frames of reference, have specific and discrete patterns of neurological activity associated with them (Buchsbaum, 1983).

Language is an interesting behavioral and psychological phenomenon which interfaces directly with brain structure and function and plays a major role in changing frames of reference. Group therapist Hyman Spotnitz says:

> I first learned in the course of my neurological research the rationale of talking cures. Speech affects the mind and through the mind's physical structure — the nervous system — and the chemistry of the body . . . (T)he body has its own chemical laboratory; and the psychotherapist, through his words and attitudes, tries to stimulate it to produce these chemicals (Spotnitz, 1961, p. 25).

Bateson (1972) believed that frames of reference are modified through verbal communication with people who are operating out of different frames. He points out that, in the psychotherapy process, much jockeying for control of the frame is taking place between the client and the therapist, even though paradoxically the objective is for the client to learn to think for himself.

The most skillful practitioner in the area of changing clients' frames of reference was Milton Erickson, psychiatrist and master of clinical hypnosis, who lived and practiced therapy in Phoenix, Arizona, where he died at age 80 in 1980. Due to crippling physical illness, Erickson traveled relatively little late in his life and it remained for Ernest Rossi, Jay Haley, Paul Watzlawick, Richard Bandler and John Grinder, Stephen and Carol Lankton, and others to make the work of this brilliant psychotherapist known. He is considered to be the father of "strategic therapy," which is at the heart of most modern schools of family therapy. He was a friend and admirer of Bateson, who was to be the keynote speaker at the first Milton Erickson Congress in 1980. Unfortunately, both men died in that year before the conference.

Erickson often created and used clients' confusion as a useful tool in the therapy. Breaking apart their stultified frames of reference, Erickson capitalized on the new perspectives that would emerge. Erickson also used the vehicle of hypnosis to deepen concentration and enhance suggestibility. Erickson's hypnotherapy included techniques to minimize the involvement of the conscious mind in the treatment, thereby bringing forth more of the resources of the unconscious.

It is my contention in this book that group therapy is an "altered state of consciousness" or frame of reference which is similar in many respects to Erickson's induced trance states. In group, the moods, rules, goals, and ways people perceive each other are in constant flux, creating at times an almost dream or trance-like situation. The unclarity that results works on clients in a way similar to Erickson's induced "confusion states," in that it stimulates their unconscious processes and creativity. In both environments, trance and group, old frames of reference are destroyed and new ones generated.

Two phenomena that greatly accelerate the process of change in frames of reference are paradox and metaphor. They will now be explained.

PARADOX

Bateson says,

> . . . as we see it the process of psychotherapy is a framed interaction between . . . persons in which the rules are implicit and subject to change. Such change can only be proposed by experimental action, but every experimental action in which a proposal to change the rules is implicit, is itself, a part of the ongoing game (1972, p. 192).

Bateson's words aptly describe the contract of the therapy group, where, with respect to influence and frames, changing the rules is part of the game. The Alice in Wonderland dilemma of how to play croquet when the wickets, the mallets, and the balls are all alive aptly describes the core paradox of group therapy. While talking about and trying to learn about who we are and what we think, we are constantly changing who we are and what we think. The process is the content and the medium is the message.

The notion of paradox rests on Bertrand Russell's Theory of Logical Types. Mathematically speaking, the totality of a collection of "things" is called a class and the components of the class are "members" (Watzlawick, 1974, p. 6). Russell's observation was that a class cannot be a member of itself. Mankind is a class of all individuals, but it is not itself an individual. The difference between the class and its members is one of degree of abstraction. If we blur the distinction between the class and its members, we come up with puzzling or bizarre conclusions. For instance, if a soldier were considered identical with the army, one could conclude that to make more soldiers we should chop up the soldiers into subdivisions as we do with the army.

"Classes" are on different logical levels from some other classes and on the same with others. Sisters and brothers are on the same logical level. They are classes within the larger class of "siblings" or "children." By contrast, the class of operations required to drive a car in a certain gear are on a different logical level from the class of operations involved in switching gears. Switching gears is an operation that will determine a whole set of operations on a lower logical level. Switching gears is *meta* to (outside of and on a higher logical level than) the operations of driving within a particular gear. The members of a therapy group are part of the entity known as "the group," but are not identical with it. The group is more than the sum of its parts. The group-as-a-whole's activities are meta to those of the individual in most instances.

In his seminal book, *Change,* Watzlawick puts forth the concept of first- and second-order change. The distinction between the two is based upon the Theory of Logical Types. First-order change "occurs within a given system which itself remains unchanged" (Watzlawick, 1974, p. 10). Second-order change "is one whose occurrence changes the system itself" (p. 10). In other words, second-order change is "change of change" (p.11) and involves a change "meta to" the ongoing changes of the members of the subgroup. Second-order change requires a shift of frame of reference to a higher level of abstraction and an operation on the class of things which exists at a lower logical level.

Therapeutically, first-order change is symptom relief, while second-order change involves change in frames of reference. Medication, behavior modification programs, and direct suggestion hypnosis are examples of first-order change techniques. They are useful when no system changes are needed and the problem is completely straightforward with no inherent secondary gain. If the problem needs to be seen in a wider context in order to be understood and dealt with, then a frame of reference shift becomes necessary which brings us into the area of second-order change. All psychodynamic psychotherapy, including group therapy, strategic methods, and Ericksonian hypnosis, while accepting the value of first-order change in the few instances when it is sufficient, are oriented toward second-order change.

The premise of this book is that what needs to change for clients in therapy is their inadequate frames of reference. As a therapist my objective is to help each client generate new frames of reference and a frame of reference from which he can further develop more new frames of reference. With this agenda, anything that causes shifts in logical levels, in my own thinking as well as in the clients', becomes a valuable tool in the psychotherapy. It is precisely here that paradox comes into play.

Wilbur defines a "real" paradox as a situation in which "two mutually contradictory occasions are known to occur simultaneously and equally," giving the example of "it is both raining and not raining on my house" (1982, p. 283). In rational-conceptual theory, a paradox is any (linguistic) situation in which the Theory of Logical Types is being violated and a class is, in fact, a member of itself. Consider the statement "All Generalizations are False." If you think about this contradictory statement carefully, you will inevitably experience some confusion. This is because it forces you repeatedly to leap out of one frame to a wider level of generalization, as you fruitlessly try to encompass the concept of *all* generalizations (class designation) being *part* of the subcategory (member designation) "false."

It is impossible to stay in the same logical framework and grasp the "All Generalizations are False" statement at the same time. We see here how paradox forces us out of our traditional assumptive mode and to jump around from one logical level to another. We can also see how such a dislodging of habitual thinking patterns might be beneficial in psychotherapy, where the goal is to ferret out crippling frames of reference and change them.

Paradoxes cast us into internal search process. We first are thrust into confusion, a sort of "huhhhhhhhh?" type of experience. We then go inside our head and try to find meaning. Stimulated by paradox, the right hemisphere begins to percolate pictures, words and sounds, ideas, even memories — anything that might stop the confusion, give us clarity. Somehow we get to some conclusion that makes sense for us, that stops the buzzing. This is called a new frame of reference.

One thing we may do to try to resolve the dilemma posed by a paradox is to create pictures in our head. Bateson was the first to point out that the schizophrenic uses hallucination to resolve a problem posed by contradictory commands (paradox), which cannot be discussed (Bateson, 1979, p. 223). The schizophrenic is in the situation that, in obeying one parental instruction, he violates another one of equal importance (same logical level). He breaks out of his double bind into a psychotic frame of reference where such inconsistencies are the rule rather than the exception, and therefore create no internal dissonance.

Hallucinations are only considered "psychotic" if the person who is having them has no recognition of their being mental constructs as opposed to external reality. "Normal" individuals have such mental imagery all the time, and particularly creative people more than most. Erickson and others recognized the utility of the "hallucination" or mental imagery as a conductor, in the sense of an electrical conductor, of new frames of reference and creative solutions to problems (Erickson, 1980, Vol. II). In his hypnotherapy he would create therapeutic double binds to ignite the processes of mental imagery in the client's mind.

Group therapy is inherently a paradox. For one thing, it exists to study itself, which is a clear violation of Logical Types. There are other interesting paradoxes endemic to the therapy group which are described in detail in Chapter VI. The paradoxical structure of the therapy group is very therapeutic, sparking off new ways of thinking that could not exist in a more straightforward behaviorally-oriented modality.

Group deals with paradox on the content level as well. Many of the difficult life dilemmas facing group clients are framed as paradoxes — two equally weighty ideas or values that are related in a contradictory way to one another, such as: freedom vs. responsibility; death anxiety and fear of life; the need for boundaries and the need for closeness. Such themes are grappled with continuously in group therapy, as we shall see in Chapter V.

METAPHOR

Stephen and Carol Lankton term "metaphor" the "saddlemate" of paradox (1983). A metaphor is a non-literal description of something. The metaphor, an analogy of some sort, whether it be in word form (a phrase, word image, story or poem), in pictorial form, or in tonal form, exists on a different logical level from whatever it is describing. Making the metaphor linguistically equivalent to the "thing" or "event" or "relationship" it describes is necessarily a paradoxical event and generates frame or reference shifts. It is for this reason that metaphor is so frequently used in psychotherapy.

When clients enter therapy their limited frames of reference are denoted by their metaphors. "I feel like a fat pig," one of my clients said during her first session. "I am a raging cauldron under the surface," said another — a more literal, but still metaphorical, statement. All therapies, whether explicitly or not, try to replace the self-deprecating, pessimistic, narrow-minded metaphors with ones that are more positive, valuing, and interesting. Some modalities bring their own metaphors to the client. Transactional Analysis, for example, endows patients with a Parent, Adult, and Child ego state, and encourages them to think about which part of them is operating in different interactional situations. This is useful for many clients, but it can become tiresome if clients or therapist forget that it is only a metaphor — not a reality. In their "treatment principles," Stephen and Carol Lankton include the admonition that the metaphor of the person should not be confused with the person himself (1983, p. 14). Richard Bandler jokingly emphasizes this when he reminds his audiences at Transactional Analysis conferences that the only people who "have" a Parent, Adult, and Child part are TA therapists and their clients (Bandler and Grinder, 1979). Psychodrama, Ericksonian hypnotherapy, Gestalt therapy, all the creative arts therapies, psychosynthesis, Jungian analysis rely heavily on the development of the client's *capacity* for metaphor as part of the healing and growth process.

Group therapy provides a plethora of new metaphors for the client in the form of stories, analogies, and actual events. In addition, at any given moment, for each individual, the group can "be" a number of different things, each existing on a different logical or metaphorical level. The group can function as a support group, a collection of friends, and a source of objective feedback, while simultaneously (paradoxically) having a metaphorical existence as a surrogate family, microcosm of society, a slate of transferences, or a representation of the different parts of self. Any or all of these can occur for any one person singly or in a combination (see Chapter II).

In group therapy the many levels of metaphor that exist help to create the paradoxical structure of the group. Together paradox and metaphor facilitate thinking on many different logical levels. In group therapy the client is given plenty of practice in switching and adjusting frames of reference and in the process he learns to think far more creatively and spontaneously.

CHAPTER II

New Maps: Change on the Psychological Level

INTERNAL MAPPING

A major determinant of frames of reference is the way one constructs one's experience in one's mind. As humans we have two sets of tools for coding our experience internally: *representational* and *linguistic*. Each of these will be explained briefly, and ways in which they might be affected by group therapy will be suggested.

Representational Modes and Patterns

The components of subjective experience are the "representations" we make in our head of perceptions acquired through the five senses. Information received by each sense is coded in the brain in a form discrete from the information collected by the other modes. The "pieces" of experiences are called by Grinder and Bandler (1976) "internal representations." Bandler and Grinder, in their workshops and writings on Neuro-Linguistic Programming, have shown how subjective experience is changed through changing and rearranging internal representations (Grinder and Bandler, 1976; Dilts, Grinder, Bandler, DeLozier, and Bandler, 1979; Lankton, 1979). For example, if the content or the order of the internal representations — pictures, words and sounds, feelings, smells and tastes — associated with a certain event in our minds and memory banks, is altered, our subsequent internal representations are different in response; hence, our entire experience of that event is completely transformed. Such a change in internal representations constitutes a fundamental shift in frame of reference.

In Neuro-Linguistic Programming workshops I learned to cure phobias rapidly and completely. The first step of the process is to figure out what internal *representation* (internal picture; word or sound; or feeling) triggers the phobic response. The second step is to isolate what has to happen in the environment or in the person's mind (*stimulus*: external or internal) to produce *that* particular internal representation (stimulus→representation→response). The objective is to get the person to have a different internal representation in response to the stimulus so that he may have other choices of ways to respond. The new representation might be of the same category (visualization→visualization) or it might be one of a different category (visualization→auditory). In either case, if the old phobic-response-producing representation is obliterated by another representation of comparable intensity, the phobic response will not be activated.

I mention the "phobia cure" because it demonstrates that the tiniest change on the level of internal representations can often change an entire frame of reference. Bateson, in his laudatory introduction to Bandler and Grinder's *The Structure of Magic* (1975), notes that the five modes of internal representation (visual, auditory, kinesthetic, olfactory, and gustatory) are on discrete logical levels.

> We did not see that these various ways of coding — visual, auditory, etc. are so far apart, so mutually different even in neurophysiological representation, that no material in one mode can ever be of the same logical type as any material in any other mode (Bandler and Grinder, 1975, pp. x–xi).

Bateson was excited about this discovery because it provided a simple and effective option for changing frames of reference: changing representational systems.

Every time there is a switch from one representational mode to another, there is a paradoxical breaking of the barrier between two different logical levels, an occurrence which, as we have explained in Chapter I, always creates a frame of reference change. Changes in internal representation can be made on the conscious or unconscious levels. Occasionally we can decide to change the pictures in our head and give ourselves "a new perspective," or to replace the negative auditory "tapes in our head" with messages which are more positive. More frequently, however, changes in internal representations take place automatically and effortlessly. Suddenly, everything "snaps into focus" (visual), "falls into place" (kinesthetic), or "clicks" (auditory) in our mind. Even as we utter these phrases, we are not aware of how literally we mean them. They refer to the internal representations which, in changing ever so slightly, are radically altering our entire perception of a situation or a problem.

The direction in which someone's eyes are cast when he is paying attention to his internal experience and not actually looking at something in the environment can tell the trained observer what mode of internal representation is occurring in the person's mind (Grinder and Bandler, 1976). Most people look upward when they are in the visual mode, down and to the left when they are in the auditory, and down right when they are in the kinesthetic. Other cues besides language and eye scan patterns also suggest a person's current mode of internal representation. Gesturing in toward the body often indicates kinesthetic experience; hands in a telephone pose suggest auditory (Lankton, 1979). Rapid high-pitched speech and shallow breathing may mean the person has pictures in his head (Dilts et al., 1979).

Bandler and Grinder's techniques are helpful in understanding and communicating with a person's unconscious as well as conscious mind. As a group therapist using these methods, I establish a much stronger degree of rapport and empathy with all group members than I might otherwise be able to, because I am able to divine their internal representations and speak to them in the language of the representational mode they are using at the time. For example, when I think a client is visualizing (either because her metaphors are visual, and/or her gaze is upward), I will use visual verbs and metaphors ("I see from what you're saying that, in your view, no one has a clear picture of what the problem is . . . "). I will also ask clients what they are picturing. If they are in an auditory mode, I will use auditory metaphors ("That rings true" or "the two of you are not in harmony"), and talk to them about how things sound, what people said. If they are in kinesthetic experience, I will speak in kinesthetic terms ("Do you feel you have a handle on it?"; "this problem is pulling you in many directions"), and ask them what they are feeling in their bodies or what their hand movements or body position might be telling them.

During the course of participation some clients in group therapy seem to actually change their habitual patterns of internal representation. For example they may begin group feeling all of their feelings (kinesthetic) very intensely and not being able to make clear pictures in their head. By the time they terminate two or three years later, they may have acquired the ability to dissociate from their feelings when need be and go into a visual mode. In the visual mode they can "create new perspectives" and "see new options" not available in the kinesthetic system of experience. Others undergo the change in reverse: They come in split off from their feelings and are always seeing pictures in their head. Through the group experience they learn to become aware of body sensations and automatic motor behaviors (kinesthetics) and to appreciate the information these experiences and gestures communicate to them from their unconscious about their underlying, or unconscious, thoughts and emotions. People who talk in their head too much (auditory) may learn to "shut off the sound" when they want to and become more adept at seeing pictures or experiencing kinesthetics.

In addition to switching habitual modes of representing, people can learn to change the content of their pictures or internal messages from negative to positive. In their work on "self-image thinking," the Lanktons (1983) teach people to make pictures in their heads of what they would like to portray to others, develop compatible auditory components for these pictures, step into the pictures and build in the desired kinesthetics. In this way they can create entire new roles for themselves. Useful changes of this sort occur naturally through the group experience. Needed improvements in ways of representing are lodged within each person, waiting to be tapped. The clients themselves are not always as aware of these changes as was 35-year-old Elizabeth, whose report of what she derived from her three-year group experience is a glowing testimonial to the powerful and therapeutic effect group can have on a person's way of representing, and hence, her model of the world. She recounts:

For me the whole group was about changing pictures. When I joined the group I didn't use the part of me that could visualize except to remember bad experiences. I saw lots of bad pictures and had lots of bad feelings about them, like remembering pictures of when I was raped and feeling terrible, scared and angry. Group helped me develop new pictures to replace the old ones. For example I had no pictures of men being sensitive and feeling. The first time Ron talked about his scary dream and cried was the first time I saw that men have feelings—a whole new set of pictures of men were built for me in group. Other people's solutions to problems similar to mine created new pictures, and I learned to find all the permutations and combinations with a particular picture through discussion. I can make pictures of where I want to go and go there, rather than proceed blindly according to my feelings, and this makes me feel more in control. Learning how visual I am in group helped me release energy to go ahead and be myself—not fight myself.

Language

Transformational Grammar

Bandler and Grinder remind us that "there is a necessary difference between the world and any particular model or representation of the world . . . " and that "the models of the world that each of us creates will themselves be different" (1975, pp. 7–8). Indeed, the "map" is "not the territory" as Korzybski (1933) put it. But what *is* the relationship of the "map" and the "territory" and how do people's "maps" relate to one another? In the previous section we touched briefly on Bandler and Grinder's notions of how we take in information and code it in our minds in patterns made up of auditory, visual, kinesthetic, olfactory, and gustatory components. We look next to the contribution of psycholinguists, particularly Grinder, to help us understand a bit about how we then go about representing our experience through language.

Transformational Grammar is the tool of psycholinguistics that offers actual rules for the representation of experience in language. It is:

> an explicit model of the process of representing and of communicating that representation of the world. The mechanisms within Transformational Grammar are universal to all human beings and the way in which we represent our experience. The semantic meaning which these processes represent is existential, infinitely rich and varied. The way in which these existential meanings are represented and communicated is rule governed (Bandler and Grinder, 1975, p. 37).

There is far more in our environment to hear, see, feel, smell, and taste than we can possibly process. Since we are bombarded by more input than our brains can handle, the primary task of language is to synthesize most stimuli *out* of awareness. As Huxley says,

> to make biological survival possible, Mind at Large has to be funneled through the reducing valve of the brain and nervous system . . . to formulate and express the contents of this reduced awareness, man has invented and endlessly elaborated upon those symbol-systems and implicit philosophies which we call languages (Huxley, 1954, pp. 22–23).

In order to make use of data, the computer must have a program through which to feed it. Similarly, the human being creates "models" (Bandler and Grinder, 1975), mental vehicles through which to manipulate symbols. The ability to create and recreate models determines the amount of information that can be absorbed and what kind of sense is made of it by the brain. The reader will notice the inherent similarity between the concept of "model" and "frame of reference." What kind of models one uses will determine how one communicates, as our example of Joseph a little later on will demonstrate.

Linguists have discovered three cognitive mechanisms by which humans reduce, organize and code experience via language:

Generalization: "the process by which elements or pieces of a person's model become detached from their original experience and come to represent the entire category of which the experience is an example" (Bandler and Grinder, 1975, p. 14).

Deletion: "the process by which we selectively pay attention to certain dimensions of our experience and exclude others" (Bandler and Grinder, 1975, p. 15)

Distortion: "the process which allows us to make shifts in our experience of sensory data" (Bandler and Grinder, 1975, p. 16).

The processes of generalization, deletion, and distortion are the "transformational" principles, the universal rules of Transformational Grammar, common in every human language. When an experience is stated in a sketchy but recognizable form in a particular language, it has undergone a number of the above transformations and is said to be represented in Surface Structure. When the full linguistic representation is included, the statement is said to be in Deep Structure. A person's idiosyncratic way of using and combining these rules in "transforming" what he perceives from Deep Structure to Surface Structure is an essential component of how he thinks.

If the tools of deletion, generalization, and distortion are wielded too liberally in the linguistic representation of experience, the result is a Surface Structure sentence that does not denote the Deep Structure. When one person is misunderstood by another, it is because essential details have been left out, too much has been generalized, there is a distortion somewhere, or some combination of two or three of these processes has occurred.

Linguists approach scientifically the task of deriving the intended meaning (Deep Structure) of poorly-formed Surface Structure utterances of others. In Transformational Grammar, a "derivation" is a series of transformations which connects the Surface Structure with the Deep Structure. We will now take a look at how group members informally learn to perform derivations in order to make sense of one another's words.

Developing Precision in Language

The following piece of transcript is from a new group, all of whose members joined together about three months earlier. Though it may not sound it, these are well-educated people. The imprecision and vagueness in their language are a function more of their lack of cohesiveness as a group than their intelligence or mental health.

Barb: Well, my life is a mess and it's weird.
Janet: That's why I wanted to call you when I was sick.
Therapist: What kind of problems are you having?
Barb: My boyfriend got a job.
Hank: When are you going to realize he is just out for himself?
Janet: He hasn't shown you nearly the caring you've shown him.

Generalizations, deletions and distortions are rampant in this conversation. There is no indication here that anyone knows what anyone else is talking about, but everybody proceeds as if they are all aware. Mind-reading occurs, assumptions are made, and advice is given, when, in fact, no one is in the same model of the world. No one seems to be thinking. The therapist tries to obtain some information without much success.

Now note the questions asked by another group of a client, Hannah, whose opening line, like Barbara's, is in Surface Structure and gives little idea of what is going on with her. The educational level of this group is comparable to the first one, but most members have been in the group for two years or more. One can tell by the clients' questions that they are attending closely to language and know how to track down relevant information about a member's experience.

Hannah: I'm having some problems I'd like to discuss with the group tonight.
    I've been feeling very weird.
Joan: What problems specifically?
Hannah: Problems concentrating—at work mostly.
Lilly: Did you want to talk about this with anyone in particular in the group?
Hannah: No—I'd like everybody's feedback.
Terrence: You said you were feeling weird. Are you feeling this weird feeling
    at work?
Hannah: Yes.
Ted: What specifically do you mean by a weird feeling?
Hannah: It is a tugging at the pit of my stomach. I think I'll call it "dread."
Joan: *When* precisely do you feel this dread?

Hannah: When I think of my boss quitting.

Lilly: What about your boss quitting would make you feel dread?

Hannah: I don't know. I'm really glad he's quitting. He's such a pain. . . . Oh my. I think it reminds me of my brother quitting work to go into the hospital.

Jason: How are the two situations similar and how are they different?

(Conversation continues in the same vein . . .)

We can see that all the crucial questions are being asked in a logical order. As she answers each one, Hannah's particular internal experience becomes better defined. Through her dialogue with the group she is not only improving her communication, but is actually learning to think more clearly.

In individual psychotherapy the therapist asks questions designed to help the client organize and understand his thoughts and feelings. In group therapy, clients learn to ask these questions themselves. While they may not be aware of the linguistic principles involved, clients in group learn to listen for deletions, generalizations, and distortions in speech, and to query logically to obtain Deep Structure information. This finely developed precision in the use of language serves them well in many areas where thinking and communicating clearly are important.

Changes in the Structure of Language

The rules governing a person's idiosyncratic employment of linguistic structures, such as syntax, ratio of verbs to nouns, relative use of metaphors, and sentence construction, are key to the way he thinks. Any change in frame of reference that occurs in therapy will be reflected in a change in the client's language. Interestingly, the reverse is also the case: An intentional change in linguistic structures can produce a change in the individual's frame of reference. Group therapy is a place where rigidities in a client's language will be challenged, confused patterns straightened out, and alternative language patterns made available. Group therapy may be, therefore, an optimum setting in which to change cognitive structures by changing language.

When Noah, a 50-year-old philosopher, entered group, he had a tendency to be pedantic. He repeatedly used certain phrases, which were indications of how he thought. His very first response to most questions was "I don't know." He would then proceed to answer the question with two answers which were in direct opposition to each other. These answers were preceded by "on the one hand" and "on the other hand." The "I don't know" meant "I do not have just one answer," but it was heard by the listener as "I do not have an answer," so most of what followed from Noah would not be carefully attended to. His "I don't know" was functioning as a signal for the listener to tune out. Noah's two oppositional answers ("on the one hand . . . on the other hand") left little opening for dialogue, since he was covering both polarities.

The group became very frustrated with Noah's communication. It was suggested that Noah bar himself from the use of "I don't know" and limit himself to one answer to a question. Noah did a lot of biting his tongue at first, but was able to accomplish both changes. Almost immediately his communication became much more direct and spontaneous. He used more metaphors and fewer abstractions. His eye contact improved and his voice took on a more assertive and musical tone.

Changing two very simple but highly limiting language patterns opened up new avenues of thought and expression for Noah, as similar shifts have done for many other group therapy clients.

Changing the Metaphors

In Chapter I it was stated that metaphors are inherently paradoxical. The phenomenon of metaphor fuses the processes of internal representation with those of language. Since these exist on more than one logical level, the receiver of a metaphorical communication is receiving a paradoxical message. In processing the metaphor, therefore, the listener may undergo a frame of reference shift.

Everybody's mind is a jumble of metaphors, but we all have a few "pets" which form the cornerstones of our frame of reference, our perception of the world. In the case of therapy clients these may be quite negative (e.g., "Men are beasts"; "I am a lost child"). Every group therapy session is replete with metaphors: narrations, memories, word pictures, dreams, nonverbal expressions, analogies, comparisons, new word combinations, puns and jokes. During the therapy group, through the interaction, the client not only develops new metaphors, but changes some of the basic ones that have contributed to and reflect her neurosis or interactional problems.

When she entered group, Jeanette was trying to separate from her alcoholic husband. At that time, her earliest memory was from the age of five. In this memory she and her little brother are standing on the driveway crying as her alcoholic father is drunkenly trying to drive out of the driveway; her mother is trying to stop him by holding onto the car door. The father suddenly jams the car in reverse and runs over the mother's foot. This was a "screen" memory, which means it was selected unconsciously as reflective of her current situation. The scene was a metaphor from her unconscious, depicting all the ambivalence, guilt, fear, anger, and pain she was associating with her impending marital separation.

In group, Jeanette gradually learned to be close to some adults who were not alcoholic. She learned to confront herself and others directly without cowering and, by seeing others succeed, to develop some hope for her own future.

Jeanette's progress in therapy and her connection to the group were evident through the change in her metaphors. In the spring, a year after joining group, she shared a waking fantasy she had had: She and another woman in the group, Melissa, would give an elegant party. They would be dressed beautifully, and there would be bowls of tulips on all the tables. The next week, to reinforce the positive metaphor, and to symbolize that I believe such dreams can come true, I brought Jeanette and Melissa each a tulip. The tulip metaphor often gave Jeanette courage in the months that followed as she proceeded to separate from her husband.

REFRAMING

There is an adage in sales that says, "The sale begins when the customer says 'no'." For the canny salesman, the "no" is not a signal to be discouraged, but rather an indication of some emotional involvement on the part of the customer and, therefore, the possibility of a deal. This is an active version of seeing the "half-empty" glass as "half-full." Through an interactional group experience, clients are exposed to a similar approach to life and solving problems. They learn either consciously or unconsciously to "reframe" problems or, quite simply, to turn liabilities into resources (Lankton, 1979).

Bandler and Grinder (1982) classify two major types of reframing: reframing of meaning and reframing of context. Both are described here, with examples of how these processes are learned in group.

Reframing of Meaning

Sometimes something seems like a problem because we are not perceiving the situation correctly. A new view and a simple *relabeling* of the problem are often all that are needed to turn what seemed like a terrible situation into a benign circumstance or, in some instances, a resource.

In group a reframing of meaning occurs when two people are mis-communicating. For example, Hilda's way of showing that she found a man attractive was to talk baby talk. Stuart's unconscious association with such behavior on Hilda's part was to his mother, who used the same tone of voice when she was trying to make Stuart feel guilty. Stuart's automatic response to Hilda's baby-talk seduction, therefore, was to withdraw without explanation, which left Hilda feeling hurt and rejected.

After seeing this unfortunate interchange a few times, another group member, Sandy, asked Hilda what she was *trying* to communicate to Stuart when she spoke to him in baby talk. Hilda blushed and said, "That I *like* him, of course!" Hilda's peculiar speech pattern was thus instantly "reframed" into an attempt to communicate sexual interest. As such, the message was received warmly by Stuart. Hilda, no longer frustrated and embarrassed, now understood how her earlier messages had been misunderstood and was happy to learn new ways to show men that she was attracted to them.

Reframing meaning becomes a natural response for group members as they try to improve their communication with one another. What is he (am I) trying to express? How can I do or say it another way? This positive framework for understanding one's own motives and those of others opens up creative solutions to problems, circumventing many so-called "blocks" and "resistances."

Contextual Reframing

Reframing of context is necessary when reframing of meaning is insufficient, when a correct relabeling of the problem does not in and of itself create the desired outcome. In these instances the problem must be viewed in a different context.

Inherent in the process of reframing is a belief that all behaviors and symptoms have a *"positive connotation"* (Palazzoli, Boscolo, Cecchin, and Prata, 1978). It is a generally accepted notion in family systems therapy today that any symptom or behavior will be shown to have a value for the larger system. The "system" may be a family, group, or an individual "self" system. It is assumed that any problem can be solved if its "positive intent" (Bandler & Grinder, 1982) is satisfied some other way. The therapy process involves coming up with the core positive intent and finding ways to satisfy it more fully and gracefully than the original behavior or symptom does.

Contextual reframing occurs in group all the time. The secrets and insecurities that have plagued clients for years become, when shared, the links between members. Feelings, no matter how painful or prohibitive they may have been for clients, are the currency of group therapy and are highly valued.

In group therapy, in contrast to the "real" world, problems and struggles are not considered anachronistic. Difficulties within or external to the group are seen as fodder for the group process, while people's problems are just a small part of what make them unique. As one client said, "I went from seeing myself as just messed up to seeing my messed-uppedness as part of my human-ness." This realistically broad perspective frees people to address and solve their problems instead of torturing themselves with them.

The Ongoing Group Structure as a Reframe

The ongoing group provides a forum in which to reframe and solve problems, while its continuous format insures that there are always unresolved issues. The realization that personal growth and therapy are unending processes need not be discouraging. As Watzlawick says,

> The effect of leaving an unresolved remnant is twofold: It lifts the whole idea of change out of the all-or-none utopia of either complete success or total failure, and it enables the patient to go, on his own, well beyond the change that the therapist considers possible (Watzlawick, 1978, p. 73).

The therapy group reframes problems into opportunities for learning. Self-sufficiency is defined as acceptance of one's limitations and ability to make use of internal and external resources when needed. As client Joan said, "At the end of group, people have accepted parts of themselves that need to be taken care of. They know how to get these parts taken care of and look after themselves."

USING THE RIGHT SIDE OF THE BRAIN

Research and experimentation have validated the hypothesis that our dominant and nondominant brain hemispheres have discrete and equally important functions, as Watzlawick explains:

> In the typical right-handed person, the *left* hemisphere is the dominant one, and its main function appears to be the translation of perceptions into logical, semantic, and phonetic representations of reality, and the communication with the outside world on the basis of this logical-analytical coding of the surrounding world. It is therefore competent for all that has to do with language, and thus also with reading, writing, counting, computing, and generally, digital communication. . . .
>
> The function of the right hemisphere is very different. It is highly specialized in the holistic grasping of complex relationships, patterns, configurations and structures. Most of the clinical and experimental evidence seems to suggest that this ability must be somehow akin to the technique

of holography, for the right hemisphere not only masters the perception and recognition of a Gestalt from the most diverse angles and consequent relative distortions (a natural ability of the brain which still presents great problems for computer simulation), but it may manage to perceive and recognize the totality from a very small portion of the latter. This enables us, for instance, to recognize a person although we may see only a tiny part of his face, very much as a musician may identify a concert or a symphony on the basis of one single bar or even just one chord. This ability of the right hemisphere seems to be based on a pars-pro-toto principle, that is, the immediate recognition of a totality on the basis of one essential detail (Watzlawick, 1978, pp. 21–22).

Each brain has its own language. The left brain's language is "objective, definitional, cerebral, logical and analytic; it is the language of reason, of science, explanation and interpretation" (Watzlawick, 1978, p. 14). The right brain's language is "of imagery, of metaphor, of *pars pro toto,* perhaps of symbols, but certainly of synthesis and totality, and not of analytical dissection" (Watzlawick, 1978, p. 15). The right brain can quickly perceive quantity, but cannot count or add beyond 20. The right brain perceives and constructs totalities through a mixture of pictures, words and sounds; its language, not organized chronologically or logically, but rather poetically and by analogy, reflects the potpourri of right brain thought processes. When fabrications and compilations are commented upon in the analytical language of the left brain, more often than not, much is lost in the translation.

The theme of this book is that most psychological and emotional disturbances are related to inadequate frames of reference. Watzlawick states that anyone seeking the help of a psychotherapist suffers from the discrepancy between his "image of the world" (1978, p. 40), and his image of what the world should be. Watzlawick identifies "image of the world" as a right-brain function. To change world images or frames of reference — or simply to understand them — right-brain thinking and language are the correct tools, not the analytic, quantitative left-brain methods so often used in traditional "talk" psychotherapy. This provides substantial validation for group therapy. In each group session there occur many levels of paradox, metaphor, transference, and rapid time frame shifts, all of which keep participants' right brains in continual activation.

One of the ways that the right brain is activated is by the shutting off of the left brain. We explain how this works in our section on paradox and metaphor. When logical levels are mixed up, the conscious mind or left brain takes a mental vacation, and the right brain comes in to generate new concepts that will attempt to explain or reframe the confusion. This is one principle of Milton Erickson's hypnotherapy. Erickson would keep the conscious mind very busy while communicating directly with the unconscious by means of metaphor and nonverbal signals. The person might be told to "count backwards from one hundred" (left-brain function); at the same time he would be directed to make pictures in his mind (right-brain function), and listen to a story and make whatever meaning seemed relevant to him (right brain). Group therapy similarly keeps the conscious mind focused on particular problems and issues, while a great deal of other things are going on that may be creating changes in right brain thinking patterns.

The second way right hemisphere action is stimulated is by hearing right-brain language. If a person is spoken to in metaphors, imagery, puns, etc., his right brain responds. Creative group methods such as psychodrama, Gestalt, and psychosynthesis explicitly work to generate right-brain thinking. These therapies reverse the process of traditional therapies, which try to turn right-brain utterances into left-brain interpretations. Through "fantasy exercises," stories, and metaphors, creative therapists begin early in the treatment to activate the imagination of the client. They learn to understand their client's right-brain communication, listening carefully to the client's metaphors and attending to all nonverbal messages. Such therapists also use their own internal imagery and metaphors as a guide to what might be happening for the client or in the therapist-client relationship. The metaphors are shared with the client in non-literal form, rather than translated into "left-brain" insights or interpretations.

I find creative methods invaluable in my work as a group therapist because of the tremendous boost they give to the production of clients' right-brain, subconscious material, and the options they present for richer communication. Even without the aid of such techniques, however, interactive group therapy automatically fosters right-brain thinking via its inherently paradoxical structure. People's metaphors and imagery spark those of one another, in a kind of chain reaction. As the natural language of sessions becomes more and more metaphorical, more connections are made among the people in the room and parallels are perceived between past and present time frames.

Right-brain thinking and language are the media which produce two important group therapy phenomena: the group as microcosm and the corrective emotional experience. These metaphorical therapeutic events constitute two of the most valuable aspects of group treatment, for they are highly influential in the changing of clients' cognitive "maps."

CHANGE THROUGH THE MICROCOSM

Almost all group therapists concur that the group is a microcosm for its members, but there is not much agreement within the field as to what this really means. The first thing that theorists do not all see eye to eye on is "a microcosm of *what*?" Some conceptualize the microcosm simply as a slate of transferences for each individual, a replica of the member's family of origin or current relationships outside the group. Others view the group much more broadly, as being a representation of society, and still others see it as a replication of global and universal phenomena as well.

The second thing that group therapists vary on is the relative importance of microcosm-related aspects of group therapy, which are highly *symbolic,* as opposed to the (for lack of a better word) *real* things that go on within the group. Yalom (1975) and Bach (1954), for example, clearly consider the support, feedback, and empathy clients receive from one another to be a major value of group therapy; they point to ways in which these factors lead to increased self-esteem, diminished loneliness, and a more realistic perspective on one's problems. Many psychoanalytic group therapists, however, see these real-life benefits of peer interaction as "gravy" compared to the "meat" of the therapy, which is considered to be the learning that takes place as individuals' personal dramas arise out of the interpersonal transferences.

Finally, group therapists differ as to the amount of attention they pay to the group as a whole and to group dynamics, compared to the emphasis they place on the treatment of the individual within the group. Alexander Wolf wrote and stated many times that "group dynamics never cured anybody" (quote from panel at annual conference of the American Group Psychotherapy Association, Feb. 1982). Foulkes (1948, 1957), Bion (1959), and Whitaker and Lieberman (1964) strongly disagree. They believe that the stages the group goes through, the ways that a group selects and deals with themes and resolves conflict, and other group dynamics feature strongly in the therapy of the individuals in the group. Appreciating how profoundly group phenomena affect the psychological map of the individual, they assess the microcosm and often gear their interventions in terms of the group as a whole.

I will outline and comment briefly on some specific ways a few theorists have developed of viewing and utilizing the microcosm in group therapy. I will point out how each of these does or does not attend to the "real," as well as the symbolic, occurrences in treatment, and note whether or not they attend to group dynamics.

Freud's theory of transference directed psychotherapists' attention to the patient's unconscious tendency to superimpose his relationship with his parents onto the relationship with the therapist. Freud also advanced the notion of repetition compulsion, a proclivity to replicate specific interpersonal struggles until root internal conflicts are resolved. All group therapists, with the exception of behavior modification specialists, acknowledge, and in some way use, the concepts of transference and repetition compulsion in the therapy. Sooner or later, for each member the group takes on aspects of his present or past life. "A freely interactive group with few structural restrictions will, in time, develop into a social microcosm of its participant members" (Yalom, 1975, p. 29). While some strictly psychoanalytic therapists might limit the microcosm to a replication of the family of origin or parent-child situations, most transference theories would hold that the group is a microcosm of any and all the significant groups in the client's life. It is a stage for the simultaneous reenactment of individuals' unresolved problems, with group members taking the roles in one another's scripts.

Wolf and Schwartz (1962) view the microcosm strictly from the perspective of what it symbolizes to the individual client. They are interested in the intersecting transferences within the group as they relate to each person's developmental issues. In the Wolf-style psychoanalytic group, each member is seen at some point to replicate through the transferences the particular problematic interactions that occurred in his childhood. These regressions are then analyzed by the therapist. Hopefully, the perspective given by insight allows the client to give up his maladaptive ways of seeking gratification, love, or approval. Through interaction with fellow participants and the therapist(s), the client may even be able to redo the developmental and social lessons he failed to complete. He at least will become disabused of his infantile fantasies and expectations and prepared to deal with life more realistically. As mentioned, Wolf's model places little importance on the "real" value of the members to one another, and even less on group dynamics.

Fritz Perls (1969) originated Gestalt psychotherapy based on the concepts of internal mapping put forth by Gestalt psychology. The emphasis in Gestalt therapy is on the personal awareness of the individual. Gestalt techniques — "talking to the empty chair," for example — are designed to help a person become aware of exactly what he is thinking, picturing in his mind, or feeling at any given moment in time, without slapping on labels or judgments. Perls moved away from the notion of transference, not because he did not believe it could exist, but because the idea of it predisposed therapists and clients to think in certain set ways, and to move out of the here-and-now where the curative experiences of human contact and spontaneity are to be found.

To oversimplify, Perls saw the group as a collective blank screen for members, one on which they could continually project their ever-changing feelings and internal images. In Perls' model of group therapy, one member's comment to another is considered practically irrelevant to the receiver of the communication. Much more attention is focused on what the remark meant in terms of the speaker's own perceptions and feelings, and what parts of himself he might be projecting onto the other person.

Perls' concept of the group is very sophisticated and highly useful for clinicians. Unfortunately, because he ignored group dynamics and the therapeutic possibilities of group interaction, and because he himself tended to monopolize the groups he ran, his contribution to the field has not been recognized by group therapists to the extent it should have been.

Eric Berne developed a derivative of and alternative to individual psychoanalysis, called Transactional Analysis, which employs a group, rather than individual, format in an attempt to make therapy economical and non-elitist. Such democratic ideals notwithstanding, Berne used an authoritarian model of group therapy and had a cynical view of the value of peer interaction in psychotherapy. He said that the "organizational structure of a therapy group consists of only two roles, therapist and patient" (Berne, 1966, p. 153). In Transactional Analysis groups clients take turns "doing their work" with the therapist in front of the group; and the group interaction consists of other clients' sharing with the client after his "piece of work."

Although it could be argued that Berne's therapist-centered model misses the whole point of group therapy, he did develop a powerful microcosm theory, "the group imago" (Berne, 1966, p. 154). He said that each individual comes into the group with a mental construction of what the group will be to him, his "group imago." The imago has specified roles for people or parts of himself with whom he currently has "unfinished business." The member will unconsciously select people in the group to fill all the slots in his group imago. He will engage in "games" (Berne, 1964) and other maneuvers with these stand-ins in an effort to continue or finish the "business." Berne's theory is exciting because it suggests an explanation in terms of internal mapping for the cross-transferences in the group, a refinement of the "blank screen" concept. Both Berne and Perls did believe that the feedback, support, contact, and understanding people received in the group were highly beneficial to them, but they greatly minimized the therapeutic value of group-as-a-whole phenomena.

Philip Slater (1966) views the group as a microcosm of civilization. His theories are based on Freud's *Group Psychology and the Analysis of the Ego* (1951) and *Totem and Taboo* (1950). Slater observed students in experimental classroom groups in which the leader/teacher was extremely nondirective. Slater was fascinated to find that, when left to their own devices with a leader whom they experienced as passive and withholding, these groups frequently engaged in certain angry rituals which were highly reminiscent symbolically of the rites of totemism and cannibalism practiced in primitive tribes. His work is a favorite of leaders of what are called "Tavistock" groups, which are used for training in group dynamics. In these groups, and in some therapy groups based on a Freudian model, the therapist or consultant is present for purposes of interpreting the group process only and gives the group very little structure or direction. Leaving the group to establish its own rules and purposes, the leader simply makes interpretations which focus on how members' infantilism, greed, irrationality, and rage are displaying themselves. Needless to say, this kind of group tends to be anxiety-provoking and does little to promote humanistic behavior and improved self-concept; however, much can be learned in such groups about infantile conflict and emotion and about how people deal with power and authority.

It was mentioned earlier that J. L. Moreno, founder of psychodrama and sociometry, conceived of the group we carry around in our mind as the "social atom." The social atom theory was Moreno's version of a group transference theory; however, the social atom was only a small part of what Moreno felt the group represented. He saw the group as a microcosm of the cosmos, of life itself:

> The objective of (the group) was, from its inception, to construct a therapeutic setting that uses life as a model, to integrate into the setting all the modalities of living — beginning with the universals of time, space, reality and cosmos — and moving down to all the details and nuances of life (Moreno, 1966, p. 460).

Foulkes (1957), a British group analyst, developed an impressive microcosm theory — "group matrix" — that pulls together the various interpretations we have mentioned and many others. Foulkes saw the group as representing not only the emotional patterns and relationships of all individuals, but all possible communication and organizational patterns. Individuals invest the group structure with the properties of many contexts besides family — class, workplace, forum, playground, stage, community, society, humanity, reality. The interaction within the group at any given moment is related to the total "group matrix," which is "the total transpersonal network of communication that becomes laid down" (de Mare, 1972, pp. 176–177). It not only contains past events and communications, but also refers to the present and future. The social microcosm of the group is a changing backcloth to the foreground figures (in a stage production) . . . "where the backcloth (matrix) determines the stage (structure) and the stage determines the script" (de Mare, 1972, p. 176).

Foulkes' group matrix theory is a blend of all the best microcosm theories, fully utilizing the slate of transferences theory along with the blank screen concept. He taps into the group as a source of spiritual as well as emotional awareness, without neglecting the healing value of the real relationships and communications among members. He espouses the use of the group-as-a-whole, without in any way discounting the value of considering members as individuals in their own right. Like Moreno's social atom, Foulkes' notion of the microcosm extends beyond the normal dimensions of space and time, encompassing realms of what *might be* as well as what *is* and *has been*.

Each one of the microcosm theories is useful in explaining ways in which the group might be seen by individual members. Understanding a given client's internal mapping of the microcosm greatly assists the therapist in monitoring the frame of reference changes taking place in that group member's mind, and helps the therapist plan interventions to facilitate further therapeutic shifts in thinking.

THE CORRECTIVE EMOTIONAL EXPERIENCE

The "corrective emotional experience," a concept introduced by Franz Alexander (Alexander and French, 1946) in reference to psychoanalytic cure, is useful in understanding how therapy groups are effective for individuals. Loosely defined, "the corrective emotional experience" is the reenactment with satisfaction and favorable consequences of an emotional situation which in the past was painful and/or ended unfavorably. Research reported by Yalom (1975) indicates that the corrective emotional experience is a primary curative factor in group therapy.

The corrective emotional experience takes place in group therapy in two modes: ongoing and situational. The overall experience for the group client of being treated with consistency, respect, caring, objectivity, and sensitivity is certainly a corrective one. Beyond that, however, therapy clients have their own specific and painful scripts that they bring to the group. More often than not, the parts of their life drama that caused them the most anguish and most influenced their subsequent self-concept and ability to form relationships occurred in childhood. The most powerful corrective emotional experiences in group, therefore, involve reexperiencing traumatic or unhappy childhood experiences — first the way they actually happened, and then the way they should have happened.

The corrective emotional experience in group rests on the transference phenomenon. The fortunate tendency of group clients to conjure up the microcosm stimulates the spontaneous reenactment of past struggles, with group members being unconsciously summoned by one another to play key roles in their scripts. With the help of the group under the leader's direction, such dilemmas are resolved in a new way.

The corrective emotional experience may occur spontaneously through the group interaction, or the process may be hastened and intensified by means of techniques such as psychodrama. Either way, it is a highly emotional experience for the client, involving, at some point, a *catharsis,* a purgation of feeling. The catharsis may be very dramatic or of the quieter "aha" variety. The client may not always be able to articulate *what* has happened through the corrective experience, but he knows he has changed in some way. As a result, he experiences a renewal of energy and is more spontaneous. With the true corrective emotional experience, some form of cognitive restructuring takes place.

In the first two cases below, the corrective emotional experience occurred for the clients in the natural progression of the group — one was dramatic and one was more gradual. A third instance will be described in which psychodrama was used to enhance the verisimilitude and intensity of the corrective emotional experience.

Case Examples

Lenny

Lenny, a homosexual man in his early twenties, joined group with a complaint of severe anxiety. Lenny was underemployed at the time, working at a factory although he had a bachelor's degree, was fluent in several languages, and had secretarial skills as well. When he first entered group, Lenny was so nervous that he could not understand most of what was going on. Lenny has a slight hearing problem, which is aggravated when he is anxious, but he seemed to exaggerate the number of times he had to ask people to repeat themselves. He would blurt out information about himself, but was not connected with any feelings about what he was saying.

Lenny's parents were both actors. Lenny's mother was a beautiful and accomplished woman who had great ambitions for Lenny, her only child. She sent him to lessons in almost every kind of athletic and performing activity and expected him to be the best performer in all of them. Lenny devoted most of his energy to trying to please his mother, which seemed to be impossible. Lenny's parents' relationship was fraught with jealousy and rage. Both mother and father drank heavily and Lenny witnessed vicious fights between them all during childhood. When Lenny was 17, his mother committed suicide with pills and alcohol.

As a teenager Lenny was physically slow to develop and was very self-conscious. Having no brothers or sisters as models, he behaved in awkward and silly ways that generated merciless teasing from his peers. Both at home and at school Lenny felt the spotlight was always on him, continually exposing his many inadequacies.

After his mother's death, Lenny's father buried his grief and guilt in alcohol and sexually promiscuous behavior. Since sexual issues had been prominent in the couple's conflict, Lenny was already nervous about sex in general and his own sexuality in particular. Lenny's father's inappropriate sexual behavior only served to cement this confusion.

Like most group members, Lenny acted out within the group most of his historical conflicts with parents and peers. He developed a love/hate transference with me, frequently imagining that I was feeling critical or angry at him when I was not. He responded to group members superficially, tending not to remember anything about their lives and problems and taking as much group time as he was allowed, without consideration of the needs of others. His employment problems persisted. He would apply for jobs that were totally wrong for him, such as sales, and ignore possibilities in multi-lingual secretarial work for which he was uniquely qualified. He would solicit group advice and patently ignore it, leaving members frustrated with him.

Lenny was not in individual therapy concurrently with group. One reason was that he could not afford it; another was that I felt he needed to make some changes on the behavioral level in the group before he would be ready to deal with the explosive material of his childhood. The first two years, therefore, were spent with Lenny learning to manage his anxiety and to listen to other people. By the end of the second year Lenny was fairly appropriate in his interactions with people most of the time.

Throughout his life Lenny had felt very vulnerable and frightened. His father did not protect him from his mother's demands and her rage; his parents did not protect him from the assaults of his peers. Lenny always perceived himself to be in danger, even in the group. As a result, he could not even begin to express his emotions freely. A dramatic group encounter afforded Lenny a crucial experience of being protected which unlocked years of pent-up feelings and advanced Lenny's growth considerably.

Lenny had messed up another job interview and felt terrible about it. I thought the group had learned not to engage in criticism of Lenny on the matter of employment, since he would then use it as fuel to sabotage himself further. Suddenly, however, Daniel, a man close to Lenny's age, leveled a quiet but scathing attack on Lenny, stating, among other things, that Lenny had brought all of his problems on himself. Daniel's attack was startling since he was usually very generous with other members; it was also significant in that Daniel himself had vocational troubles similar to Lenny's. Feeling that Daniel was projecting unfairly, I turned to him, and, using my best "firm parent" voice, emphatically confronted him:

"Daniel, I think you're out of line on this one. For one thing, you yourself have plenty of issues of your own about getting and keeping a job commensurate with your education. But even if you didn't, why are you so invested in Lenny's vocational success or failure? Where do you get off criticizing him for having the problems he is in therapy to address? Everyone is in the group because they have particular problems out there in the world, and it seems unfair for you to put him down for exhibiting his problem!"

Daniel had not even had time to respond before we looked over and saw Lenny dissolved in tears in the arms of the two members sitting beside him. Sobbing for minutes on end, he exclaimed that no one had ever "stuck up" for him in his life before now. Lenny was overwhelmed with appreciation and relief. In these moments Lenny was experiencing some important things that had almost never occurred when he needed them during childhood and adolescence. Lenny's parents were always pushing him to accomplish and succeed. They paid no heed to the teasing and humiliation he was receiving from peers at school. In group, instead of ignoring Daniel's attack, I, as the parent figure, intervened on Lenny's behalf, more concerned about Lenny's feelings of comfort and safety in the group than about whether he would get a job that week. This sense of safety allowed Lenny to let himself be accepted and comforted by the two other group members. He then was able to talk about the unspeakable loneliness and isolation he felt most of the time in his life. For the first time he began to realize that, through his repeated vocational failures, he was trying to make his parents feel guilty for not helping him. His attempts to frustrate the group in *their* efforts to help him were a displacement of his need to punish his parents. Lenny began to see how this behavior was an obstacle to his growing and learning in the group, as well as a useless and painful process for everyone concerned.

After his corrective experience that night, Lenny began to do a number of things he had never done before. He began to call other group members for advice before taking vocational steps. (A few months later, he began to listen to and sometimes even heed their suggestions!) As he felt safer in the group, his anxiety diminished and concomitantly his inappropriate comments and deafness decreased. His natural perceptiveness and sensitivity to others began to show prominently in the group, and he became appreciated as a very understanding member, rather than a distraction and a bother. He has since learned to use the group productively to deal with the painful issues of his childhood rather than destructively as a vehicle for perpetuating his dependency and resentment.*

Margaret

Margaret, mentioned in our Introduction, is an example of someone who had a prolonged corrective emotional experience in group, a creative redoing of a very painful and destructive family situation.

Twenty-five years old, Margaret entered the group soon after being divorced. She had had a brief affair and told her husband about it, upon which he left her and never spoke to her again. She had been totally banished from her family when she married him, so when her husband left, she had nobody. Margaret's mother and father were very disturbed and physically violent people; hence, even though she was lonely and frightened, Margaret sensibly decided it best to stay separated from them.

Upon entering group Margaret began worrying that the other group members would consider her promiscuous, since she was involved in meeting men and dating. Nothing the group members said could reassure her that they were not judging her. On some level, Margaret was aware that her feelings about the group were distortions based on her experiences with her parents, whose worst brutality had emerged whenever one of the children reached the age to become sexually active. In her life Margaret was reenacting her attempt, cruelly thwarted by her parents, to take responsibility for her sexuality, and to make her own decisions about whom to date, go to bed with, and so on. Perhaps her affair and subsequent confession to her husband had been an attempt to do the same thing, but her husband's reaction had been the same as her parents—to cut her off completely.

One night fairly late, Margaret called a fellow group member, Sam, the only male parent in the group. She asked him to come over to her house and change the lock on her door, because she was worried about some vague threats made by her recent boyfriend. Sam's wife objected and Sam did not go. Feeling guilty for not helping her, Sam reported the incident in group the next week. Upon questioning it became clear that Margaret's anxieties about the boyfriend were unfounded, and the call had been unnecessary. Sam felt

---

*This case is described in more detail in my article entitled "The Narcissistic Personality in Group Therapy" (1984).

annoyed and Margaret was terribly embarrassed. My sense was that she thought the group believed she was trying to seduce Sam, which was not the case. Her confusion and anxiety increased and she began to miss sessions. She asked the "violent" boyfriend to move in with her, which caused the group to express some concern. Naturally, Margaret read their worries for her as censure, and pulled away further. Finally, one night the group congruently expressed to her that they believed in her right to make her own decisions and run her own life—that they would not judge her or be angry, even if she made mistakes. They simply wanted her to attend group regularly and try to learn to trust them.

Margaret began to believe that people could care without controlling or victimizing her. Her attendance was perfect for months on end, and she frequently called members to offer and obtain support between sessions. She began to recognize distortions in her own thinking and instances when she was confusing the group with her family.

Corrective Emotional Environment

The corrective emotional experience of group therapy for an individual does not occur in one cathartic moment, although, as with Lenny, one incident may be the culmination. The construction of a therapeutic family of substance which heals wounds incurred in the family of origin is a complex process that may take years to be accomplished. Fortunately, however, the time spent in the process is also therapeutic. While an elaborate redoing of each member's personal history is taking place, each individual is afforded the experience of being in a consistently warm, sane, and supportive environment, which in most cases is quite different from the homes of their childhood.

In group therapy, members are accepted without regard to their failures and other imperfections. Frank mentions that the therapy group is similar to Robert Frost's concept of the ideal home—"something you somehow haven't to deserve" (Frank, 1974, p. 275). The most corrective emotional experience of the group may be the nurturing environment it makes available to the client on an ongoing basis.

Psychodramatic Corrective Emotional Experience

Moreno was the first to clearly articulate the relationship between theater and group therapy. He invented the term and the modality of psychodrama, a process which creates within a group the stories and dramas that exist in the minds of the members. Psychodrama makes the phenomenon of the corrective emotional experience far more accessible for therapy clients.

As a trained psychodramatist and group therapist, I know that the therapy group is an ongoing drama at the group and the individual level. As mentioned earlier, people in group are constantly attempting unconsciously to use the people in the group as stand-ins for persons in their outside or past life. In doing this they are groping to understand and resolve internal conflicts which are in some way associated for them with these figures.

Group leaders who know psychodrama can use techniques within a regular therapy group session to highlight or intensify the evolving personal dramas within the group. A psychodrama can begin with a group issue or with a client's discussion of an outside problem. Either way, the content of the problem and the action of the group become joined in the psychodramatic process. The central person of the psychodrama is someone in the group whose problem is somehow representative of that of others at the time, or whose emotional energy is very high and can draw other members into his internal world. Somehow that person emerges as focal in the group session, perhaps by the group's attention naturally turning to him or by the group leader singling him out. The group leader then becomes a psychodramatic director. He helps the subject, called the "protagonist," organize persons in the group to play the roles of important others in the "story" or problem he has been discussing with the group. The others can be parts of the protagonist himself as well as other people in his life. The protagonist has an opportunity to play all of the roles himself, which gives him perspectives on the situation that he could not have otherwise.

The psychodrama often involves a dramatic redoing of a personal situation that was or is painful or traumatic for the protagonist, followed by an enactment of how the protagonist would want it to have been or to be. This is, in essence, a corrective emotional experience of the type discussed earlier.

A poignant psychodramatic episode took place with Dorothy, a 37-year-old divorced woman, who was extremely isolated in her life. Even though she was outgoing, funny, and warm, she had few friends, a situation of her own making. Dorothy was afraid to get close to anyone because of a deep fear of rejection and abandonment, something she had experienced from her father, her brother, and others in her childhood. Dorothy, whose parents had divorced when she was a young child, had once had a younger stepsister, Beth, of whom she was very fond. Dorothy's mother had divorced the father of the stepsister when Dorothy was 15 and Dorothy never saw Beth again. This loss was particularly painful for Dorothy, whose only real sibling, a brother, was much older than she and highly abusive toward her. Dorothy's early life was further disrupted by her mother's two other divorces and several moves to different towns and schools.

Meanwhile Deanne, a slightly younger, shy woman, was contemplating leaving the group. Dorothy was very upset that Deanne was leaving and adamantly insisted that Deanne would never contact her, Dorothy, after her termination. Seeing a similarity between Dorothy's situation with the stepsister in the past and now with Deanne, we decided to amplify the stepsister issue by staging a psychodrama in which Deanne would play the stepsister. We first reenacted events from a period of her life that Dorothy described as "the only time" she was "ever happy" — when she was with Beth. The group enjoyed playing out scenes of Beth pulling Dorothy on a wagon when she had proclaimed herself "Queen for a Day" and of the two girls messing up the kitchen while making Christmas cookies. We then did a scene in which Dorothy actually says goodbye to Beth, something she never did in real life. This brought many tears from Dorothy, Deanne, and the rest of us. The group urged Dorothy to try to find Beth in real life and reunite with her. We hoped this would help her connect with a part of herself that was joyous and funloving, a part she uses in her work but rarely for her own personal benefit. When Deanne did leave the group, she carried Dorothy's good wishes rather than her resentment, and the two women did keep in touch, at least for a while. Dorothy did contact Beth, with all the hoped-for results.

In my view the psychodramatic process occurs spontaneously in the therapy group whether or not psychodramatic techniques are used. The reality of the involved group member is expanded and intensified as real bodies spring forth to fill the shoes of the important people in his life. Moreno called this heightened intensity "surplus reality," the intangible dimensions of intrapsychic and extrapsychic life, the invisible dimensions in the reality of living that are not fully experienced or expressed (Moreno, 1966).

When Yablonsky (1976) writes the following about psychodrama groups, he could just as well have been discussing therapy groups:

> Everyone at some time has an inner drama going on in his mind. In this confidential setting you are the star of your session and play all the roles. . . . (it is) a unique opportunity for externalizing the internal world (pp. 3–4).

In group therapy the psychodramatic recreation of an individual's conflict and the spontaneous development of new solutions and alternatives is a curative factor. Often the protagonist will not be able to verbalize what the psychodramatic experience meant; yet, he will feel relieved and clearer about his problem, while other group members will see substantive positive changes in his attitude and demeanor in subsequent weeks. Profound insights emerge through psychodrama, but they arise out of the group experience and not from interpretations made by members or therapists. Psychodramatic learning is "transformational" in character, generating more options and changes in frames of reference for the protagonist and others in spontaneous and effortless ways.

CHAPTER III

The Group as Learning Laboratory

When I taught elementary school in the early seventies, we would set up a learning environment, or "learning laboratory," in the classroom, with materials and instructions for each subject clustered in corners of the room. The children contracted with the teacher to learn a certain skill or body of material, and the teacher would provide them with a variety of tasks and projects, all of which would lead to the mastery of that step.

In many ways the therapy group is a "learning laboratory" for clients, where the curriculum being taught is communication. The overall objective is to help members learn to get along with one another and use the resources of one another for mutual benefit. Like students in the learning lab classroom, group members are continually being presented with new learning opportunities and challenges; each person selects avenues to follow and tasks to master based on her own personal needs and interests. In both the learning lab class and group, the teacher/group therapist is, by and large, considered more as a resource than an authority figure. Success is measured less by grades and teacher evaluation than by peer feedback and degree of self-satisfaction. In both settings, mistakes and conflict, often considered negatively in most traditional education, are reframed as "grist for the mill" — opportunities to learn something new. In the learning lab and in group therapy, the subject matter emerges from the actual experience of participants and, after it is studied, is related back to the real lives of participants in a relevant way. The emphasis is on learning *skills* more than content and on teaching participants to think for themselves — to question and confront, rather than simply swallow information.

Two of the major life skills learned in the therapy group laboratory are *spontaneity* and *role development*. This chapter explains what these are, why they are necessary for coping and creativity, and how they are taught in the therapy group experience.

SPONTANEITY

Spontaneity is one of the most important of human assets or skills. Without spontaneity we cannot love, communicate, make decisions, or be creative. Without spontaneity we cannot cope. We fail to recognize problems, to see alternatives, to make choices or to act on them. At times an inability to respond spontaneously can endanger survival. This is true on both the personal and societal level.

The importance of spontaneity has not been adequately recognized in the field of psychology and the mental health professions. It is underestimated in its role in personality functioning and intelligence, and overlooked as a component of emotional well-being and successful adaptation. Enhanced spontaneity is often referred to after the fact as evidence of therapeutic success, but it should be a priority in treatment. The use of spontaneity — the therapist's as well as the client's — is the *sine qua non* of the therapeutic process, and yet, it is only minimally discussed in the literature.

Moreno and his followers are among the few who have given spontaneity its rightful emphasis in the behavioral and social sciences. Moreno's "theory of spontaneity," discussed below, leads the way to teaching spontaneity in the "learning laboratory" of the therapy group.

Moreno's Theory of Spontaneity

Spontaneity is novel response to a new situation or a new response to an old situation (Moreno, 1946, p. 50).* Spontaneity is the ability of a subject to meet each new situation with adequacy. Spontaneity is coping; spontaneity is adaptation. It is also an energy to live.

Spontaneity is, for Moreno, the basic life force — the catalyst for our emotions, thoughts and acts, and for our creativity. Spontaneity is neither strictly a hereditary factor nor strictly an environmental one (p. 51). It is most

---

*All quotes in this section, unless otherwise noted, are from Moreno, J.L., *Psychodrama,* Vol. I, Fourth Edition, 1977.

present at birth and during infancy, when the baby is continually faced with totally novel situations and must have spontaneity to survive.

The root of the word "spontaneous" is *sponte*, the Latin for "free will." Spontaneity is experienced by a person as "his own state, autonomous and free — free that is from external influence and free from any internal influence that he cannot control" (p. 81). It is a factor which helps man to move beyond himself (pp. 50–51). It is a readiness to respond as required. It is a "condition — a preparation for free action" (p. 111).

Spontaneity is in the here-and-now. "It functions only in the moment of its emergence just as, metaphorically speaking, a light is turned on in a room and all parts of it become distinct" (p. 86). It is the factor "animating all psychic phenomena to appear new, fresh and flexible" (p. 102).

Moreno's theory of spontaneity flies in the face of Freud's idea of psychic determinism. For Moreno not all emotion and behavior are motivated by a chain of events and associations from the past. Spontaneity determines the course of the present and the reporting of past events; in this sense the present determines the past rather than the other way around. According to Moreno, the results of spontaneous moments are relegated not to history, but to a different corner of time and space called the "cultural conserve" (Moreno, 1966, p. 468). Books, paintings, plays, and completed therapy sessions are part of the cultural conserve, finished products of spontaneous moments and creative acts gone by.

Spontaneity has an important and quixotic relationship to intelligence. Moreno says spontaneity can and should be measured by psychologists, as the presence or lack of it can actually influence intelligence and memory. Adults with a high degree of spontancity actually appear smarter than their IQ tests may show. Spontaneity is present at birth, while memory and other aspects of intelligence are still latent. Throughout the development of the infant and child, even as various cognitive functions emerge, they never obviate spontaneity as a necessary tool for thinking and learning.

Spontaneity is the opposite of apathy and passivity; however, it is not to be confused with either impulsivity (spontaneity gone awry) or simply being active. One can be quite spontaneous sitting quietly in a chair. Spontaneity is related to timing and to "warming up," which will be discussed later in this chapter.

Moreno identified four characteristic expressions of spontaneity that can exist relatively independently of one another (p. 89). The first is the *dramatic quality of response*. This is the quality which gives a feeling of vivacity to feelings, actions, and verbal utterances. This characteristic of a person has great practical importance in energizing and unifying the self. However, a person who demonstrates this kind of energy or intensity may have no feeling behind her animation and may, in fact, be repeating words and behaviors for the thousandth time (a discrepancy often noted in "borderline" personalities); in this case, spontaneity makes the individual look more youthful, intelligent, more "together" than she is. It makes dissociated automaton-like acts look like true self-expression. It is, Moreno says, a "cosmetic for the psyche" (p. 90). While it may not be sufficient, the dramatic quality of response is necessary for good interpersonal functioning. It is the factor that infuses life into routine communications. A person with "the dramatic quality of response" is the "life of the party" and contributes important energy to a therapy group as well.

While the first form of spontaneity serves to activate and perpetuate cultural conserve and social stereotypes, the second form of spontaneity is the kind that goes into creating new organisms, new forms of art, and new patterns of environment (p. 89). This is *spontaneous creativity*—the *eagerness* to express oneself and *do*—"to create the self and change the world" (p. 91). A generally "creative person" might have a plethora of imaginative ideas, but, without the spontaneity factor, there will be no response or activity to bring these ideas to fruition. For creativity to be mobilized it must be "warmed up" by spontaneity.

The third form of spontaneity is that of *originality*. "It does not contain any contribution significant enough to call it creativity, but, . . . is a unique expansion or variation from the cultural conserve as a model" (p. 91–92). The drawings of children are often original in that way. Eccentricities or efforts to "be different," such as mediocre attempts at avant-garde art, may be original, but not creative. Of course, a piece of art that is original, creative, *and* dramatic is one that will make its mark and is likely to become part of the cultural conserve.

The fourth form of spontaneity is *adequacy of response*. An adequate response is appropriate. It is enough but not too much, and it is well-timed. All kinds of examples come to mind from groups and elsewhere of creative, original, and dramatic responses that fall flat because they are inadequate—too little, too late, too much, too soon or some combination of these. Moreno gives examples of inadequate responses: no response to a situation—when a person has given up his old response and not yet substituted a new one; using an old response to a new situation; or employing a new, but wrong, response to a new situation. This form of spontaneity has the most to do with coping and adaptation.

Moreno equated mental health with spontaneity. Other group therapists echo this, using their own words. Spotnitz says, "The mature person is emotionally versatile . . . that is, he has the capacity to act spontaneously in socially desirable ways and to respond appropriately to the behavior and emotions of other people" (Spotnitz, 1961, p. 198). Communication theorists, such as Jay Haley and Paul Watzlawick, systems theorists, cyberneticists, and George Kelly in his "psychology of personal constructs" (1963) — among other theorists of various persuasions — equate spontaneity with increased choice. They subscribe to the notion of the Law of Requisite Variety (Kelly, 1963) — that the person with the largest number of choices in the system will control the system (Lankton, 1979). They would agree with Moreno that the goal of therapy is to build spontaneity on the individual and group levels, thereby guaranteeing increased choice.

Therapeutic change is not possible without spontaneity. It would therefore seem to be necessary for psychotherapists to *teach* spontaneity. This seems a ridiculous contradiction, doesn't it? Yet, it is consistent with the nature of this book to embrace such paradoxes. We will now take a look at how "spontaneity training," as Moreno conceived of it, occurs in group therapy.

Spontaneity Training

"Put the subject into a life situation and see how he acts" (p. 101) was Moreno's advice to therapists. This sounds a little like the briefly popular method of teaching two-year-olds to swim by throwing them into the pool, and to a certain extent this is what Moreno meant. For spontaneity training, he put students in stimulus-free situations and told them to "act as if they had no past, and were not determined by an organic structure" (p. 83). The students were observed as they fumbled around trying to make structure out of unstructured situations, sometimes with others, sometimes alone; they were then given feedback on their "performance." The most striking therapeutic effect was the general increase in flexibility and facility in meeting life situations outside of the training situation (p. 84).

The birth situation is the one where the most spontaneity is demanded of us. Moreno felt that conditions that duplicated infancy in terms of a total lack of preconceived notions or "cultural conserves" were highly conducive for the ignition of latent spontaneity, and this belief provided the rationale for the first crude and probably rather dangerous spontaneity training techniques. While he learned from these experiments, Moreno was aware that conditions other than novelty were necessary for the development of spontaneity. There needed to be structure and protection for people, as well as freedom and a certain amount of unpredictability in the environment. As his work evolved, Moreno developed a setting and a structure for spontaneity training through psychodrama. He conceived of the psychodramatic situation as a paradigm of the undetermined, script-free environment. If one is playing a role in another's psychodrama, one simply enters "and the plots, the persons, the objects in it, in all its dimensions, and its time and space — are novel to him. Every step he makes forward in this world on the stage has to be defined anew" (p. 53).

Each meeting of a therapy group presents a totally novel situation to all participants. At each session people, situations, ideas, feelings, and opinions are "defined anew." The development of spontaneity in each person and the group is both the cause and the result of the many changes in frames of reference that occur in the group.

While development of spontaneity should be a priority in group therapy, "throwing group members in the pool" is not at all advisable. For spontaneity (instead of terror!) to grow in a group, clients must be treated gently and respectfully. They must be allowed to "enter the action" of the group drama in any way they choose and only when they feel ready, whether this means putting a toe in shyly or leaping in right away. The greatest teaching tool for the enhancement of spontaneity in group members is the leader's own spontaneity. It is enormously helpful for group therapists to obtain training in psychodrama and other creative therapy methods even if they do not wish to use the techniques per se in their groups. The therapist's personal participation in group modalities that emphasize spontaneity will help him learn to stay in touch with his feelings, his sense of humor, and his intuition when he is leading his own groups.

Spontaneity on the Group Level

Moreno (1971), Yalom (1975), and others have connected spontaneity on the group level with cohesiveness. (See, also, Chapter V.) Bion's (1959) notion of a "work group," one that is in a reality-oriented state, free of infantile "assumptions," presupposes a condition of spontaneity.

In their "focal conflict" theory, Whitaker and Lieberman (1964) deal with the interplay of spontaneity and anxiety on the group level. According to their theory, which I have always found apt and useful, themes in group always emerge and are dealt with dialectically. In every session a "disturbing motif," a feeling or thought that is new or uncomfortable for the group, is presented by at least one group member. The anxiety level of the group rises, and instantly, in response, there begins to emerge from the group remarks that contradict the "disturbing motif," reflecting an unconscious attempt by the members to restore equilibrium and diminish anxiety in the group. This is known as the "reactive motif." Through elaboration on the "disturbing" and "reactive" motives, the group will work through the conflict to one of the two following conclusions: a "restrictive solution," which binds the anxiety, but does not satisfy anyone completely and has an inhibiting effect on the group; or an "enabling solution," which creatively synthesizes both polarities and satisfies everybody. The "enabling solution" represents spontaneity on the group level. It meets all Moreno's criteria for spontaneity: It is dramatic, creative, original, and adequate. The "enabling solution" also liberates the spontaneity of individuals, increasing the therapeutic effect of the group and increasing the potential for more enabling solutions.

Spontaneity is definitely a therapeutic frame of reference for the individual and the group. We will now touch on how spontaneity operates in group therapy, how it affects and mobilizes people in constructive and creative ways.

When a Group is Spontaneous

When a group is "in spontaneity," everything is different from when it is not. When one looks around the room in a spontaneous moment, one sees flushed faces, full of expression, and people making eye contact. There is frequent laughter, and sometimes tears or anger. Bodies are relaxed, with arms that move freely in space. There is motion; it may be subtle or bold, but it makes some sort of coherent sense. People may unintentionally be mirroring one another's body positions or gestures, or their movements may be synchronized in some way. People may literally reach out to touch one another, or even move across a room to embrace. The room seems bright and warm.

When the group is anxious, people are alternately frozen and jittery. There is little meeting of the eyes and hardly any touching; if there is physical contact, it is not received well—one person may touch and the other recoil. People's faces are slack or tight, their color subdued. Their movements are jerky; arms are plastered to their bodies or shooting out awkwardly. There is a coldness and tension in the room.

When we "turn up the sound," we notice other differences between the group that is being spontaneous and one that is trapped in anxiety. In spontaneity the group members speak clearly, with greater modulation, and many shifts in voice tone, pitch, volume, and tempo. There is a broader distribution of verbal contributions. People interrupt freely and their timing is right. In spontaneity, people's gestures and facial expressions tend to match the content of what they are saying; in other words, they are *congruent*.

The group that is experiencing anxiety will tend to be dull or very tense. One person or dyad may dominate the conversation, with others reticent to contribute. Things move slowly and there are frequent yawns. Everyone's timing seems off. The conversation does not flow; non sequiturs creep in; people talk vaguely and abstractly. They do not always seem to mean what they say or they give double messages. Often they are not at all congruent.

One of the most curious and exciting aspects of group therapy is how quickly a group can change from the uptight, impotent anxiety state to the powerful and creative state of spontaneity. A single remark from just one person — an expression of dissatisfaction with the current state, a confrontation, an admission, a joke — if it is what the group needs at that particular moment, can change the group from deadly to lively in no time.

The cumulative moments and experiences of spontaneity in groups are the essence of the group therapy "cure"; and the more spontaneous times there are, the more likely the people in the group are to get well.

Spontaneity Training and Dealing With Resistance

Strictly psychoanalytic group therapists might disagree with much of what I have written about the value of spontaneity in the therapeutic process. Some group therapists refrain from interventions that relieve the group's anxiety, believing that the anxiety reflects resistances which should be confronted and analyzed, not avoided. I agree that elicitation, confrontation, and analysis of resistances are vital in group therapy, but from my experience I have found that group anxiety beyond a certain point is counterproductive to that end. If the spontaneity is very low, people express less and are not willing to explore resistances. People are much more likely to talk about their anger and dissatisfactions toward one another and the therapist when they feel safe than when they feel anxious. Moreover, unconscious material is more likely to be revealed in the heat of the spontaneous moment than in the anxious times when clients are highly defended. Moreno's psychodramatic and sociometric techniques are incredibly effective tools in helping group members connect with their feelings and with each other.

"Spontaneity is energy that must be spent" (McNamara, 1982). For the individual, the more spontaneous moments she experiences the more energy she has, and the more her own spontaneity becomes available to her for use in the group and outside. If the group is lively, supportive, and relevant to her, she learns to warm up to her own assertiveness, expression of feeling, humor, sensitivity, and capacity for loving. If the group is dull and inauthentic, or, worse yet, hostile and critical, the individual will only warm up to her resentment, her fears, and her modes of fleeing, the neurotic or fixed responses which she probably knows all too well already.

ROLES AND ROLE DEVELOPMENT

Moreno's Role Theory

Moreno said the most important single factor in determining "personality" was "role," claiming that "the tangible points of crystalization of the 'ego' are the roles in which it manifests itself" (Moreno, 1971, p. 471). We are the roles we play. From birth to death, we accumulate roles which we perform either satisfactorily or not: infant, son or daughter, marriage partner, student, hippie, parent, tennis player, professional, grandmother, group member, therapist, and so on. Our roles are defined by our interaction with others. The more rewarding the roles we play, the greater our life satisfaction; limitations in relationships and all other endeavors are a function of inadequacies in our repertoire of roles.

Roles are the ingredients of "self." Moreno said, "Roles do not emerge from the self, but the self may emerge from roles" (Moreno, 1946, p. 151). (Note he says "may" rather than "does"—a coherent integration of roles is necessary to insure adequate ego functioning.)

The roles we play throughout life or in any given moment are influenced by the other roles we have been playing, the roles others are playing, the "hidden" roles of ourselves and others, the task at hand, and environmental factors. The ability to take on new roles and to switch roles easily and appropriately is part and parcel of spontaneity.

Moreno's theory offers a taxonomy of roles (Hale, 1981, p. 137): Our first roles as infants are *somatic* (eater, sleeper, crier), and we adopt new somatic roles throughout life. *Psychodramatic roles* are roles referring to a specific person's perception of the role; these roles emerge from the person in response to life and are tied to a personal definition of the role, such as *a* son, *a* teacher. Beginning later in childhood are the *socio/cultural roles,* which have a collective definition (student, club member, American) and are related to cultural stereotypes (Jewish mother, black militant). Other differentiations of roles include active roles, once active but now past roles, ideal roles, fantasy roles, and future-projected roles.

The process of creating new roles is spurred by life's physical and emotional demands at each developmental stage and in the many situations in which we find ourselves. An impairment in the ability to change roles or develop new ones is a serious liability in coping. *Role fixation*, the inability to get out of a certain role, impedes growth in relationships and in other areas as well. The impetus for personal growth and creativity is the desire to embody more than just the assigned or traditional roles — to try many new roles and to find many variations within the same roles. Moreno (1971) speaks of "act hunger," the craving to play a certain role in a certain life situation. When we have "unfinished business" with somebody, we have a real need to play out a particular role with them — not in the manipulative sense, but in the sense of needing to express ourselves more fully and in a different kind of way than we have before.

In group therapy the individual is trained in *role development*. She learns to play her current roles with more awareness. She may learn to become a better friend, spouse, team member, employer, employee. She may expand her role repertoire, acquiring totally new and unfamiliar roles: A man may learn "mothering," or a wallflower may experience the role of being popular. She may be allowed to play roles that were forbidden or interrupted in childhood. She becomes aware of social roles, deciding for herself which ones she finds meaningful and wishes to adopt, and which she chooses to reject as empty or destructive for her. She also learns to reverse roles, to step into the shoes of the other person, simply for the purposes of understanding that individual's experience, or, in some instances, to learn that role so as to use it in her own life. She becomes aware of fantasy and future projected roles and learns to reactivate past roles when appropriate, as well as to let them go when necessary. In a group situation the client is *tested* in many roles. The therapist and other group members can easily distinguish the ones the client performs capably from those which are problematic for her; the latter then become targets in therapy.

While spontaneity is the fuel for the process of role development, spontaneity is also the result. The more roles we can play, the more spontaneously we can respond in any given situation.

Roles: Other Theories

Milton Erickson believed that we all have all the resources within us to be or do whatever we want in life. Ericksonian hypnotherapy involves helping the person obtain access to these resources within herself or in her environment. Generally, Erickson accomplished this by communicating directly with the unconscious mind of the client. He might bring forth the desired part of the client by telling her a metaphorical story that would inevitably remind her of a time when she had the resources she needed, or he might structure a situation in the environment that would give the client no other alternative but to behave in a new way. Erickson's objective was to teach the client new roles to play in her social world.

In Assagioli's *Psychosynthesis* (1965) the client takes a much more active part in conjuring up the new roles to be played, but the process of making the richness of the unconscious available for enhanced role development is similar to Erickson's. Elaborate techniques involving the use of mental imagery, movement, and writing are used to help the client contact her subconscious or "not-quite conscious" parts. While sometimes a group is used, group dynamics are ignored, and the work is almost entirely intrapsychic in its orientation.

Moreno, Erickson, and Assagioli all see growth as a function of role expansion and role development. Erickson and Assagioli conceive of roles more structurally; Erickson calls them "parts" and Assagioli calls them "subpersonalities." Moreno conceives of roles interpersonally and dynamically. He believes roles are taken in from the outside; we gather them from our experiences with others. Moreno believes the group to be the most effective catalyst for the creation of new roles and the optimum environment for role training. While it is doubtful that Erickson, Assagioli or any of the other therapists mentioned in this section would *disagree* with Moreno in his notions of how roles are developed and played out through contact and relationships with others, only Moreno had the vision to use group therapy as a vehicle in the reparation of role difficulties.

Jung (1964, 1971), like Moreno, Assagioli, and Erickson, viewed the unconscious as a powerful resource. For Jung, the psyche is an almost infinitely plastic phenomenon, capable of reaching realms far beyond the immediate, material, and interpersonal. Jungian analysis presses one way beyond one's individual psychological past into the cultural, spiritual, artistic, and mythological realms of a world in which everything and everyone are believed to be connected. Jung, like Moreno, conceived of human growth in terms of the development of a richer consciousness and fuller utilization of all the different parts of ourselves. Jung pointed out the existence cross-culturally of certain universal "archetypes" (Jung, 1964), metaphorical figures such as the "hero" and the "shadow," whose images are depicted in various forms throughout art and mythology. These "roles" have a spiritual dimension in that they are shared by all mankind through the collective unconscious. Jung's "types" (1971) — the "introvert" and the "extrovert"; and his "intuitive," "feeling," "sensation," and "thinking" dichotomies — are ways of characterizing people's modes of being in the world, which might be seen as relevant factors in their choice and performance of roles. One would think that Jung would have viewed the group as a likely forum for clients in their efforts to emancipate these parts and express themselves in new roles. Unfortunately, Jung looked on group therapy in a much more pedestrian way than that. He saw its value for social education and adjustment, but feared the dependency and lack of individuation he assumed it engendered in patients (de Mare, 1972, pp. 50–51).

Adler (1927) saw people as having life goals of a social nature, a notion which fits with the social orientation of Moreno's role theory, and would speak to the potential for learning about and resolving role problems in group contexts. Adler began to look at interactional phenomena in a sophisticated way. He thought in rudimentary systems terms, and experimented with the idea of family group treatment; however, when it came to group therapy, Adler, like Freud, Jung, and others of the Viennese tradition, was limited by the *Zeitgeist,* which lauded the individual analytic hour as the only pure therapeutic form (de Mare, 1972, p. 49). It is unfortunate that Adler never even explored the obvious possibilities of group therapy in his therapeutic work.

Sullivan, like Adler, rebelled against Freud in favor of an interpersonal view of personality. His view sounds much like Moreno's role theory when he says "the person is not an isolated entity, that personality is revealed and has its being in interpersonal relations, and is observable only in interpersonal relations" (Sullivan, 1940, p. 146). It is another sad inconsistency in the history of psychotherapy that Sullivan, who believed that the self was created and repaired *solely* through interpersonal validation and reinforcement, could not see the obvious usefulness of group therapy toward this very end.

Because of the short-sightedness of the first few generations of psychiatry and psychotherapy about the relationship of role development and group therapy, it remains for today's therapists to put their ideas into practice in the most natural of therapeutic milieus, the therapy group. The therapy group is an optimum environment for role training and role development. The mechanisms of the therapy group process — feedback, positive reinforcement, modeling, the microcosm, and the corrective emotional experience — create and enhance new roles in clients continuously and naturally. The ongoing group gives clients the time to tailor and integrate these roles.

"Living Life in Mini-Phases": Joan's Role Development Through Group Therapy

"I think when I leave this group, I will have gone through my life in mini-phases." When Joan made this statement, she had been in group for three years. Upon entering group at age 23, as intelligent as she was, she was vastly deficient in her role repertoire. There were a few roles she played well: student, employee, professional (real estate agent), and soon, group member, but in most other areas of her life she was in trouble. For one thing, although she was sexy-looking, she had great difficulty with the role of "woman" in the sexual sense. While she seemed to have conservative values, she was quite promiscuous. She felt very guilty and out of control with regard to sex. Her body image was negative and quite confused. She was considerably overweight, and yet, strangely, she worried little about that, and instead obsessed continuously about some almost invisible acne scars on her back. Joan's role as "friend" needed work as well. She occasionally lost friendships with women by somewhat unintentionally seducing their boyfriends. She did not have male friends because she did not know how to relate to men in any way other than to seduce them.

When Joan first entered group, she went to bed with a male member after the first meeting. She subsequently tried to get almost all the other men to have sex with her as well. It was Joan's escapades that prompted my "no-sex" rule, a device which is explained in some detail on pp. 77–78. Simply being told to refrain from sexual interactions with group members greatly helped Joan gain control over her sexual acting-out; there were no further incidents with group members and such behavior on her part outside the group was reduced.

The reason Joan was having such difficulty in these adult roles was that, during childhood, her "child" and "daughter" role had been sadly contaminated with pseudo-adult components. The following sad story not only explains Joan's role conflicts, but illustrates how role restrictions and deficiencies can cause the destruction of a family.

Joan's parents were both ambitious without the training, self-discipline, and direction they needed to be successful. They pinned high hopes on bright and pretty little Joan, who showed talent in many areas, including art and athletics, both fields of great interest to her parents. They encouraged/pushed many lessons to develop her considerable abilities. Her father's role as "coach" to Joan seems to have given both him and Joan considerable gratification until Joan's adolescence. The mother's role was "costumer," making elaborate frilly dresses for all occasions, including school, as well as stunning outfits for skating and ballet performances. Mother's role, though it had its narcissistic rewards for Joan, left Joan dissatisfied and feeling a little guilty. She remembers wondering anxiously whether she was taking her father away from her mother, and whether her once pretty, now obese, mother resented her success. In the shadows was Joan's younger brother, who clearly had not been picked for a starring role by the parents. Troublesome, rebellious, and never getting the attention he craved, the little boy early on laid the foundations for roles he would play in adolescence — "drug dealer," "drug abuser," and "dropout."

When Joan reached age 11, she developed physically very rapidly and almost overnight went from a Shirley Temple-type child to a sexy woman (in looks only, of course). Joan was paralyzed with fright at the changes occurring in her body and at the aggressive sexual responses she was getting from men. She needed reassurance, explanations, role-modeling, structure, and understanding that only parental figures could provide. Her father's "coach" and mother's "costumer" roles no longer met Joan's needs.

Unfortunately, the "coach" and the "costumer" were playing the only roles they knew! They did not know how to be parents, particularly not to a teenager who was no longer the "little doll" of whom they had been so proud. What is more, they had been so busy as "coach" and "costumer" that they had not had to face the fact that they did not have a clue about how to be "husband" and "wife." The presence of the father's psychotic mother living in the house with them during the early years of marriage had also contributed substantial distraction from the basic problems in the marriage.

The pathetic choice these parents made as their daughter entered puberty is a perfect example of the tragic consequences of *role fixation*. Continuing the coach-costumer-star roles, the father clad Joan in sexy lingerie and got her a modeling job. Live shows would be held, and men would cheer and whistle at 12-year-old Joan dressed in scanty underwear and negligees. Father, as her agent, continued as "coach," and mother as "costumer." Joan was understandably mortified and confused. She internalized her rage at her parents and men, and began to hate herself and her body. Mother was not enthusiastic about the modeling project, but failed to take a stand against it to father. Joan was afraid her parents would reject her if she refused to do it, and part of her liked the attention given her by the men. Finally, her unconscious got her out of this terrible predicament. She got fat.

"Coach" and "costumer," lost without their roles to play, both began to drink. The father already had a drinking problem, which had been kept under control somewhat by the demands of his role as "coach." Now he was drunk all the time. Mother switched from food to alcohol abuse, and sat home practically comatose most of the time. Joan took on the roles of "maid" and "parents to her parents," roles for which she received little appreciation. Not surprisingly, it was when Joan went away to college that her parents finally split up, at which point the mother recovered from alcoholism almost immediately. The father attempted to stop drinking periodically without success and lived a haphazard and lonely life. Joan's brother then took the spotlight in the family. He became as antisocial as his sister had been "goody-goody," continuing to deal and take drugs and periodically getting himself arrested or involved in automobile accidents. Joan, wisely relegating herself to the shadows in the family, began a slow process of separating from their toxic influence.

Joan's participation in group has been a process of creating in sequence the roles she needed to flourish as a woman, a professional, a friend. The first roles were all daughter-related. With my co-therapist, a new kind of father figure, she developed a completely nonsexual, unexploitative relationship in which she got unconditional nurturing and respect. She found in me a female role model for professionalism and self-confidence, someone who appreciated and was not threatened by her creativity and intelligence, but respected her choices about how she wished to use and develop her many talents. During her four-year participation in group Joan has been through many escapades and tribulations (many of which are described later), all resulting in some way in her learning more about the responsibilities of friendship and using one's sexuality. These roles had developed initially for her in such a warped context that she needed to start all over in learning the parts, with a different cast of characters in the supporting roles. Incidentally, she was able to develop lasting, rewarding, and nonsexual friendships with males — including the man she went to bed with her first night in group.

"Nebbish" and "Mensch"

In her book *The Possible Human* (1982), Jean Houston describes two roles that human beings often play — the Nebbish and the Mensch. The Nebbish can best be described as "a drag." The Nebbish has no sense of humor, is self-pitying, cloying, and never satisfied, always miserable. As she says, "When a Nebbish leaves the room you feel as if someone just came in." The Nebbish misconstrues everything nice as a problem or a slight against him. ("So why are you phoning me? Are you trying to avoid ironing?")

The treatment of choice for Nebbishes is group therapy, provided the group leader is a Mensch and there are some potential Mensches among the membership. The following quotes are from Houston (1982, pp. 120–121):

"A Mensch is the antidote to the Nebbish."
"A Mensch sees the Mensch in you."
"A Mensch loves to learn, loves to laugh, loves to listen."
"A Mensch, when the Nebbish comes to the door, tells him a joke."

In my years as a group therapist I have seen many a Nebbish blossom into a Mensch, or pretty close to it, over a period of two or three years in group therapy. For instance, Walt, an overweight repairman, was out of a job. His second wife was filing for divorce, I think on grounds of his being a Nebbish. Walt had no interests, few talents, and did not seem very bright. He had the most horrible laugh, which he never used when things were actually funny, but as a nervous response to a greeting or a question about himself. I saw Walt for several individual sessions, which I experienced as pure torture due to his whiney voice and help-rejecting complaints. His hostility toward women seemed to be coming out in his relentless, though unintentional, attempts to bore me to death.

At that time, Walt really wanted me to help him make friends and get a job. He had no idea of how his mannerisms offended people. I felt the group would help him by giving him feedback and modeling new modes of behavior. I was surprised at how quickly Walt made changes in the way he interacted in the group. He was a good imitator and quickly picked up new behaviors from watching and listening to other members. Although he always responded with hurt and self-pity to the considerable negative feedback he received, he never failed to change what needed to be changed, for which he received much positive reinforcement. He stopped whining and became a good listener. He lost weight, changed his hairdo, and smiled more often. The last thing to change was the inappropriate laugh, but he even traded that in for a suitable replacement.

Besides feedback, the Nebbish benefits greatly from the nurturing in a supportive group. As the only son of a bitter single woman, Walt had been deprived of touching and affection, probably even in infancy. The tremendous oral neediness I had felt from him in the individual sessions was considerably gratified by a group that cheerfully gave him all the hugs he asked for after sessions. Like most Nebbishes Walt was an oral character type, who needed lots of holding and nurturing.

The other particularly helpful aspect of the group therapy for this Nebbish was the mental stimulation it provided. Walt had had minimal formal education and had led an insular, conventional life. He became fascinated with people's stories and the dynamics of the group. His eyes lit up whenever I told the group a bit of theory or stories about Milton Erickson's astonishing cures. He loved psychodrama and learned to play roles very well.

When he left the group after four years, Walt was handsomer and more solvent, having been employed for over a year. He was living with a competent and intelligent woman, a teacher with several teenage children. Walt was coping well with the enormous demands of being a "stepfather," a role for which he needed his newly developed sense of humor. I would not be surprised if Walt's stepchildren see him as a Mensch.

The Assertive Role

A major goal of most group members is to become more assertive. In the group, they are taught to analyze responses and discriminate between assertive and non-assertive behaviors. One member, Fred, who is mentioned many times throughout this book, created a totally new role for himself as an assertive person over a period of two years in the group. He said:

> I like the way I am when I am there (in the sessions). Before group, and still a lot on the outside, I am whimpy, but in group I confront people. I'm attractive, perceptive, sensitive to others, but objective at the same time. It's taken a long time of group telling me that I am these things for me to believe that "the group me" is real, and can operate outside of group as well.

In group therapy, the assertiveness training that takes place is very similar to the kind offered in organizations and communities during the last several years. Behavior modification, role-playing techniques, and ample positive reinforcement for being assertive are all used to help clients who are learning assertive behaviors. But, as Fred suggests, there is a difference between a bunch of behaviors and a "role." The ongoing group provides a kind of continuous "role rehearsal" that prepares the client to play the new role congruently, comfortably, and forever. This will be illustrated in subsequent chapters.

The Warm-up

Moreno believed that each person has her own way of warming up to roles — of activating her own spontaneity. He said each human being has an individualized manner of preparing to respond emotionally, intellectually, physically, or spiritually. The process occurs swiftly and unconsciously. While we are born with almost perfect warm-up mechanisms, they are sometimes impaired through socialization experiences. Some of our paths for expression become blocked, leaving an unspontaneous response and an inability to respond adequately. We may have difficulty "warming up" to certain feelings, such as anger or love, or we can become blocked from most feelings. We may not be able to cry, dance, make noise, or have sex because we cannot warm up to the feelings necessary to generate these behaviors. Some people can warm up to feelings but fear the consequences — perhaps rejection or isolation — of behaving spontaneously. People encounter problems in their communication when their warm-ups to whatever responses they need in the communication are incomplete or cut off. All defensive maneuvers, whether singular or interpersonal, can be seen as poor warm-ups which eradicate rather than promote spontaneity. We can see, therefore, that the therapy of the individual in a group involves learning adequate warm-up processes (Moreno, 1966; Yablonsky, 1976).

Tony, an extremely talented musician, had a particularly difficult warm-up problem that profoundly affected his personal and professional life. The only way he could get in touch with what he was feeling was to get angry first. Since he could not sing unless he was in touch with his feelings, he had to get angry before each performance. Needless to say, this was hard on his wife, who got the brunt of his hostile warm-up most of the time. It also made therapy difficult for Tony and the group, because Tony had to get furious before he could get into working on anything significant. Not surprisingly, we learned that in Tony's family quiet expression was not recognized and vulnerability was rewarded with humiliation. People could not talk about their anxieties and diffused them in the only way they knew how — by fighting. The task for Tony in group became one of developing other warm-ups that were more direct and less interpersonally expensive, but that would still satisfy the positive intent of the original one in helping him feel safe and preserve his dignity.

Many people take circuitous routes to certain feelings. Some have to be threatened with being left before they realize they feel love; some can only feel sexual passion in conjunction with anger; others warm up to rage by experiencing hurt and anxiety first. Berne (1966) suggested that feelings can be "rackets," authentic to some extent, but serving also as a cover for other less acceptable emotions. A good question for a therapist to ask when a client seem mired in a "rackety" feeling is: "What would you be feeling if you weren't feeling ____?" This clears away the racket, which is really a labored and ineffective warm-up, and gets right to the underlying emotion.

Hunger for action leads people to seek out consciously or unconsciously people to "warm them up" to certain feelings or states of being. This may or may not be a good thing, depending on what the hidden agenda is. Tony's wife did not enjoy warming him up to singing, since it involved his having to get angry at her first, but there is a possibility that she was good at getting him angry, and that was one of the things that attracted him to her!

Moreno mentions that the longer the warm-up, the less the spontaneity (Moreno, 1971). The group helps people shorten their warm-ups, make direct contact with their emotions, and avoid unproductive detours.

Moreno began almost every psychodrama and group meeting with a structured warm-up. These were exercises and activities designed to bring the group together around a certain emotion or theme. His "empty chair" technique has become a standard warm-up technique in many group settings. In this exercise a chair is placed in front of the group and members are invited to imagine a person who is important to them in some way to be sitting in the empty chair. They are then instructed to have a dialogue with that person, first in their minds, and then out loud, playing both the role of themselves and the other person. Another standard Moreno warm-up was a sociometric exercise, designed to put members in touch with their spontaneous reactions and intuitions about others in the group: "Walk around the room and find someone whom you trust . . . (or don't trust . . . or have unfinished business with . . . or believe has something distressing them, etc.)." More sociometric exercises are described on pp. 98–101.

Since Moreno, practitioners of group therapy have invented hundreds of group warm-ups. Many involve ways to get the group members interested and involved with one another. Some involve physical activity, playing a game, exchanging backrubs. Others are fantasy trips, much like hypnotic inductions, designed to bring forth unconscious material to be worked on in the session or to activate creativity and spontaneity.

In an ongoing group, I usually let the group warm up naturally rather than engage in structured exercises. All pre-session behavior, the chatting by the coffee pot in the waiting room, casual remarks about the traffic coming in or the seating in the room are part of the group's warm-up for the night. An important aspect of my role as facilitator is observing the specific difficulties of each group and individual with respect to warming-up, and devising ways to help them improve their warm-ups through the group experience.

Mechanisms of Role Development

Modeling

A major vehicle for role development throughout life is modeling. A large percentage of what children learn derives from watching other people. In therapy group clients benefit greatly from watching other clients model both problems and potential solutions. As group client Terrence said, "It's a chance to be together with peers who are going through similar developmental things and see how they handle them. Also, it's nice to know you are not the only one with these problems."

Group members provide each other with a variety of behaviors and responses to imitate and incorporate into their repertoires. The vivacious flirt can become a model for the plain, self-conscious person; a nurturer in the group can show someone who has difficulty with parenting how to give positive "strokes" and provide safety and caring to others. A client who has difficulty trusting himself and others sees another with similar difficulty taking risks and opening up, and he finds the courage to follow suit. The manipulative or insincere person sees the group responding positively to someone who is authentic and begins to give up some of his "games." A divorced member shares experiences with the recently separated client and models effective ways to cope with the stress and new roles associated with being single.

Frequently, group clients "take pages from one another's books" and avoid making some of the mistakes of their co-members. Sam, whose wife would not have sex with him, was considering an affair. He happened to be in the same group as Margaret (discussed in Chapter II), who, under similar circumstances a year prior to entering therapy, had gone ahead and had an extramarital liaison. She had decided to tell her husband, drastically overestimating his tolerance. He refused to talk to her ever again and promptly divorced her. Sam knew that his wife, although appearing aloof, was as rigid and vulnerable as Margaret's husband had been. He did not want to destroy the marriage or her, which he probably would have done if he had not learned from Margaret's experience. He opted not to have the affair and to try instead to get his wife to go with him to couples therapy.

Modeling and sharing are far more effective tools for role development than advice. As Fred put it, "Advice-giving is usually a tease. People make you feel good by pretending to listen, but you wind up frustrated because they hardly ever follow your advice." In group therapy advice is often given by people when they are avoiding their own issues or feelings about something.

The majority of clients have had losers as role models. Most group members who stay with the group one or two years see plenty of people "win" and are inspired to become "winners" themselves. There is enormous reward for all members in seeing a person come through the group experience with renewed energy, happier lives, and better relationships. As Joan put it, "seeing other people's successes helped me a lot."

Feedback

Group member Lenore said, "I remember being confronted by Bob and Wendy. They said I was whiney, and told me how it was affecting them. I didn't like what I heard from them and I stopped whining. Since then my relationships at home and at work have improved."

Lenore's example is typical of the kind of specific behavioral change that can occur for a group client as a result of feedback from other members.

Her fellow group member, Bob, took a broader view of the importance of feedback, particularly constructive criticism. He eloquently connected the feedback process with the development of trust and new roles.

The neat thing is, whatever the feedback was, it was well-intentioned. At first I didn't know that and it really hurt, but I learned to take it in. What I know now is that in the world, *what is important is not how well-intentioned you are, but how others see you. If you come off like a jerk, you're a jerk.*

Sullivan (1953) stressed that "consensual validation" from other human beings of one's reality and self-perception is a vital factor in mental health. Such consensual validation happens in many ways in group therapy, but particularly through interpersonal feedback. In any group feedback is continual, whether it is consciously noticed or not and regardless of how it is used. In a therapy group the natural processes of feedback are turned into a major therapeutic tool.

All research reviewed by Yalom (1975) on the effectiveness of therapy groups suggests that feedback is of vital therapeutic significance in group therapy. Lieberman, Yalom, and Miles (1972) created a questionnaire for persons who had completed a 30-hour marathon group and who had felt positively about the experience. Of the 14 items deemed most important to group members in the learning experience, intermember feedback was cited most frequently. Yalom, Tinklenberg, and Gilula, in an unpublished study reported in Yalom's book (1975), examined the curative factors in the group therapy of 20 clients who had successfully completed long-term (one to two years) group psychotherapy. "Interpersonal input" was determined to be the number one mechanism of positive therapeutic change.

From Moreno's perspective the process of feedback is important in helping the individual decide which roles to keep and which to cast off or improve upon. Feedback from others is a guide in the process of building and tailoring new roles. In my view, the more feedback flowing back and forth within the group, the more change takes place within the group as a whole. Honest feedback is the catalyst of group therapy. It is the mechanism by which positive reinforcement is given, self-examination is sparked, and behavioral change is promoted.

The general systems theory definition of negative and positive feedback illuminates why and how these phenomena are so important in the process of change for the individual. Negative and positive feedback are two kinds of information taken in by a system. The former initiates change; the second continues the action of the system. Paraphrasing the glossary of Durkin (1981, p. 343): negative feedback uses "the error signal" to force the action of the system back to the ideal or set point, while positive feedback drives the action of the system "to the limits of its functioning and beyond." Negative feedback nudges the system to stop its direction and reorient itself toward its homeostatic balance; positive feedback drives current behavior to continue. "Neurotic cycles of crisis and exhaustion are positive linear feedback configuration because they do not transform themselves as a result of their experience" (Durkin, 1981, p. 343). In other words, neurotics tend not to pick up error signals and are not sensitive to negative feedback. Therapy group members are exposed to considerable negative feedback, which interrupts the runaway ("positive") linear thrust of their problematic behavior. Once they have made a needed change, they then receive positive feedback, which keeps them progressing in the new direction.

In colloquial psychotherapy terms "negative feedback" generally means criticism and "positive feedback" means positive reinforcement. The glossary in Kaplan and Sadock (1971) defines feedback in group as "an expressed response by one person to another person's *behavior*" (p. 839, emphasis added). Constructive feedback refers to something that the receiver of the feedback can and might want to do something about; it is neither an attack on her whole personality nor a criticism of her beliefs or values.

Giving and taking feedback are among the most difficult and important skills taught in group therapy. In giving feedback, one must learn not to project one's own problems onto the other, not to attack, not to make unwarranted assumptions. In taking feedback, one must learn to accept criticism thoughtfully, adopting a non-defensive attitude. Much of this is very hard for most people. Clients who were brought up in environments where hostile put-downs, derision, and physical abuse constituted the only mechanisms of feedback may be so bruised that at first they hear even the mildest of well-meaning criticisms as attacks. Those from families where subtle indirect communications — pained looks, sarcastic comments, raised eyebrows and the like — were substituted for verbal feedback may also feel devastated at the slightest negative comment; they also cannot speak their minds and give straight feedback, because they project their hypersensitivity onto the other party and assume that that person will be destroyed or hate them if they say anything negative. An important role of the group leader is to model appropriate ways of giving and taking feedback. She should be willing to confront whenever necessary and should be as open to criticism as she expects her group members to be.

Sometimes a person in group receives valuable feedback through a psychodramatic technique known as *role reversal*. This is when two people literally switch roles for a few minutes, each trying as best she can to talk and behave, even feel, like the other. This is done not to poke fun, but to give each person the opportunity to see and hear for herself how she is coming across to that other person.

Terrence, a civil engineer in his twenties, was new to the group and was generally garrulous and approval-seeking. One night he was gently rebuked by another member, Bob. Hurt and angry, Terrence fell into a morose silence, and group members' attempts to draw him out were unsuccessful. I asked if anyone wanted to reverse roles and be Terrence. Bob volunteered. Other members chuckled, knowing Bob might play this part well, since he had acted the same way when he first came into group. Bob sat in Terrence's seat, sprawled out against the pillows, assuming the same pitiful expression Terrence had been wearing. Terrence, as Bob, tried to get Bob's Terrence to talk, and was responded to with monosyllables and grunts. When back in his own role, Terrence expressed disbelief that he had been "as bad as that." Everyone confirmed that Bob's portrayal had not been exaggerated. Terrence readily relinquished his "sulking" act, when, through the feedback of the role reversal, he saw for himself how unbecoming a role it really was.

Other feedback comes in the form of *positive reinforcement.* Endless examples come to mind of members' recognition of one another's attempts to change both inside and outside the group: kudos for shy Gwen when she gave a party; awed appreciation for Jason in his courageous, loving efforts to reach out and help his parents, even after they had rejected him; praise for Lily when she finally told Henrietta to stop snubbing her. As Tom put it,

> I needed to hear stuff about myself to reinforce positive stuff not reinforced by my parents. When you hear good things about yourself from five or six people who aren't being paid to tell you, you begin to believe it. After being out of group a year, I still fall back on nice things people said about me.

Terrence also named positive reinforcement as a major value of group therapy, saying,

> A principle of group therapy is to build self-concept and positively reinforce people for just being real human beings. Positive strokes from the therapists and the group are very important in this.

Many group members need a lot of practice before they can trust the sincerity of the group's positive reinforcement. As Bob said, "It took a long time to accept compliments—to believe people when they said I was nice, smart, and caring."

Permission to Express Feelings

Part and parcel of developing new roles is having the spontaneity to express feelings. Most people have difficulty getting warmed up to and/or expressing at least some of their innermost feelings. Some may be afraid to feel their feelings, lest their feelings overwhelm them. Others might feel the need to hold their feelings in, lest they be misunderstood or used against them by others. Group provides ongoing permission to feel and to express emotions in a safe, caring, and respectful environment.

Group therapy clients consistently report that having one's true feelings heard, understood, and accepted by the group is a major value of the group therapy process (Yalom, 1975). Group members are continually experimenting with expressing deeper levels of feeling. If the risks they take bring them understanding and acceptance from the group, they will begin to allow themselves to be more spontaneous and feeling in other contexts.

One of my group therapy trainers, Bob Singer, said to me,

> The value of group is that people talk about things which they have loaded up with shame and guilt; they express those feelings and all the others beneath, and they find that people are not overwhelmed. The result is a detoxification of those areas.

A group member, Tom, put is more graphically. "I remember the feeling of getting everything out, and afterwards feeling like I had just thrown up. It was out. It was okay." Terrence said, "Self-worth comes from being cared about by people you have dumped all your garbage to. It's okay, because it's all a part of you." From the language and metaphors used here, we can see that expressing one's feelings fully in group is a form of unconscious regression — to the "somatic" roles in Moreno's vocabulary, to pregenital stages of development in psychoanalytic terminology. Group clients frequently talk about "holding onto shit" versus "letting go of it." The dilemma of the two-year-old in trying to decide whether to retain or let go of feces is unconsciously recalled as the group member is faced with the possibility of releasing herself from the pain of holding on to her feelings. The terrible fear of loss of control and of the emptiness that she might be left with should she let go may stop her from revealing her innermost feelings for quite some time. When she does give in, she learns that, in fact, she has more, not less, control because she has her spontaneity and flexibility. She also has the warmth and caring of the group to fill up the empty spaces.

CHAPTER IV

Change on the
Interpersonal Level

INTERPERSONAL LEARNING

The goal of group therapy is "interpersonal learning" (Yalom, 1975). Given that no one transcends the need for human contact, acceptance, social intercourse, and being noticed, the therapy group is an optimum environment in which the individual can have some of his need for people met while, at the same time, acquiring vital skills in the area of managing interpersonal relationships.

Sullivan (1940) emphasized the therapeutic importance of the reconciliation of the individual's self-concept with the view others have of him. He stated that psychiatric cure is the "expanding of the self to such final effect that the patient is known to himself as much as the patient behaving to others" (p. 237).

A crucial aspect of interpersonal learning in group therapy involves bringing the individual's frame of reference into alignment with the world's view of him. Such alignment is necessary for reduction of cognitive dissonance and, therefore, of anxiety. It is also a necessary condition for one to be able to use the human resources in one's environment. For example, if one has the idea, based on childhood experiences, that one is not at all lovable, one will probably fail to even see, much less avail oneself of, potential nurturing from others, and emotional starvation will be the result. Only a correction of the original cognitive distortion will open up pathways for gratification for this individual.

Interpersonal learning in group therapy occurs through powerful emotional experiences that serve to break apart the individual's rigid and limited views of his environment and render him accessible to more expansive possibilities for interaction. Our multifarious assumptions, desires, and fantasies regarding our importance to others, how lovable we are or aren't, and all our ideas about what others mean to us, can give us, or expect from us—all are subject to challenge and reevaluation in group therapy. Interpersonal learning in group therapy, then, becomes synonymous with changing frames of reference.

This chapter will explore ways in which interpersonal learning occurs in groups. First, we will look at *"contact operations,"* the ways people go about making contact with one another authentically and inauthentically, and how these change through group therapy. Next, we will study the phenomenon of *contact* itself—the magic of interpersonal electricity. We will examine ways and situations in which people do and do not make contact, showing how group members can learn to increase the quantity of contact in their lives. We will see how people in group learn to *communicate* clearly and effectively in the group. Finally, we will point out some important skills and concepts group members absorb through the group experience, having to do with *relatedness* and *relationships.*

"CONTACT OPERATIONS" AND THE INTERPERSONAL FRAME OF REFERENCE

"Contact operations" is a phrase used by Bach (1954) to encompass the ways people have of making contact with each other and the motivations and experiential determinants of these efforts. Contact operations are determined by "the cognitive field" (Lewin, in Bach, 1954), the perceived possibilities for contact in any given moment. The cognitive field is the interpersonal frame of reference out of which contact operations, modes of being with people, are developed.

That internalized experiences often are externalized at a later time was one of Freud's greatest discoveries. Through repetition compulsion, the human being recreates unresolved interpersonal conflicts in his present environment. Bach (1954) suggests a reason for the urge to do this: "the contact drive," the need to seek a particular kind of contact for purposes of emotional and biological tension reduction (p. 219). The type of interaction that caused difficulty to begin with is replicated by the person again and again, motivated by the unconscious desire to obtain the needed response that was not forthcoming in the first place. The contact drive is a necessary spur in the "keep-on-doing-it-'til-we-get-it-right" compulsion.

Healthy contact operations are those by which a person interacts with another in the here-and-now, without transferential distortion. Such operations involve paying attention to and using the feedback of the other in order to obtain a desired response. Obtaining a desired response from another requires that the "cognitive field" (perceived contact possibilities) and the "social field" (actual possibilities) match.

From a general systems theory point of view, contact operations could be seen in terms of boundary function. In this frame of reference the individual is seen as a system with the capacity to open or close its own boundaries to include or exclude information or emotion. Helen Durkin (1981) sees healthy boundary functions as those which enhance or restore a person's autonomy. Healthy contact operations for Durkin would then consist of those which maintain healthy boundaries for the individual, keeping the system nourished but discrete (separate). Unhealthy contact operations for Durkin would be transferential responses, which represent resistances: she describes resistance as "a case of dysfunctionally closed boundaries across which patterns of interaction could not effectively be transported" (p. 14). People who are embroiled in transferential patterns are unable to take in new information and emotion. Recognizing and analyzing transferences helps to restore healthy boundary function, and leads to an internal reorganization of the system characterized by more spontaneous and adaptive responses in interactions.

Upon entering a therapy group, clients are less likely to engage in *unhealthy contact* operations. They carry in agendas from a different time and place, which cloud their vision and prevent them from seeing others as they are. Unhealthy contact operations play a part in, but are not identical with, *transferences*, unconscious attempts by one person to superimpose a *relationship* from the past and outside of the therapy setting onto the relationship at hand. Faulty contact operations hark back to other *interactions*, not whole relationships. They are maneuvers which are motivated not by what is going on in the here-and-now, but by an anxious need to either recreate or avoid a particular kind of interaction. In unhealthy contact operations, objectives are confused; the person is operating out of two time frames simultaneously. Unhealthy contact operations never bring the desired response and rarely any other response which is satisfactory.

Unhealthy contact operation patterns start for a person when he experiences an interpersonal interaction or contact that causes him great pain. That experience is stored in the person's unconscious (as well as, perhaps, his conscious) mind, from which it serves to motivate him from then on *to avoid*, at all costs, a recurrence of this circumstance. Since the contact drive persists, however, the risk of a repeat performance of the "critical" contact is continuously present. For example, if, in a person's family, someone getting angry meant he was going to be hit, he might go out of his way to be ingratiating, to manipulate people out of any anger they might feel, while still seeking their approval, love, and admiration. In doing so, he engenders in them exactly the response he so desperately fears: frustration and hostility. The attempt to get the positive contact is generally foiled by the anxious need to avoid the critical contact.

In unhealthy contact operations one attempts to influence the behavior of others without attending to how one's own behavior is affecting them. A great deal of group therapy involves becoming aware of one's conscious and unconscious motives in the process of contacting others. Usually the "critical contact incidents" must be faced; what must be learned is what genuine need existed that was not met as a result of the catastrophic contact incident. When this need is filled, the compulsive striving and avoidance can cease.

Clearing past contact experiences out of the way through the group interaction allows group members to approach each communication with freshness and spontaneity. They learn to attend to external cues in communication, rather than to operate only out of their "internal maps." They begin to get the responses they seek from others and to deal with — even benefit from — threatening encounters.

"SET-UPS" AND "THERAGNOSIS"

Ruesch and Bateson (1951) comment that the "neurotic creates a stage in his environment in an unsuccessful attempt to communicate certain messages and obtain certain responses" (p. 88). The context in which this happens most obviously (and not just with "neurotics," but with people in all diagnostic categories) is in the therapy group. Bach (1954) noticed how people in therapy groups set each other up to play the programmed role in their dramas. He calls these unconscious co-manipulations *"set-up operations."* The analysis in group therapy is, in large part, a continuing assessment of the collusion of members, via their interlocking scripts, to play the roles called for in one another's dramas.

A question never fully answered in psychoanalytic theory or in Bach's or Moreno's work is exactly *why* set-ups in group are mutual. Why, when a role is vacant, does someone in the group almost always come forth unconsciously to fill it? This mysterious phenomenon is illuminated by examining it in the light of the general systems theory model of group therapy. Therapy clients by definition have inadequate boundary function. They take in and give out information in ways that are inappropriate and maladaptive. They readily respond to pressure to behave or feel in ways dictated from the outside rather than from inside themselves. The group, like any other system, seeks to maintain a balance within itself. If a role in one subsystem (individual client's "social atom" or "group imago") is crying to be filled, the whole system is thrown off kilter until someone takes the role. Given the presence of a group of people who are prone to respond to the script demands of others, the therapy group will readily stabilize via the mechanism of mutual set-ups. H. Durkin (1981, p. 23) says that analysis of the transferences is itself a "boundarying" mechanism which "prepares the members for opening and closing their boundaries more functionally on their own." As individual members' boundary functions improve, they more often maintain their identity in response to set-up demands. This destabilizes the group system, forcing it to reorganize in patterns based on autonomous individual functioning and healthy interdependence.

Bach (1954) points out that, in group therapy, diagnosis, analysis, and therapy are inextricably woven together. He terms this "*theragnosis*." Theragnosis involves the monitoring and reframing of set-up operations, as well as the creation of a new interpersonal frame of reference. First, the client is literally caught in the act of trying to manipulate people into playing roles that either were played or were failed to be played by people in the past. He then becomes aware that these maneuvers on his part have never really worked, and have, in fact, caused him, as well as others, great frustration, so he becomes motivated to change the defensive behaviors. The group can then help him analyze the original meaning, or "positive intent," of the problem behaviors. What purpose did the defense mechanisms serve? From what did they protect him? What is the underlying threat or need that must be addressed in order that the maladaptive patterns may be dropped? When these questions are answered, the client can find a way to get that need met, either in the group or outside; he lets go of the unhealthy contact operations and develops new ones to replace them.

A "Perfect Set-up"

It is easier for a client to leave his symptoms at home in individual therapy than in group therapy. While a client might be able to avoid playing out his pathological behaviors in a one-to-one relationship with the therapist, it is unlikely he will be able to do so in group therapy, given the large slate of transferences available and the intensity of the situation. Even though the ultimate goal of group therapy is for each client to be able to be authentic and spontaneous in his communication, we welcome unhealthy contact operations and set-ups when they occur, for it is then that the theragnosis can begin.

Treatment had been pokey and not very effective for Sarah in her six months of participation in group. Then she contracted hepatitis and was absent for three months. During this time she talked with all group members on the phone frequently and received visits from many of them.

Sarah, an employment counselor, age 36, had recently divorced an immature man after a 14-year marriage. She was resentfully engaged in an ongoing rivalry with him for the affections of and influence over their 13-year-old daughter. She was struggling to support her daughter and herself financially, while also trying to embark on life as a single woman, having little social or sexual experience to go on. Sarah was the oldest of two daughters. She seldom spoke with her parents, but still felt the very high expectations they had placed on her.

The set-up occurred when Sarah returned to group. Her first night back she rather jubilantly walked into the meeting carrying a huge bowl of strawberries, whipped cream, sugar, cups and spoons. Almost immediately, she began dishing out the delicacy, taking great care to ask each person how much he or she wanted. It took 25 minutes, during which time one young man tried in vain to talk about a problem. The only comments from the group, directed to Sarah, were "how nice, how delicious," and so on.

In the next session, people's true feelings and fantasies about Sarah and her strawberries tumbled forth. Most members had been annoyed with Sarah for disrupting the meeting and now were angry at themselves for not saying so at the time. This was the here-and-now level. As the discussion continued, it became clear that Sarah's gesture had sparked reactions from other levels of people's psyches as well. Here are just a few of the responses.

Henry said that he had been furious at Sarah the night she returned to group, before he even saw her. "I know it's irrational, but I feel you abandoned me by being sick." Henry's response to the strawberries at the time had been to very pleasantly refuse, saying he was allergic to them. In fact, he told us, this was a lie; he *loved* strawberries! But he did not want Sarah to "get away with buying herself back into the group."

Henry's response to Sarah had much more to do with his relationship with his mother than with Sarah. The response he wanted from Sarah was guilt, which he had been good at getting his mother to feel, in order to mitigate his fear that she would abandon him, as she had done for a few months when he was two.

Cindy, who had spent most of her 25 years taking care of alcoholic parents, said Sarah's bringing the strawberries made her feel guilty for not having visited Sarah enough when she was sick. Consistent with her childhood crusade to find love and appreciation, Cindy's response to Sarah's strawberry set-up was to make further demands on herself to show Sarah how much she cared about her.

John, who had gotten in some trouble in his life by being seductive with his friends' wives, sheepishly told us that he had had an immediate sexual response to Sarah and her strawberries, but had not wanted to share his lascivious thoughts for fear he would be considered crude. "Not at all!" was the general reaction to John's admission. "After all, what could be more seductive than a luscious bowl of strawberries in the middle of winter!"

Sarah herself realized some unconscious goings-on in her that had motivated her effort. She said that, while sick and immobilized, she became aware of how much she relied on physical modes of expression. Specifically, she realized that "doing things" for people represented one of her few ways of making contact. Bringing the strawberries was a perfect example of that particular faulty contact operation. Sarah had brought the strawberries out of guilt and anxiety. Never thinking about what *she* had missed by being absent, she was worried that people would be angry at her for not being around for *them*. She was "going for" the group's forgiveness and approval, and all she got from them was confusion, anger, and guilt.

I felt Sarah's endeavor had another meaning as well. It felt like Sarah was competing with me in a struggle similar to the one she and her ex-husband were engaged in for their daughter, only this time Sarah was going to be the "good guy." She seemed to be saying to me, as a stand-in for her ex-husband, "I will entice this group (these children) away from you. I will be the nice fun parent, the one that the kids like, and you can take my usual role of being the spoil-sport, the one who has to be realistic and grownup and is never appreciated for it." She was also implying that she was a better "parent" than I, when she said she felt guilty for not being around to take care of people.

In addition to all the other things it communicated, Sarah's bringing strawberries was a sincerely generous act and was recognized as such. No one level of meaning of a communication invalidates any other. It must be remembered that "set-ups" are unconscious; furthermore, they are usually harmless. If they are intentional and/or malicious, the people involved in them must be held accountable for their actions, but otherwise, the underlying hostility of a set-up can be dealt with without the perpetrator(s) having to feel guilty or blamed. After all, engaging in set-ups is part of the client's task—showing the group what his problem is.

The strawberry incident marked a turning point in the group in two important respects. First, the group realized that choosing not to speak about their reactions to Sarah right away was indicative of the kind of lack of assertiveness and spontaneity that they usually demonstrated in their lives. Realizing in retrospect that no negative consequences would have been forthcoming had they confronted Sarah immediately, they became irritated at their own passivity, and became more motivated to change it. Most members began to speak their minds much more readily in the group after that.

Secondly, the group had, up to that point, been very superficial in their analysis of their own behavior. Shunning the notion of unconscious motivation, many of them would giggle and shake their heads if it was pointed out to them that they were behaving in ways that revealed other thoughts and feelings than those that they were verbally expressing. Sarah had been particularly resistant to looking beyond the most literal interpretations of behavior. The strawberry set-up made clear to everybody, including Sarah, that there is plenty going on to which our conscious minds are oblivious, and that, whether we accept it or not, we are constantly communicating to one another unconsciously via our actions. This idea, which had previously been very threatening to Sarah, now began to intrigue her and she became more curious about the mysterious inner workings of herself and others. She began making observations in the group that were quite insightful. Her new awareness helped her make a little more sense out of her interpersonal experiences in the group and out, which gave her more confidence in her relationships with her daughter and the new men in her life.

Set-ups Outside the Group Meeting

Some group therapists impose rigid rules against socializing and telephone contact among group members, on the theory that such association will breed resistance and dilute the quality of the therapy sessions. I find exactly the opposite to be true. The set-ups that are generated outside the group during social contacts are as transferential in nature as the ones generated inside. Analysis of these set-ups is extremely productive, as the case of Erica, Joan, and Terrence, discussed below, illustrates. In order for this to happen, the therapist must be extremely alert and tuned in to her group. Group members will usually let the therapist know what's going on outside the group, one way or another, but sometimes their ways of informing are ambiguous and indirect. A requirement for set-ups to be effectively analyzed is a commitment from the group to work on any issue that comes up, including incidents that occur outside the meeting. The fortitude necessary to handle outside set-ups, which can be anxiety-provoking or embarrassing, can only exist in a group that is cohesive. It is less likely to be present, at least on a consistent basis, in a group that is still in its early stages of formation or undergoing crises in membership (see section on Cohesiveness in Chapter V).

There are other reasons why I do not impose rules against extra-group contact:

1) Part of the purpose of a therapy group is to teach people how to build support systems in their environment; it seems contradictory to stress that interdependence is healthy and then turn around and tell clients not to use the interpersonal resources of the group during the week.
2) Another function of the group is to teach socialization skills. After-group get-togethers afford some members their first opportunities to learn to be with peers in unstructured contexts. At meetings following group events, such clients can obtain encouragement and positive reinforcement for their social efforts, as well as feedback regarding ways in which they might improve their social skills.
3) Finally, to forbid clients to see each other outside is to practically guarantee that they will do so out of rebellion; such furtive meetings lend themselves to sexual liaisons among members, a situation which presents a number of problems in group therapy, as the following section will explain.

Sexual Relationships Within the Group and the "No-sex Rule"

It has been my experience that sexual relationships between group members tend to have a destructive effect on the group as a whole in a number of ways. First, one or both parties will probably be embarrassed to discuss the sexual encounter and will quit the group so as not to have to deal with it. If they do bring it up, and the sexual partners stay in the group, it may present problems in that the sexually-linked pair is more exclusive than other subgroups. Other members may feel left out and jealous and, depending on the stability or maturity of the group, may even drop out. When the relationship peters out — which such liaisons usually do, since they often have their origins in resistance to the therapy — the pair and the group have to deal with the breakup. At this point divisive allegiances may be formed. Again, one or both parties might drop out at this stage, because they do not want to take responsibility for ending the affair or to face being rejected in front of the group. Group therapy sexual pairings which survive tend to take up an inordinate amount of group time, becoming a handy vehicle for the resistance of other members.

The individuals who become sexually involved rarely benefit from the experience, and in some instances the sexual affair can destroy their therapy.

For one thing, the people who are most likely to have a sexual encounter with another member are, in all likelihood, the clients who most need to work therapeutically on issues relating to sex and relationships. If they act their sexual problems out, and then are inhibited from talking freely because of the presence of their sexual partner, they may defeat the whole purpose of being in group. A set-up is only useful if it can be discussed and analyzed fully.

Since the 1960s there has developed in our society a permissiveness with regard to sexual intimacy which has engendered a pressure among many single adults to go to bed with almost everyone they date. Most adults today must at some time struggle with issues regarding their sexuality and how freely they wish to use it. For many, moral strictures have been intellectually cast aside, but inhibitions and guilt about sex linger on. The need to discuss feelings about all this is very great, and actual sexual relationships within the group greatly inhibit everyone' from speaking freely.

About five years ago, after a few negative experiences with intragroup affairs, I made a "rule" against sexual contact among members. The policy is that, if two people agree that they want to have sex together, they are asked first to discuss their attraction for one another with the group, or at least with me. If they are sure they want a sexual relationship, then we will arrange for them to be in two different therapy groups, or they can be seen individually or as a couple. In this way, both the couple and the group are relieved of extraneous responsibilities having to do with the relationship. The "no-sex" rule is explained at the beginning of a new group or whenever a new member joins.

In the past five years no sexual liaisons have occurred in my groups. While many have considered having affairs, after thinking it over and discussing it with the group, all pairs have opted for continuing as co-group members rather than becoming lovers. In interviewing my clients about how they feel about the rule, they unanimously agree that it is very useful. They say it is a great relief to be in a group of male and female peers, where one is relieved of the responsibility of having to seduce, reject, or be rejected. They find it comfortable and informative to discuss sexual matters with members of the opposite sex without having to worry about turning off potential partners.

People do seem to be much more relaxed in discussing sex in group than they were before the "no-sex" rule. Delicate matters such as sexual dysfunction and sexual perversions are discussed openly for the first time by many group members. Members feel comfortable expressing their sexual feelings for one another, without having any compulsion to act on them. Important information is exchanged about birth control and venereal disease. As they become more relaxed with the topic, group members begin to explore the matter of sex more fully, investigating the interplay of sex with love, marriage, and children.

Sadomasochistic Set-ups

The concept of sadomasochism is frightening, conjuring up images of whips and chains. It is, however, at the root of most set-ups and must be understood if one is to do effective theragnosis within the group. Susan Schad-Somers has written an excellent book, *Sadomasochism: Etiology and Treatment* (1982), which is a synthesis of her own and others' psychoanalytic work on the subject and a useful guide to the psychotherapy of sadomasochistic individuals. She says that group therapy is an almost indispensable part of the treatment of such individuals.

Here we are looking at sadomasochism from two perspectives: as a particular form of psychopathology, and as a dynamic in interpersonal interaction. In both, *projective identification* is a key factor. Projective identification is a primitive defense mechanism that involves the psychological splitting of oneself into "good guy" and "bad guy," and placing the undesirable "bad guy" part onto another. It occurs on the individual, group, and societal level and is always pathological. Politically, for example, it is seen in the form of extreme nationalism, where countries define themselves as irreproachable and others as totally evil. The phenomena of racism and scapegoating are social forms of projective identification.

With respect to individual psychopathology, the adult who employs projective identification exaggeratedly and repeatedly has clearly never learned to accept himself as one, whole, "okay" person, with some good qualities and some that are not so good. If he does begin to acknowledge his darker side, he tends to lose the "good guy" part and to think of himself as all bad, while projecting the "good part" onto another — often the same person that had previously embodied the "bad guy" part. (Projective identification, often referred to as "splitting" is a hallmark of the clinical diagnosis "borderline personality.") When it is brought into the realm of one's actual relationships, projective identification leads to sadomasochism.

Projective identification is a device used unconsciously by the sadomasochistic individual to shift responsibility for his own inadequacies away from himself. His two divergent views of himself — as either all-good or all-bad — are both highly inaccurate vis-à-vis the way the world sees him. He has difficulty forming relationships because one part of him is too good for everybody and the other is totally unacceptable.

Sadomasochistic persons are narcissistic, but they are not, like the simple narcissist, able to just throw off unwanted parts of themselves on anyone who happens to be around. Sadomasochists are *driven* to be in relationships with people who will actually play the other roles — will be a "bad guy" to their "good guy" and vice versa.

With the sadomasochist there are a number of different packages that "good" and "bad" come in. Figure 1 illustrates the kinds of roles played by the sadomasochist when he is being the masochist and when he is being the sadist. All roles fit into the good-bad dimension *and* the weak-strong dimension. Certain masochistic roles mesh with certain sadistic roles and the result is a two-person "dance." Often the sadistic-masochistic duo are so synchronized in their interaction that it is impossible to tell who is leading and who is following.

In any therapy group one is likely to have sadomasochistic individuals who initiate sadomasochistic "dances" with others in the group. Even if there are no bona fide sadomasochists in the group, when anyone's masochistic roles emerge they are inevitably met by sadistic counterparts through mutual set-up operations. The story of Erica and her group is a paradigm of sadomasochistic set-ups in the group context, where everyone's tendencies toward sadism and masochism were tested. The case is also an example of a rigorous and successful therapeutic effort on the part of the clients, the co-therapist,

Figure 1

MASOCHIST

	GOOD	EVIL	
WEAK	VERY INNOCENT VICTIM Gets abused by: *Savage Brute* Hides: strength in victim position	DESERVES PUNISHMENT Gets abused by: *Righteous Angry God* Hides: rage and hostility	WEAK
STRONG	*I Can Take It* Gets abused by: *Biting Baby* Hides: vulnerability	XXXXXXXXXXXXXXXX	STRONG

*SADIST

	GOOD	EVIL	
WEAK	XXXXXXXXXXXX	BITING BABY Abuses: *I Can Take It*	WEAK
STRONG	RIGHTEOUS ANGRY GOD Abuses: *"Deserves* *Punishment"*	SAVAGE BRUTE Abuses: *Very Innocent* *Victim*	STRONG

*N.B. Each type of masochist meshes with his *opposite* on the sadist chart—i.e., *Good-Weak* Masochist with *Evil-Strong* Sadist; *Evil-Weak* Masochist with *Good-Strong* Sadist, etc.

and myself. Realizing and confronting our own sadomasochistic frames of reference constituted one of the most significant pieces of interpersonal learning any of us will ever experience.

Erica, Terrence, and Joan: A Case Study of Sadomasochistic Set-ups

Erica, a 27-year-old businesswoman, was attractive in an adolescent way; she was also intelligent, articulate, and perceptive. Her presenting problem was her relationship with a very unsavory individual named Jake. She said she thought she probably should break up with him—that "he was no good for her"—but she was afraid of being alone. She reported that the sexual relationship with him was the only satisfying one she had ever had. Jake was a sportscar salesman who dealt drugs on the side and carried a couple of loaded guns. He frequently endangered Erica's life by driving his car while drunk or drugged. He rarely hurt her physically, but he intentionally tortured her emotionally, humiliating her in public and teasing her by blatantly engaging in affairs with other women and frequently having sex with his wife, whom he was always "about to" divorce. Each time Jake lied, cheated, or abused her, Erica was genuinely surprised and terribly hurt. But nothing could stop her from wanting to be with him. If he called, she would jump. She was addicted to him and he knew it; he smugly told her that she was his "fish on a hook"—he would let out the line just far enough to let her think she was free and then he would reel her in.

Erica came from a disturbed family. The father was an alcoholic. Her mother was cold and depressed, with a very violent temper. Erica's mother often told the children that they were the cause of all her problems and that Erica's birth had almost killed her. The family kept a front of absolute propriety in the community, and Erica always did very well in school socially and academically. The four children were handled severely, with authoritarian discipline. They spent every Saturday morning polishing the silver; they were hardly allowed to play; the parents never took the children out or paid much attention to them. Father drank constantly; mother and the grandfather who lived with them drank frequently as well.

When Erica was 17 her father tried to rape her. After it happened, Erica did not tell anyone. A few years later her father tried to rape her younger sister. The sister told Erica and Erica told her older sister, who revealed that it had happened to her too. Erica went to her mother, who denied the whole thing and punished the girls for "lying" about their father. Erica went to a priest to tell him about it, but he chastised her severely for disloyalty to her family, and admonished her against mentioning the matter to anyone again. Thereafter, rather than holding her father, her mother, or the priest accountable for their betrayal of her, Erica blamed herself for her father's attack on her sister, believing that if she, Erica, had told the authorities when her father attacked her, she could have prevented him doing it to her sister.

Erica had come into individual therapy two months prior to entering group. At that time she was making her first attempt to split up with Jake, but was terrified and ambivalent. She was taking drugs, and alternately running from Jake or chasing after him at all times of the day and night. Finally, she scratched her wrists with a pin and was admitted to a psychiatric hospital for four weeks.

Upon her release from the hospital, Erica joined group. She seemed determined to separate from Jake. For the first several weeks of her participation, she was talkative and helpful to others, but her discussion of her own problems was superficial. She talked about herself only as a victim of Jake, trying to enlist the group's help in analyzing him. ("I don't understand how he could do that to me. Doesn't he know he hurt me? What's wrong with him?"). She did not tell the group about her father's trying to rape her, nor how she had been abused in other ways in childhood.

When the group learned what a dangerous and deceitful character Jake was, they naturally wanted to "help" Erica split up with him. This turned out to be far more difficult than it appeared. Despite her vocal complaints and their good advice, Erica saw Jake as much as ever.

The group naturally became frustrated with Erica. "We think you *like* this situation, or else you'd get out of it," they exclaimed. I made a half-facetious comment that, for Erica, "seeing Jake is like lying down in the middle of the Interstate 95." The next week she had a bad automobile accident on Interstate 95. (I learned from that experience to avoid sadistic remarks of any kind, no matter how facetious or innocuous they may seem, when talking with an actively masochistic individual.) At the point that we began to criticize her, Erica began to miss meetings, and when she did attend, she reported even more frightening stories of her involvement with Jake, as well as with drugs and alcohol.

Our efforts to promote her separation from Jake were having the opposite effect. Our frustration with her was propelling Erica to Jake. This was because, in the sadomasochistic sense, Jake was an important part of Erica that she could not part with, but could not acknowledge as her own. He was her "bad part." Erica's issue was trust. She could not trust anyone. Jake was safe because he was *so* untrustworthy that he could not really disappoint her the way someone who was supposed to be trustworthy, like her parents, could.

Group members and therapists were supposed to be trustworthy, and the possibility that she might give in to this need to depend on people and then be betrayed by us was too frightening to contemplate. It was easier to set the group up to be angry with her, and thereby maintain her isolated, but inviolate, position.

It became clear to me that the group had been set up by Erica to play the sadistic role, to take over where Jake and her parents had left off in criticizing, humiliating, and rejecting her. If we were to gain her trust and help her, we had to get out of that role and into the role of accepting, rather than critical, parents. In front of Erica I told the group that I wanted them to stop telling Erica to split up from Jake—that this was like telling her to cut off her arm. I said I would never again object to her seeing him as long as she did not put herself in physical danger. Erica promised to keep herself physically safe. All her drug use ceased at that point.

Some of the group members were more willing to take the tack I was suggesting with Erica than others. Two women took me up on the idea of helping Erica feel safe. They became close friends with her outside the group; with great forbearance and generosity they fielded her attempts to get them to criticize her about Jake. They valued her loyalty and helpfulness to them, and continued to find their relationships with her rewarding. One of the men, Jason, was sympathetic to Erica's predicament with Jake, and gave her encouragement through the year in her step-by-step process of ridding herself of her pariah.

The other group members—three men and one woman—however, had a lot more trouble with the new approach to Erica. Their own issues with sadomasochism were beginning to surface, and it had been much easier to play the "one-up" position with Erica than it was going to be to face their own masochistic and sadistic conflicts. One man, Terrence, had a mother who had physically and verbally abused him throughout childhood. She had frequent rage attacks during which she would hit and kick him and lock him out of the house. Once she put a spoon in the flame of the gas stove and burned his back with it. Her verbal onslaughts were even more devastating than her physical attacks. This mother, who, in retrospect, was clearly psychotic, was never in psychiatric treatment. Terrence was urged by his father to try to be nice to his mother and not provoke her. At the time of his group participation, when he was in his late twenties, Terrence was still confused and frightened by all of this, feeling that his mother's abuse of him was somehow his fault. Terrence had one recurring dream: His mother was drowning in a swimming pool and he could not save her. The sadistic "wish" and the masochistic "fear" were combined in the dream, as they were in Terrence's relationships with women, all of which were characterized by masochism on the woman's part. His longest and most intense intimate involvement was a two-year relationship with a woman who was anorexic. (The dynamics surrounding anorexia are classically sadomasochistic.) The breakup of this relationship, dovetailing with the end of graduate school, precipitated a two-year depression, toward the end of which he sought treatment. Terrence's experience of himself was as the victim; however, most people thought of him as angry and brash.

Joan, whose life history and role development were discussed in Chapter III, had been in the group for two years before Erica and Terrence entered. Although she was as talented, ambitious, and attractive as Erica, Joan felt vastly inferior to her. Erica became for Joan both an idol and an object of jealousy. During the first eight months of Erica's participation, Joan rarely talked of her negative feelings toward Erica, couching her statements in an admiration that was incongruous, given Erica's obvious inability to manage her life. At times Joan would even express envy at Erica's "fast and glamorous life" with Jake and his crowd, completely ignoring the seedy and dangerous aspects of it. Joan's confused perception of Erica, as well as her brewing hostility, reminded me of her mixed feelings about her mother (the "costumer"), whom she had wanted to admire, but who disgusted Joan with her passivity, obesity, and alcoholism.

Among these three people two complex mutual set-ups developed — one with Terrence and Erica, and the other with Joan and Erica. The two "dramas" had the whole group for a cast, not just the pairs who made themselves the focus. In both instances, the group's collusion made the set-ups possible, and the group's "theragnosis" helped the individuals involved and other members uncover sadomasochistic conflicts within themselves and begin to resolve them.

About a month after Erica and Terrence joined the group, Erica invited Terrence for a drink and told him that she was very attracted to him. Terrence was flattered, but sensed sabotage. Since the "no-sex rule" had just recently been discussed, Terrence wondered if Erica was trying to jeopardize both his and her positions in the group. He brought the incident up in group, and Erica was very embarrassed. She protested that she was just stating her feelings about Terrence and was not trying to seduce him. She seemed to be angry that Terrence brought it up. In retrospect, I understand that Erica was setting up the group to see her as the manipulative seductress, which would stand in contrast to her victim position with Jake. The masochistic position demands that one be misunderstood. Erica, to establish her masochistic position in the group, had to get the group to be suspicious of her, when, in fact, she was "perfectly innocent."

This was early fall. Around Christmas time, Jake and Erica were in full swing, with fights and dangerous hysterical episodes, usually involving a combination of drugs, alcohol, and automobiles. On one of these occasions, at two in the morning, Erica called Terrence in a panic, and he invited her to his house. Terrence fed her soup and tucked her in for the night — in his bed, into which he also climbed.

With great pride Terrence informed the group at the next meeting how helpful he had been to Erica in her time of need. He was particularly pleased to report his restraint in not having sex with Erica even though she was in the same bed with him! He did not get the congratulations he was seeking from the group. Naturally, the group did not accept that the incident was not sexual, regardless of the details. Erica was again insulted that aspersions were being cast on her pure intentions, and Terrence was angry that no one was giving him credit for exercising such noble restraint. Terrence and Erica were sharing a masochistic position vis-à-vis the group, whom they had set up to be unfairly suspicious and punitive. In their minds the group was "accusing them of having sex"; as Terrence said, "They're telling me I'm not allowed to feel close with a woman if it isn't sexual."

As one might predict, it was not long before Terrence and Erica began to accuse one another of seduction. They were playing what Eric Berne (1964) would call a game of "Rapo," where one party acts seductively toward another and then, when she is responded to, shouts "Rape!" Erica said, "I realize now that you (Terrence) were taking advantage of me, when I was just coming to you for help." Terrence said, "Erica set me up so that I would have no choice but to have sexual feelings for her and she just wanted to frustrate me." Each claimed to have lost trust in the other. Terrence began to relate more closely to the men in the group and grew distant from the women. For Erica it was the reverse. She hardly spoke to any of the men except Jason.

Meanwhile Joan, who was in the process of terminating individual therapy, planning to remain in group, had engaged in a number of set-ups with Erica throughout the year. She would call Erica to get together, and when she was with her, act so depressed and sullen that Erica would have a terrible time. Erica would not get angry at Joan, but would report the incidents in a whining voice to the group. Joan would explain her attitude by saying that she felt intense jealousy for Erica, but she took no responsibility for the fact that she had initiated the get-togethers.

The next May Joan gave a party to which she invited the group. Erica finally seemed to be weaning herself away from Jake and was beginning to trust at least some members of the group, mainly the women. Before the party, a friend of Joan's asked her if she could ask Erica to buy some cocaine from Jake. Joan did call Erica and ask her to get the drugs. Erica at first refused, and then agreed to ask Jake. The deal was not consummated for some logistical reason.

Joan first brought the incident up — interestingly enough, at her last individual session — in an off-handed manner. She was surprised when I was shocked and upset. I pointed out that she had seriously violated Erica's confidentiality, not to mention Jake's. (Erica's relationship with Jake and his identity should not have been told to the friend.) She had jeopardized Erica as well as herself legally and had encouraged Erica to have contact with Jake, just when Erica seemed to be breaking her "addiction" to him.

Joan brought the matter up in group in a way that said, "punish me; I have displeased Mary; she has shown me what a bad person I am and I need you to yell at me." Erica, who had not revealed the incident to anyone, was relieved to find that Joan was being blamed for the incident and not her. It had not dawned on Erica that Joan's request was an aggressive action against her, although she had been very withdrawn in group since the incident had occurred.

The response of the group when Joan "made her confession" astounded me. They fell all over themselves coaxing Joan not to feel guilty. "It was not such a big deal," they said to her. "You were just excited about the party. Don't worry about it."

Their defense of Joan amazed and concerned me. When I tried to point out what I felt were obvious issues of therapeutic safety and mutual responsibility, I was vehemently talked down, accused of trying to make Joan feel bad and of overlooking Erica's part in it. Even my co-therapist was not sure he understood what all the fuss was about, since no drugs had been bought. By now I was feeling the sadism of the group directed at me as well as Erica.

The next week it dawned on Erica what had happened. She announced that she had lost all trust in the group, and she attributed it to Joan's behavior toward her, not just recently, but all year long. Joan proceeded to get furious at me, feeling I had incited Erica. A small resurgence of the previous conflagration surrounding Joan's behavior occurred, again concluding with most of the group's adamant stance against me, saying that my point of view was moralistic. This time, however, Erica herself supported my view and was joined by her two women allies in the group. The group was then divided, with all the men supporting Joan's side more loudly than Joan herself.

Joan and Erica, sharing very similar scripts of being abused by father and betrayed by mother, had taken complementary positions in the same sadomasochistic drama. Their views of the world were really quite similar, and they easily obtained a meshing of the alternately sadistic and masochistic positions. Erica had set Joan up to work out her rage at her mother on Erica, and Joan had gotten herself punished by losing the support of the women in the group. Joan's guilt-tinged alliance with her father was reconstructed via her phalanx of support from the men in the group. Joan even had a little of her brother in the set-up, since he was heavily involved in drugs at the time. By *playing at* being the victim, Erica could avoid the pain of being victimized *and* make Joan and the men look cruel and heartless at the same time. She, like Joan, had a guilty alliance, but hers was with her "sisters," the other two women in the group, who happened also to harbor a lot of anger at men. Hidden behind their righteous indignation at Joan and the men was a strong desire on their part for revenge against men who had abused them in the past.

Part of the reason Erica did not elicit more sympathy from the men was that she did not *appear* to be upset. No matter how excited everybody else became defending or attacking her, she remained calm and rational, even making jokes and laughing periodically. Her inappropriate affect weakened her credibility and distracted from the men's blatant sadistic reactions to her. The men, with the exception of Jason and the co-therapist, were clearly furious with Erica; one even said that Erica "deserved" what Joan did to her. It seemed they wanted to punish Erica for not having let them rescue her from Jake. More importantly, however, I think they were secretly admiring and jealous of Jake for his sexual power over Erica, while their representative from the group, Terrence, had only managed a child-like quasi-sexual experience with her. Unconsciously, they were identifying with Jake as the aggressor as a defense against their own feelings of powerlessness, which Erica was triggering. Each of these men had had his share of frustrating and painful childhood experiences as the victim of sadistic behavior by parents or older siblings.

To spell out the transferences more clearly: By asking Erica, her supposed "friend," to procure drugs from Jake, who was known to be the instrument of Erica's destruction, Joan was committing an aggressive act that, within the context of the group, was symbolically equivalent to Erica's father's attempted rape of his daughter. (This is not to say that, outside of the group situation, Joan's behavior could be deemed particularly malevolent toward Erica.) Joan's was just the kind of seedy and manipulative maneuver that Joan's own father (the "coach" in Chapter III) would have pulled on her when she was a teenager (sending her off to model negligees for pay and then "borrowing" the money she made for liquor and not returning it). Joan was also squarely in the role of Erica's mother, who would constantly betray her. Joan had placed Erica in the role of *her* mother (the "costumer" in Chapter III), whom she wanted to admire but whom she was encouraged by her father (played by the men in group) to disdain and mistrust. Joan's father had frequently said to her, "I guess your mother doesn't love you very much since she hardly ever holds and hugs you the way I do."

The men in the group put me in the role of their sadistic mothers; they assumed I, like their mothers, would be so involved in punishing Joan that I would fail to see her side of the story. Terrence particularly was reliving his childhood in his identification with Joan against the "bad mother," who had not just punished, but tortured him, when he misbehaved. Terrence, more than the others, addressed the situation as being almost entirely my fault. If I would just "lay off of Joan," then things could "get back to normal." It was almost ludicrous to hear him rage at me, as if I were advocating beatings and capital punishment for Joan, when, in fact, I was merely suggesting that everybody look at the situation closely. The men were acting a lot like their own fathers had in situations of conflict at home, voicing the passive "why-don't-you-give-the-poor-kid-a-break" position to me rather than looking at the emotional and moral issues.

The two women who were supportive of Erica were no less mired in their life scripts, which is why their defense of her was virtually ignored by others in the group. They were feeling mistrustful and abandoned by the co-therapists — by CT for not being more forcefully protective of Erica, and by me for not paying them much attention during this time. This mirrored their usual state as younger children in their families where the parents' energies were always focused on their trouble-making siblings. They clung to each other and to Erica as they had to their sisters, as if their survival depended on it. To Erica, of course, the two women fit in nicely as her two sisters, for whom she risked a great deal trying to obtain protection, her efforts frustrated to the last.

The flurry about the Joan-Erica controversy was just beginning to die down, after a month of the group talking about little else, when Erica walked into group one night and announced that she was leaving. She said she had just now fully realized how betrayed she had been by Joan and the group. Her announcement created a fresh burst of hostility against her from the men. They complained that the Joan issue was over, that she was "beating a dead horse" (an apt expression in referring to sadomasochistic interaction). Joan archly suggested that maybe *she* should leave, because the group would surely punish her if Erica left on account of her.

At that point Erica told the group for the first time about her father's trying to rape her and her sisters, and the mother's and the priest's refusing to protect them. She told the story clearly, with intense feeling, and an awareness of how it paralleled what had happened in the group. The group then began to understand how the situation of the last month in the group had replayed the themes of abuse and betrayal that so characterized Erica's childhood. They could see that her slowness to react and defend herself stemmed from a passive, masochistic response pattern developed through years of being frustrated in her attempts to obtain love and support. They realized how neatly they had fit themselves into the roles of her family and the priest. They also began to grasp how they each had been reenacting some of the painful conflicts of their respective childhoods, as well as Erica's.

The group leaders and the two supportive women managed to persuade Erica not to leave the group permanently, but to take a two-month leave of absence and decide after that how she felt about it. Everyone in the group agreed that it was healthy for Erica to finally be in touch with her anger, and to hold the group accountable for their part in hurting her; yet, they hoped she would return and give them a chance to deal with her in a different way.

Erica continued to see me in individual therapy. While her tangle with the group had caused what trust she had in the group to disintegrate, it strengthened her confidence in me; she realized that I had consistently had her best interests in mind, even when she did not. A week or two after leaving group, Erica stopped seeing Jake for good. It seemed that standing up for herself in the group had given her the last bit of confidence she needed to step out of the sadomasochistic relationship. Meanwhile, in group, the other individuals with sadomasochistic conflicts gradually began to admit their feelings of rage toward their parents and themselves, realizing how much they had displaced those feelings onto Erica. They began to realize how unsupportive they had been to one another; they admitted that they did not feel safe in the group. This came through very clearly a few weeks later when one of the men, Ted, underwent a serious brain operation, returned to group, and received barely any acknowledgment that he had even been away, much less had major surgery. Ted was furious, stating vehemently that he now knew how unsupported Erica must have felt in the group. The group felt ashamed, and became determined to change their withholding and hostile attitudes.

They began to recapture the spirit of concern and friendship they had abandoned. They realized they wanted the protection of the confidentiality rule and the reassurance of a group that was dedicated to working for the best interests of each individual. I was pleasantly surprised when Erica appeared unannounced at group exactly two months after she left. She and the group were then able to begin a healthy therapeutic alliance. Erica let herself really feel her vulnerability, and the group simply accepted her, without trying to "fix" her. She did a lot of crying and let herself be held by the two women, my co-therapist, or me. She let us know how frightening life was for her every single day. Joan began to blossom professionally and personally. By beginning to accept her own sexuality and attractiveness, she was able to laugh at herself when she found herself envying Erica; she lost weight and became more confident and flirtatious. While Erica and Joan never became friends, they learned to respect their differences and to be genuinely helpful to one another in therapy. As a result of these experiences, Terrence began to face his deep-seated anger toward his mother and women in general, and to work on these feelings directly in therapy rather than act them out in sadomasochistic struggles.

The set-up ordeal that Joan and Erica put the group through helped everyone face and renounce their own sadomasochistic tendencies. As a result, the group became a very strong and humanistic environment, which facilitated substantive and lasting changes in the lives of each of its eight members. In fact, throughout this book, this group is noted for its positive qualities: its cohesiveness, high levels of self-disclosure and psychological sophistication, and ability to use language efficiently. Ironically, the biggest group fiasco I have ever experienced seems to have produced the most resilient and therapeutic group I have ever led.

One might wonder how a therapy group survives such divisive and stressful periods. Many do not, because the leadership is not experienced and strong enough. During a period of multiple set-ups the leader must be clinically skilled enough to perceive them, autonomous enough to avoid playing into them, articulate enough to make the process of what is happening clear to the group, and confident enough in herself and the group to convince members not to give up and quit when the going gets rough. Even high-quality leadership, however, does not totally explain why clients put up with long unrewarding stretches of time where the tension in the group is high and the trust is low. Again we look to general system theory for an explanation on the systems level. Durkin (1980, p. 26) points out that the group, like any other system, has the capacity to exchange energy and information across permeable boundaries. It therefore has the inherent ability to structure and restructure, as well as regulate itself. Because of the enormous number of options it has for internal reorganization, the group can and does adapt to and survive tumultuous stresses from within and without.

CONTACT

In this section we are dealing with contact — not in the sense of "contact operations," but simple contact. What is it? Why is it so important in psychotherapy? How does it change frames of reference? How does the therapy group foster contact? What are people's ways of avoiding contact, and how can group help them to overcome their barriers to it?

"Contact is the lifeblood of growth, the means for changing oneself and one's experience of the world" (Polster and Polster, 1973, p. 101). The Polsters appreciate the value of contact as a vehicle for changing frames of reference, saying "contact is implicitly incompatible with remaining the same. Through contact one does not have to try to change: change simply occurs" (p. 101). In the Gestalt framework, contact has an intrapsychic as well as interpersonal connotation, meaning contact with one's environment and with self as well as with other people. The Polsters, like Bach, say that healthy contact can only happen between two people if they are separate beings. If two people are tangled in some way, out of mutual need, or if they have frames of reference which necessitate a distortion in their perceptions of one another, then they can only overlap or mirror. They cannot truly contact one another as themselves. ·

Tele and Choice

It is curious that while we have many names for transference, we have so few for authentic contact. Moreno employed the term *tele,* a Greek word meaning "over distance" (as in *tele*phone), to describe "a feeling which is projected into the distance; the simplest unit of feeling that is transmitted from one individual to another" (1946, p. 84). It is also " 'insight into,' 'appreciation of,' and 'feeling for' the actual makeup of the other person" (Allport, 1957, p. 307). Tele is a healthy contact operation, which involves no transference or distortions of any kind.

Tele "acounts for what seems to draw people together. . . . It is responsible for reciprocity, mutuality and cohesion in groups" (Hale, 1981, p. 10). It is the glue of any group and, combined with spontaneity, its energy. When people immediately "hit it off," when they come to a mutual understanding, when they are sexually attracted to each other, or appreciate each other's sense of humor, tele is operating. To a certain extent, tele is magic. It often occurs between the most disparate of people, completely unexpectedly. Tele cannot be manufactured—it is a spontaneous occurrence. On the other hand, what the leaders in the group do or do not do greatly influences the amount and intensity of tele in the group.

Tele has a lot to do with choosing. The focus of Moreno's science of sociometry is the interpersonal choices made in groups. The sociometry of a group at any given time is a measurement of the subjective repulsions and attractions of people toward one another. The measuring can be done on paper by the leader or the members, or it can be cone in the form of living sculptures, in which people put their hands on the shoulders of others in the group whom they feel attracted to, trust or distrust, are curious about, or whatever. Moreno's therapy of society, "sociatry" (Moreno, 1953), and of the individual as a social being, "socioanalysis" (Haskell, 1975), involve the facilitation of spontaneous interpersonal choice-making, which he considered a cornerstone of the mental health of the individual, the group and the society at large. Moreno would have agreed with Bach's conviction (1954, p. 219) that development of healthy contact operations is the first order of business in the psychotherapy of the individual. Moreno went further than anyone before or since in developing methods by which the individual could improve his ways of relating to others. He helped people experience the satisfaction of *choosing* others on the basis of tele rather than transferential distortion.

The neurotic usually believes he has fewer choices than he does with respect to what to do and how to behave, think, or feel. Group is a constant exercise in making choices. One chooses whether or not to attend, where to sit, whether or not to speak, how honest, self-disclosing, or assertive to be.

In the process of group interaction, members choose each other consciously and unconsciously, actively and passively. Members choose others with whom to chat, identify, joke, commiserate or argue; they choose whom to ask questions of, or give or seek advice from. Shy or depressed members tend to make fewer choices than aggressive members, and instead wait to be chosen by others.

As time goes on, each member is made aware of his unconscious processes of choosing and begins to think about whom he chooses for what in his life. Does he choose a "mother" for a wife? A seductress for a friend? Does he make good choices in his head, but not have the social skills to follow through on them? A group member who traditionally makes poor interpersonal choices can learn skills to help him assess people more accurately, as well as effective mechanisms for communicating his choices appropriately.

Moreno's work in the study of the patterns of choices in groups confirms what we may intuitively realize—that the spontaneous member who makes the largest number and greatest variety of choices is usually the most often chosen by other members as a person to be valued, liked, appreciated, and so on. A person who is noncommital will tend not to be chosen on these criteria. The therapeutic objective for such a client would be to increase the number of times he initiates contact and to broaden his repertoire of ways to do so. Sometimes a person's first act of "choosing," or making contact, is a tearful outburst to another member about how rejected he feels by that person.

Initial choices made by new members or a new group are generally based on familiarity or superficial similarities. For example, an older member will seek out one near her age, while persons with alcoholic spouses may want to compare "war stories." Some choices reveal overlapping pathologies, such as when the hysteric becomes rapidly infatuated with the seductive psychopath.

Interpersonal choices are a great measure of individuals' psychodynamic patterns and are targets for change in the therapy. As the individual gains the ability to choose spontaneously, wisely, and frequently, his experience of tele increases. This, in itself, greatly enhances his spontaneity, which, in turn, builds more opportunities for telic interaction. It is this phenomenon, far more than the problem-solving aspect, that gives group therapy meaning and value for the clients over the years they participate.

Encounter

Encounters are exciting and highly charged moments of interaction between people, in which everyone present knows that what is happening is authentic. They happen frequently in cohesive and well-functioning groups, and occur in all intense relationships, whether loving or hostile. Moreno, who first used the term "encounter," translated from the German "Begegnung," conceived of it as a sort of ultimate role reversal.

A meeting of two: eye to eye: face to face. And when you are near, I will tear your eyes out and use them instead of mine, and you will tear out my eyes and use them instead of yours; then I will look at you with your eyes and you will look at me with mine (translated from "Einladung zu Einer Begegnung" by J. L. Moreno, in Hale, 1981, p. 95).

Moustakas sees the encounter as essential to living fully in the world:

The "encounter" . . . is a joyous experience of self-discovery, a real meeting of self-to-self. It contains an exciting flow of feeling from the union of being lonely while at the same time feeling connected with life. It includes a sense of harmony and well-being. Both encounter and confrontation are ways of advancing life and coming alive in a relatively dead or stagnant world; the repetitive habits of communication and the social, filial, and professional roles and games that people play (Moustakas, 1972, p. 21).

The dramatic moments that seem so pivotal in the psychotherapy of an individual usually involve an encounter. Lila, a psychology student in her twenties, had a habit of whining and acting obsequious with me in the group. I sensed some hostility under her smiles and constant questioning. One night she unexpectedly said that she believed I didn't like her, expecting some reassurance. I thought for a second and said, "You know you're right. I don't really like you. As your therapist I care about you, but I don't really like you. You whine too much and I doubt your sincerity a great deal of the time." The look on her face was one of absolute astonishment. Suddenly, she straightened up in her chair and said with total conviction, "Mary, I don't think I like you either." We stared at each other for a moment and then we both burst out laughing, feeling free and clean, and each appreciating the other's honesty. That exchange was the beginning of a new Lila — much more assertive and less concerned with obtaining others' approval. Not surprisingly, we began to like each other at that moment.

Gestalt and systems theorists have a mechanistic but useful explanation of the encounter phenomenon, which permits full recognition and understanding of the separateness of self and the otherness of the other. The encounter or "contact episode," as the Polsters (1973) call it, takes place between organisms at the "contact boundary." When two people encounter one another, they are meeting at the plane of contact between them. When people meet at the contact boundary, there is no fusion; information travels freely from one organism to the other across the boundary, but the structure of the boundary of each remains intact.

Encounter or "contact . . . inherently involves the risk of loss of identity and separateness. In this lies the adventure and the art of contact" (Polster and Polster, 1973, p. 103). Because the contact episode or encounter threatens the equilibrium of the organism or person, making him highly vulnerable for change, it follows that persons oriented toward change would seek to encounter, whereas individuals resistant to change would seek to avoid it.

Jerome Frank (1974) and Carl Whitaker and Thomas Malone (1981), among others, talk in their writings about *kairos,* moments at which a person is ripe for profound personality change. These moments are usually accompanied by very intense emotional states or emotional flooding. Frank suggests, and later research begins to substantiate, that during such dramatic moments there is a "temporary disorganization of the person's psychic structure, sometimes enabling him to achieve a new and better integration with relief of symptoms" (1974, p. 250).

Very often instances of *kairos* happen in conjunction with an encounter. During these powerful and potentially therapeutic moments, a person's habitual patterns are suddenly interrupted as he is confronted in a moment of mutual understanding with another human being. The therapy group provides many opportunities for the encounter, for *kairos,* and for subsequent changes of frames of reference of a profound and lasting nature.

Contact Avoidance

Even though it is a life-giving and life-sustaining experience, contact, under certain circumstances, is experienced as frightening. Many individuals avoid contact because it brings up strong emotion and makes them feel vulnerable or out of control. Contact avoidance operates on a group level and an individual level, and is something group therapy seeks to correct.

In a therapy group, members may have ease or difficulty in making contact with one another relative to such factors as the level of group development, cohesion, trust, the theme under discussion, individual and group resistance, the therapist's role as a contact model, and the therapist's attitude toward intermember contact. Baruch Levine (1979) suggests the earliest stage of a group to be the "parallel relations" phase, one in which member-member contact is minimal. He likens this stage to "parallel play," the pervasive mode of interaction among children between the ages of three and seven, when children often play *next to,* rather than *with,* one another. In group therapy it means the group members "do their therapy" next to each other. They tend to talk mainly to the therapist and not to each other. There is little closeness and no conflict.

In parallel play, children do not compete, nor do they really have an understanding of "others" as separate from themselves. Instead, they see each other as objects of gratification of their individual needs and assumptions. The parallel relations phase in group therapy is one in which the transferences are developing rapidly, and there is little simultaneous authentic contact to counteract them. The group is still developing a feeling of acceptance and safety and is not yet ready to deal with individual differences and separateness, the prerequisites of contact.

A more mature group can also go through periods of resistance where contact is avoided. There may be a shared anxiety about dealing with a certain issue that has begun to emerge; people may be angry at the leader or each other and be afraid to speak up; they might be suppressing sexual feelings; or they may have slid into a posture of dependency, waiting for someone else to stimulate or "feed" them things to do. Regardless of the reason behind it, group members in such a state of passivity and withdrawal are not making contact; in fact, they tend to look and act rather like a bunch of dead fish.

Sometimes the group needs to go through its resistance and learn what it means — how the group's behavior is reflective of the members' behavior in real life. My co-therapist, CT, and I once had a group that was growing more passive by the session. The members would not talk to each other, only to CT and me, and they continually tried to set us up to do individual therapy in the group. When we focused on this resistance, they talked to us about it, exacerbating the problem. It was hard to know when to facilitate and when to let them bore themselves into taking some responsibility. One night, CT lost patience. Abruptly and loudly he exclaimed, "I feel like you're all in telephone booths making long distance calls somewhere else!" Everyone thought this was a great comment, but it had very little effect.

In our meeting together after this session, CT and I decided we would force the group to deal with each other. In the next session we announced to the group that we would not be participating for the first two-thirds of the session. We proceeded to move to the back of the room away from the group circle. The group sat quietly for a while and then a corporation executive, Steve, suggested they pick a topic and talk about it. Before they could decide what to talk about, Marian, a depressed young graduate student, started to cry. The group sat helplessly. Finally Nate asked her what was wrong. She sobbed a long story about failing an exam or something. Marian cried and cried and cried. It seemed no matter what the group did, it had no effect on the intensity of Marian's flood: They listened; they questioned; they tried to get her to breathe deeply; they brought her water. Nothing worked.

When two-thirds of the group time was over, CT and I resumed our places in the circle. Marian was still crying. "Good God, Marian," I shouted, "Will you please shut up!" Shocked, she did so. She also burst out laughing.

The group was furious — at Marian, CT and me, themselves, and each other. One man said he thought it was terribly irresponsible of CT and me to leave them alone like that, and several of the group loudly grumbled their agreement. This was really funny, CT and I pointed out, since we were right in the room the whole time and would have handled any emergencies.

"Did you know Marian was all right?" they asked.

"I've seen her do this before," I replied.

They did not know whether to be madder at me for not stopping Marian sooner, or at themselves for not trying what they all wanted to do but had been afraid to lest they hurt her. Now that they knew how tough and manipulative Marian really was, they would be ready to be more direct with her in the future.

After they had yelled at us for a while, they began to get angry at each other. Steve, the executive, got the brunt of it.

"You were trying to take over the group, Steve," said Nate.

"But you were just sitting there!" retorted Steve. Two or three others got in on the argument, some defending Steve in taking the intiative, others feeling that he had been patronizing about it.

CT and I were delighted. By withdrawing our presence we had stimulated contact among the members. By the end of that session, everyone in the group was involved and animated. The new group momentum continued for weeks. They continued to confront and interact with one another spontaneously, and never encountered another slump as deadly as the one they had been in before we did that exercise.

Mechanisms of Contact Avoidance

Gestalt therapists have pointed out five particular types of mechanisms by which contact between people is interrupted or distorted (Polster and Polster, 1973, p. 71). All of these processes are very common in therapy groups during group resistance:

1) *introjection*—investing energy into passively incorporating what the environment provides, as in accepting everything that is said without filtering or objecting. All advice, criticism and strokes are uniformly gulped down, even if they are coming from hostility, insincerity, or projection on the part of the other.
2) *projection*—the disowning of aspects of self, ascribing them to the environment, as in incorrectly assuming something about another that is really true of oneself. This is an entirely unconscious process. Group questioning and feedback help someone with such a tendency to reorient his frame of reference and see what his projections are telling him about himself.
3) *retroflection*—becoming separate and self-sufficient and abandoning attempts to influence environment; taking care of oneself at the expense of interpersonal relationships; reinvesting energy back into an exclusively intrapersonal system. This is best illustrated in the resistant group by the "telephone booth" phenomenon described above. Retroflective gestures, such as stroking one's own head or hitting oneself while talking, are important cues as to what kind of contact is being avoided.
4) *deflection*—engaging with environment on a hit-or-miss basis. This is seen clearly in a group during times of approach-avoidance conflict, when people are struggling between, on the one hand, engaging more fully with one another and with the group-as-a-whole, and, on the other, fleeing altogether. One group member, Sally, started right off in group by announcing

that she was terrified of talking in groups, an issue which she used frequently to deflect attention away from more troublesome personal worries. At times, she took the individual work that others did in the group so seriously that she would have nightmares about it. She would report these occurrences to the group; yet, the connection she must have felt with them at the previous session—and not talked about then—would have passed. The opportunity for contact was lost. At the height of her "deflecting" period, which dovetailed with the group's parallel relations phase, Sally's main mode of interacting in a session was to laugh at anything that could be remotely conceived of as funny and to rescue the first person who was criticized or confronted, usually with one loud protest ("You have no business saying that to her!"). When her statement was attended to, she would giggle and refuse to give any explanations or to share her feelings; she would then bolt out of the door as soon as the session was over, but talk to a group member about her experience on the phone a few days later.

5) *confluence*—yielding to current trends, merging, expending little energy. This is a phenomenon that occurs in a group when it is involved in a pseudo-closeness—a cohesiveness that cannot take much in the way of scrutiny or challenge before it yields to rifts based on underlying sexual feelings and hostility. Individuals and groups that are confluent resist making choices and subgrouping, since they are unable to see the difference between separateness and destruction. Instead, they *blend*. My newest group was asked to do a sociometric exercise in which group members were to stand up and put their hands on the shoulder of the person(s) they felt closest to in the group. The result was a human blob with arms reaching all over; everyone was picked twice. None of the members seemed to be discriminating in their choices. Some were buried under a pile of arms. The living sculpture represented their oneness, which was a defense against contact with one another. Real contact presupposes a differentiation, which at that point would have been too threatening for this group. Confluence was also evidenced in their passivity early in each session, their collective readiness to talk about anything that was brought up, with no individual ready to take the initiative or to direct the group's spotlight onto himself.

Techniques for Building Contact

Here are a few of the methods I frequently use to increase contact in the group.

The group members lose contact with one another when they are avoiding a certain subject or something that is anxiety-provoking within the session.

To help them reestablish contact, the leader must help them address what is being avoided. Often in these situations I ask a simple question to the group at large, one that will direct their attention to the group process. "What's happening here?" or "What is *not* happening?" This usually brings them into the here-and-now, a prerequisite for their making contact.

Sometimes I will comment on something that may be obvious to everyone but is not being addressed: "Everyone's very quiet." "There seems to be a lot of anger (anxiety, feelings) that are not being expressed." "The men and the women are not talking to one another tonight." "The group is avoiding Susan."

When there is a particular subject being avoided, often something to do with sex, anger, or death, I might simply notice that out loud: "Whatever happened to our discussion of sex?" This will usually bring forth people's anxieties about discussing these subjects. Recognizing these resistances gets them out of the way a bit, freeing the group to connect with one another on topics that hold great interest for all of the members.

If the group seems bored or depressed, I try to elicit their negativity about being in the session. As seen in the second transcript in Chapter V, when people's gripes and dissatisfactions are uncovered, their negativity soon succumbs to the positive energy beneath it and a great deal of contact is made. To get this going I might just ask people how they felt about coming to the group that night.

If the subject being avoided is sexual feelings for one another, the group will often shut down like a collection of clams. In this case I will probably become more playful, teasing them gently, being a little flirtatious and encouraging them to be so. I will congratulate them for their *scrupulous* adherence to the "no-sex" rule, to the point where they have managed to get rid of *all* their feelings for each other, not just sexual! At this point they either start laughing or get defensive; either reaction rekindles their spontaneity and gets them to talk about their feelings for one another.

We have discussed the relationship between tele and choice. A decrease in spontaneity in the group for whatever reason will always hamper members' inclination to actively *choose* either subjects or each other. As they choose less, the level of tele plummets. The absence of tele is reflected in the lack of direction in their speech as they talk in general ways to no one in particular, as well as in their inability to show feelings toward anyone or to express any preferences or strong opinions. To reestablish tele the leader must activate choice-making within the group. This is accomplished swiftly and easily by means of *action sociometry* (Hale, 1981). In these exercises the leader first tells the group to stand up and mill around the room. He then instructs them to choose somebody in the group according to a certain criteria. For example, he may say, "Choose someone in the group with whom you feel very comfortable (uncomfortable.)" He tells them to put their hand on the shoulder of this person. The resulting configuration of people joined hand to shoulder in various directions is then quickly diagrammed on paper or a blackboard. (This is called a "sociogram.") Members then return to their seats and discuss their feelings about choosing and not choosing, being chosen and not being chosen. There may be hurt feelings that must be heard and respected. Sometimes the leader may decide to have each person sit down with just the person he chose or who chose him to talk about the reasons why they selected one another. This pairing technique is excellent for building one-to-one bonds in a group where the tele is weak.

The choice criteria can be negative or positive, depending on whether the leader wants to bring forth similarities and enhance comfort in the group, or bring out whatever anxieties may be simmering that have caused the "resistance" or lack of tele. Both the negative and positive choice criteria, when explored via action sociometry combined with open and honest discussion, build cohesion and tele in the group. If people are sitting on positive feelings toward one another, these are allowed to emerge; if they are sitting on differences of opinion and negative feelings toward each other, these are made mentionable and are resolved in the discussion following the exercise.

Here are some examples of when action sociometry is useful:

1) A new group is bogged down because transferences are just beginning to form and have not yet become conscious. The group's initial pseudo-cohesion is crumbling and members no longer feel particularly supportive to one another. Group members seem irritable and annoyed with one another. The leader can explore some of the budding transferences by doing action sociometry exercises with the following instructions: "Let us pretend that you are going to be in a psychodrama. Who in this group—male or female—would you choose to play your mother?" " . . . to play your father?" " . . . to play any of your siblings?" " . . . grandparents?" " . . . an important figure in your life," etc.

2) Group members seem anxious and afraid of one another and/or of the material being discussed. The contact among them has diminished because of lack of trust. The leader highlights trust issues in the group by asking them to choose someone that they trust. Then he asks them to choose someone whom they don't trust. Through the exercise and the discussion, the group becomes informed as to exactly who in the group is having problems trusting

and who is having difficulty being accepted by the group, and more importantly, why.

3) In an active group a great deal of interpersonal "stuff" gets kicked up, some of which does not get immediately settled. For the most part, this is a highly desirable situation in group therapy, but sometimes the leader may sense that the number of unresolved issues between people is becoming overwhelming. There is so much going on that group members, not knowing where to start, begin to withdraw from one another. The leader is wise at this point to tag the various interpersonal issues by asking the members to choose a person or persons with whom they have "unfinished business." A sociogram is then made and the leader sees to it that everyone's "business" is completed in the sessions that follow.

In this exercise, group members are told that they do not have to base their choice on particular criteria; however, they are all urged to stand with the group so that they may be chosen. It is as important to notice who does not choose, as who chooses whom for what. Someone who is frequently chosen on a number of criteria is termed a sociometric "star." This does not always mean that this person is well-liked, for some of the choices of him may be on negative criteria, but it does mean he is a center of energy and emotion in the group. The group therapist needs a strong and open relationship with this person in order to have a comparably good relationship with the group. Someone consistently chosen for negative criteria and not for positive is, sociometrically, a scapegoat in the group. The scapegoat is a vehicle of the group's resistance, embodying split-off and unwanted parts of other members. The leader encourages the group to be open with the scapegoat about how he is turning them off, so that he can use this information to change his offensive behaviors. When he does so, the group usually feels more welcoming of him, having built up an emotional investment in his recovery. They can then begin to own the parts of themselves they have projected onto him. Someone who is rarely chosen and does little choosing on all criteria is a called an "isolate" and is at high risk for prematurely dropping out of the group. The leader's task is to somehow bring the isolate into the group, not only to help him, but to keep him from draining the tele out of the group, and/or splitting up the group by leaving. The leader does this by finding things that the isolate has in common with the sociometric stars, by giving him extra time in the group, and by modeling and encouraging interest, empathy, and concern for him in the group.*

---

*For more on action sociometry and other sociometric methods, see Hale (1981).

Analogical and Digital

Communication takes place in two different modes: *digital* and *analogical* (Watzlawick, Beavin, and Jackson, 1967). Digital communication is spoken and written language, a series of symbols — letters, words, and numerals which adhere to a logical system. A digital symbol is a purely abstract representation of what it stands for. The numeral "7" does not in any way communicate seven items, just as the letters c-a-t in and of themselves do not suggest a cat. Analogical communication, on the other hand, is directly suggestive of what it represents. Nonverbal messages are analogical: A waving fist conveys "I want to punch somebody"; a shaky voice connotes, "I am quaking with fear." Certain words, such as "buzzer" or "whistle," contain sounds in their pronunciation that evoke the experience of buzzer or whistle. Metaphors employ words to depict analogically, rather than logically or literally. Metaphors, therefore, are a convenient mix of digital and analogical communication, which is why they are so useful in human language.

Analogical communication is understandable only in a *context*. The shaken fist, in the context of a discussion about sibling rivalry, would likely make perfect sense to us as observers, whereas a shaken fist without an accompanying facial expression, or the sentence, "The man shook his fist," without any other information, would not be fully comprehensible. Digital symbols need no context in which to be interpreted. The word "cat" means the same thing in all situations.

Analogical thinking and language are thought to involve right-brain functioning. Through them we understand and communicate about relationships. As we have discussed, the paradoxical and metaphorical aspects of group therapy elicit this kind of thinking, which is necessary for a satisfactory comprehension of what is going on in the world of people.

In a complex communication, with conflicting analogical and digital messages, all meanings should be considered valid. Confused communications should not be assumed to be intentionally evasive or hostile. They are usually a function of too many equally important and equally true messages being delivered simultaneously.

A "metacommunication" is a message *about* another message. It is "meta to," outside of, on a different logical level from, the message on which it comments. The ability to metacomment is essential in communication, for it performs the functions of linguistic boundary-setting. Through metacommunication, classifications and frames of reference are established, and distinctions are made between what is *in* or *out* of a classification or frame. Communication without adequate metacommenting is chaotic; people who cannot metacomment verbally may have no choice but to act out (an analogical form of metacommenting). On the other hand, too much "meta" or "commenting upon" renders a conversation too abstract and unspontaneous. People who do this excessively are often considered rigid and overly intellectual.

Clients who stay in group for two or three years learn an enormous amount about communication. If they come into the group with deficits in communicating, as most do, they acquire feedback as to what their specific difficulties are and obtain help in correcting them. They learn how to vary their communication until they are understood by the other person. They also gain skill in reading nonverbal signals and in distinguishing different levels of meaning in a complex communication. An example of someone who learned some important lessons in communication through group therapy was Roger.

Roger, age 40, had a particular limitation in the area of reading and sending communications in the analogical mode. Roger was unusually inert when he spoke. His hands did not move and his face did not change expression when he was speaking or listening. In the digital mode, Roger was fine; he was capable of speaking articulately and logically on any subject, even feelings, but his language was so abstract and impersonal that some people in the group had difficulty listening to him. They told him so, urging him to loosen up a bit. Roger did not know what they were talking about.

Interestingly, Roger had married a woman, Fran (not in the group), who had the opposite limitation in her communication. Fran often could not get out of the analogical mode in order to express things logically in words. She had great difficulty discussing anything important or emotional without getting very excited, sputtering helplessly in an effort to get words out. When angry, she demonstrated rather than articulated her feelings, by screaming loudly and pounding the wall. Roger did not read her gyrations as an expression of anger. He called it "acting crazy." When he did not recognize her rage, Fran became even more frustrated, and pounded and screamed some more. Roger, mystified by what he considered very bizarre behavior on her part, told the group that his wife was psychotic, and that he was worried about the safety of his children.

Feeling concern for the family's safety, I called Fran in for a visit with the children. It was clear that Fran's communication with her children was excellent. She hugged and played with them physically. They were relaxed and expressive with her. I believed her when she said she did not have the temper tantrums with the children that she did with Roger. I realized that the most useful change for the whole family would be to teach Roger how to communicate analogically; this was accomplished in group.

Roger told the group that he and his wife were "not communicating." I explained that he was incorrect. They were giving each other excellent feedback, but they were operating in two different modes, and neither one had access to the other's channel. By screaming and pounding the wall, Fran was telling Roger analogically that she was angry at him for criticizing her. He *said* he was terrified of her when she became so upset, but she did not believe him because he was not giving her analogical proof. She needed to see gestures and expressions, and hear tones in his voice that matched the verbal message, "I'm scared." As typically is the case with couples in conflict, neither husband nor wife was aware of his or her own or the other's limitations; each assumed the other was deliberately trying to cause him/her distress.

Tryna, a member of Roger's group, was emotional and impulsive like Fran. Roger quickly developed a "Fran" transference with her and, in his first or second meeting, told Tryna rigidly that her loud, angry comments and outbursts of tears made him feel upset inside.

"You'd never know it to look at you," said another member.

"How do you expect me to believe you're upset when you just sit there!" barked Tryna, her face contorted and arms waving. Roger remained blank. "Where do you want me to go?" he asked.

I said, "Roger, I believe you're upset because you say so. Just because we attend to nonverbal communication in group more than happens elsewhere does not mean we ignore the content of what people say! But I can see why they have trouble believing you, because the expression on your face and your body posture do not match your words."

Turning to Tryna, I said, "You know, Tryna, words are a wonderful mode of communication."

"Oh yeah, heh-heh," muttered Tryna, sounding irritated.

"No, really, Tryna, I'm not kidding. Your family was very emotional, often violent. They were not able to use language to help them work through problems. You learned how to look beyond what people are saying to deeper levels of meanings expressed nonverbally, and that is a great skill. You are extremely intuitive. However, we have discussed the tangles you run into at work and in your marriage. I believe if you could learn to rely on verbal communication more, you would eliminate a lot of conflicts and misunderstandings.

Still directing my words to Tryna, I continued. "Roger, on the other hand, relies on words too much. He learned not to show his feelings, probably to keep his mother at bay. She made such a big deal out of every feeling he had and swarmed all over him." Out of the corner of my eye I saw Roger nodding almost imperceptibly in affirmation of what I was saying.

When I spoke to Tryna I turned directly to her, realizing that she needed to see me in order to get my message on the nonverbal as well as verbal level. I was aware of letting my hands move and my facial expression change, matching her way of talking. When I wanted Roger to understand what his communication difficulty was, I purposely talked about him in the third person so that he would not feel "swarmed in on," as he seemed to with Tryna and Fran.

Turning directly to Roger at this point, I said, "So Roger, you feel scared. Where do you feel it in your body?"

"In my stomach," said Roger.

"What was the feeling?"

"A fluttering."

"Can you tell me what the fluttering feeling is like?"

"Like a bird beating its wings in preparation for flight."

"Wonderful," I said.

"Wow, Roger, that's great. You're showing your feelings!" exclaimed Tryna.

"I am?" he said.

"No, he's not," said another member. "He still has no expression on his face!"

"He made a metaphor," I explained. "A metaphor is a word picture. Tryna can understand it by making a picture of the fluttering bird in her mind. Metaphor puts them both on the same wave length."

A few sessions later, Tryna was sobbing and shaking in discussing her divorce. Roger asked her why she was crying. Tryna looked up, annoyed at first; then she remembered how to talk to Roger. She said, "I feel like the last little leaf hanging on the tree in a winter wind."

"You must feel very lonely and frightened then," said Roger gently.

"Exactly," said Tryna gratefully.

I explained to the group, as I often do, the things that I had done to enhance my own communication with Roger and with Tryna, as well as to facilitate their communication with one another. I spelled out the value of using metaphor to merge the digital and analogical modes. I also pointed out how I match the behaviors and styles of speech of the person with whom I am talking, demonstrating how effective this is in establishing and maintaining rapport. I elaborated on how I got Roger to identify a bodily feeling first in order that he could then associate to a metaphor. I reminded them of the validity of all messages in a complex communication, cautioning them not to discount the verbal or the nonverbal. By highlighting and expanding on small bits of communication as they happen, I make all my communication tricks available to the group, so that members can pick up and use whichever ones are useful for them.

Roger was able to take the metaphor option into his relationship with Fran. When he wanted to tell her what he was feeling, he would identify a feeling, turn it into a word picture, and say it. She understood him perfectly. Then he taught her to speak in metaphors too, and they had a glorious time talking to each other! Fran easily refrained from temper trantrums, and Roger, no longer scared, loosened up physically as well as emotionally. The group noticed more expression on his face, and even some hand movement when he talked.

The change in Roger's communication was reflective of a drastic change in frame of reference and vice versa. Roger's unexpressiveness and rigidity had made his relationships superficial and frustrating for himself and others. By gaining access to the analogical mode, a whole new world was opened to him — one in which he could connect with others on a far deeper and more meaningful level.

Establishing Goals in Communication

Most people do not establish goals in communication (Dilts et al., 1979). They prefer to "wing it." Many are not even aware that they can do anything to influence the outcomes of their communications. Others consider it manipulative and, therefore, undesirable to have such goals.

There are two key skills in being an effective communicator. The first is to have a wide range of responses in one's repertoire, and to be able to quickly gain access to the appropriate one at the right time. We discussed this earlier in this chapter in our section on spontaneity. The second, which is equally important, is the ability to establish realistic desired outcomes in communication. For example, when going for a job interview, it is useful to decide ahead of time what kind of impression you wish to make on the interviewer. In trying to resolve a fight with your spouse, it is useful to have an idea of what kind of interaction you would like to have instead. Far from being manipulative, establishing desired outcomes in communications helps one be clear, honest, and efficient in one's interactions.

As we discussed under "Contact Operations," many therapy clients have objectives in their communications which are unconscious, unrealistic, inappropriate — or all three. A client may harbor the subconscious desire to be mothered or seduced, which gets in the way of his conscious efforts to secure a raise from his attractive female employer. Such a person needs to sort out his personal from his professional goals, establish programs to see that both are met, and tailor his communications judiciously to make sure he accomplishes what he wants in each context.

The group format gives the client time and assistance in the process of establishing communication outcomes that are desirable and achievable, both in the group and outside. The feedback process helps the client determine whether or not he is attaining his outcomes, and if not, how he might adjust his own communications for greater success.

Jack, an impetuous young lawyer, had aspirations in the direction of becoming the Perry Mason of Connecticut; however, he was having a good deal of trouble in his litigation work because of his tendency to speak before he thought. Naturally, he was the same way in group. When he associated to something someone said, which happened frequently because he was highly alert and enthusiastic, Jack would blurt out his thoughts so suddenly that the person speaking would totally lose track of what he was saying. The group quickly became annoyed with Jack, and gave him considerable negative feedback, which hurt his feelings but did not help him control himself. He continued to interrupt, get reprimanded, feel badly, and withdraw, only to repeat the pattern again the next time he got a bright idea. My co-therapist decided to tackle the problem head on and teach Jack in the group how to establish goals in his communication.

Whenever Jack began an outburst, CT would interrupt him as soon as he opened his mouth. "Stop!!" CT would yell so suddenly that it would render Jack speechless (not to mention the rest of us, who would be startled out of our wits). "Now, Jack, sit back and think for a few seconds about what you want this person or the group as a whole to get from your communication. What is your purpose? Do not speak until you are sure what that is." The conversation would resume and Jack, when he was clear about what he intended to communicate, would insert his contribution at an appropriate time. CT repeated this procedure with Jack as needed, and the number of Jack's outbursts was drastically reduced, as Jack learned to interrupt himself in the process of interrupting. As Jack incorporated this new skill into his repertoire of communication choices, his potency in the group and the courtroom was greatly increased.

Intuition and Psychic Communication

People communicate a great deal more than they realize. Through gestures, facial expressions, voice tone changes, and many other nonverbal cues, people let other people know consciously or unconsciously what they are experiencing. Often people are not aware that they are giving any messages at all, nor are they tuned into the feelings that are going on inside them that are being quite clearly communicated to others. When a nonverbal message is delivered, it may be read consciously, or it may be received unconsciously and stored in the unconscious. Often the receiver of a communication responds unconsciously to a message, even when he does not know he has received one.

The group is a complicated network of communication that is conscious to conscious, unconscious to conscious, conscious to unconscious, and unconscious to unconscious. Part of the purpose of group is to help people take control of their communications. To do this they must make conscious what heretofore was out of their awareness, so that they can build skill and precision in understanding and conveying messages to others.

Hannah, the first year or so that she was in group, was a lightning rod for the feelings of others. If unexpressed anger was lurking anywhere in the room, she would pick it up and feel scared. If someone was depressed or suicidal, she would absorb the feeling and become paralyzed with fear and anxiety herself. She was unaware that she was "catching" these feelings from others, and looked for reasons in her life outside the group for explanations. As the group members became aware of her tendency, they helped her identify from whom in the room she was attracting that feeling, and encouraged her to ask that person what was going on with him, so that she could, in a sense, "give his feelings back to him."

Hannah was a stunningly sensitive individual, but her intuition, potentially a resource, was too much the property of her unconscious. In order to keep from going completely crazy from picking up vibrations from everybody everywhere, she needed to keep in mind that she might be absorbing feelings from others, and determine exactly what cues she was reading from the other person that were suggesting the particular feeling she had tapped into. Painstakingly, we made her analyze her intuitions until she gained control over them. Gradually the process became more spontaneous and she was able to say something like, "Hey, Nate. Are you feeling sad tonight? I'm noticing your mouth is sort of turned down at the corners and your eyes are sort of droopy."

John came to the group with phobic symptomatology focusing on the fear that he had cancer. Along with a very high level of anxiety, John occasionally experienced severe stomach pains, for which there seemed to be no medical explanation.

John talked very slowly and deliberately with a wide and frozen smile on his face. Even when talking about his fear of cancer, he maintained this rigidly cheerful visage. His communication was so incongruent that group members could barely listen to him, much less empathize with his fright. I decided to

let John's stomach pain communicate with us and him, figuring it would probably do a better job of letting us all know what the problem was than John's
conscious mind had been able to manage so far.

"John," I said, "Your stomach is obviously trying to tell you something.
Zero in on the pain and let it give you its message from your unconscious."
Without even questioning the instruction, John closed his eyes and put his
hand on his stomach. A minute or so later he began to cry.

"I had a memory of my mother taking care of me when I was sick. She
is feeding me soup and giving me a warm heating pad for my stomach. I am
still so dependent on her even though I don't live with her. She won't always
be there for me. I must learn to nurture myself more."

Shortly thereafter John met a nurturing woman whom he married a year
later. The story has a poignant conclusion. The year he married, John's
mother developed cancer of the stomach. Perhaps John's symptoms were a
message from his mother's unconscious, telling him to separate from her so
as to be independent enough to survive her death. As communications from
his unconscious, John's stomach pains gave John and the group guidance on
how to proceed with his therapy, focusing on his dependency. During his
mother's illness up until her death, with the group's constant support, John
was able to show his love and share his sadness with his mother without any
somatization of her symptoms.

In *The Psychic Thread: Paranormal and Transpersonal Aspects of Psychotherapy* (1983), Mintz says psychic experiences are far more likely to happen
when they serve some useful purpose in a person's life. John needed to plan
for his mother's death. His symptom had an important meaning which was
able to be determined and appreciated in group. As a result of John's experience, all the group members had a new respect for the fine ways in which
the unconscious makes itself known to us, if only we will pay attention.

Structuring Time with Other People

Eric Berne (1972, p. 22) suggests that there are six basic classifications for
the "short-term structuring of time in human social behavior." He says when
people are in a room together, they have six possible kinds of social behavior
to choose from:

1) *withdrawal*—no overt communication occurring.
2) *rituals*—the safest form of social action, stylized interchanges, which,
   whether formal or informal, become absolutely predictable.

3) *activities*—commonly called "work"—oriented toward external reality, task-oriented; programmed by the material being worked with, not by the spontaneous wishes of individuals.
4) *pastimes*—not as stylized or predictable as rituals, but have a certain repetitive quality; cocktail party talk; acceptable subjects are talked about in acceptable ways.
5) *games*—sets of ulterior transactions, repetitive in nature, with a well-defined psychological payoff.
6) *intimacy*—candid, game-free, mutual.

Berne felt that, in order to be socially competent, one must be able to participate in all six forms of interaction. For instance, it is a real limitation not to be able to *withdraw* when one needs to or when it is socially appropriate. We see this in group with the anxious individual who cannot tolerate silences. Not being able to engage in *pastimes* would hamper one greatly at parties or in business. *Rituals* give order to our lives and structure our communication, while the value of cooperation in work or *activities* is obvious. Even *games* should not be taboo, if only because they are so prevalent that it behooves us to be aware of them.

I prefer to call Berne's sixth category (intimacy) by Moreno's term *telic communication*. Free from transference and games, it is time during which connections are mutual, spontaneous, and genuine, although not necessarily peaceful.

In a therapy group all forms of communication take place in every session. Each provides a different kind of frame of reference for the group. There are many instances of silence and *withdrawal* by certain individuals or the whole group. Not only do all groups share *rituals* like getting coffee before group or writing their checks at the end, but each group develops its own rituals. Notable in this respect was the group that insisted on a group hug at the end of each session for a whole year. *"Pastiming"* is a frequent occurrence even during the session, but even more so in the halls before the meeting or at social get-togethers afterwards, The group itself is an *activity,* but sometimes extra exercises or warm-ups are designed by the leaders to facilitate interaction or self-examination. *Games* take place inevitably, as we mentioned under "set-ups." *Telic communication* is the constant goal and challenge for the therapy group. As the group matures, telic communication takes up a larger and larger percentage of the group's time, and the other five processes recede considerably. The ratio of the time spent in telic communication relative to time spent in these other social pursuits is a good measure of participants' involvement in the group and of the quality of the therapy taking place for the individual clients.

RELATEDNESS AND RELATIONSHIPS

"What are people for?"

"Where do I fit in?"

"Does anybody really understand?"

These are questions pertaining to *relatedness*. The interpersonal frame of reference is partly a function of the way one perceives oneself in relationship to the world of people. Research has demonstrated that people who perceive themselves as isolated are more susceptible to mental and physical illness than those who see and feel themselves as connected to others (Totman, 1979). This section will explore some ways in which the therapy group teaches clients the experience of "relatedness."

People everywhere are always talking about *relationships*. Talk shows, rap groups, magazines and books spew forth information and theories about how people can "make their relationships more meaningful." In this section, we will throw in our "two cents" on the subject, suggesting ways in which group participation changes the interpersonal frame of reference in ways that positively affect the clients' relationships with important people in their lives.

In this section we are dealing with some of the curative factors in group therapy that happen almost automatically in any cohesive, well-functioning therapy group. While the skill and style of the leader are crucial in the development of such an environment (see Chapters V and VI), the group works a magic of its own. The group harbors resources for the individual that cannot be duplicated in individual therapy. The group actually *provides* relatedness and relationships for the individual.

Exposure to Other People

Georgette, at 27, had worked since she was 18, but had never been part of any "group" other than her family of origin. She still lived with her family, which consisted of her old-fashioned parents, younger brother, and schizophrenic older sister. For three years of participation in group, Georgette carefully tried to hide how little she knew about sex, politics, travel, or any other matters of the world. Participating minimally and superficially herself, she gained exposure to people who had had experiences she had never dreamed of. In group, Georgette acquired a healthy curiosity about people, some social skills, and a feeling of concern for others.

Elizabeth, as mentioned in Chapter II, had no "good pictures in her mind" of men. She assumed most of them were insensitive, like her father and the man who had raped her. Elizabeth was gratified as well as surprised to realize how vulnerable and tender the men in her group could be. Prejudices on the part of men who believe women are avaricious, domineering, or whatever, are similarly dispelled by the group experience. Homo- and bisexuals are much better understood by heterosexuals after the group gives them a chance to air their views and share their feelings. Because of the depth of the interaction that takes place, group therapy is a good place for learning to quickly move beyond professional labels, skin color, ethnic background, or religious persuasion, and to get to know people for who they are.

Group members are sometimes asked to deal with situations or people that they might never be exposed to anywhere else. Once a member of one of my groups decided to change his sex and become a woman. I certainly had no experience with transsexuals and, not surprisingly, no one else in the group had either. Our association with Mark, who later became Blanche, opened our eyes to complexities with regard to gender identity that had never occurred to us. Several people in the group had nightmares about castration during the period that Mark was in the group, but all listened as sympathetically as they could to his feelings and the reasoning behind his decision.

In group, the plethora of stories from persons of all backgrounds provides the group member with all kinds of data on everything, from the complexities of everyday living to instances of severe psychopathology. The net result is a larger frame of reference and a more refined social awareness for members and leaders alike.

Empathy

No one writes more eloquently on empathy than Carl Rogers. The following quotes are from *A Way of Being* (1980):

> Empathy means entering the private perceptual world of the other, and become thoroughly at home in it. It involves being sensitive, moment by moment, to the changing felt meanings which flow to this other person. (p. 142) . . . . In some sense it means that you lay aside yourself; this can only be done by persons who are secure enough in themselves that they know they will not get lost in what may turn out to be the strange or bizarre world of the other (p. 143). . . . Empathy dissolves alienation, at least temporarily (p. 151). . . . An empathic way of being can be learned from empathic persons (p. 150).

Empathy is the most valuable gift one can offer to the person in psychic pain. Empathy is often all that is needed to initiate therapeutic change, for it provides what Donald Bloch* terms "the right kind of discrepant information" needed to cause a crucial shift in paradigms. If someone's view of the world has presupposed his being all alone, then feeling empathy from another would contradict a basic assumption, forcing him into a new frame of reference that includes at least some component of being accepted and understood. This is a very radical change that has all kinds of implications and ramifications in the person's thinking, feeling, and behavior.

Empathy had such an effect in the case of one group client, Bruce, who for 17 years had made obscene telephone calls and/or engaged in voyeurism several times a week. He was in group for two years before he felt safe enough to bring up these compulsive practices, which he considered unspeakably shameful. The group's response completely amazed him. Everyone responded not to the deeds themselves, but to the pain and humiliation he was experiencing. One woman cried for him when she heard his story. They could see how the fear of being found out would haunt him each day, and sensed his frustration at not being able to stop a behavior so counter to his values and the way he wanted to be seen by people.

The group also helped Bruce understand how the people who received his obscene phone calls felt, by telling of their own unnerving experiences with such things. Women in the group related how just one such call could keep them on edge for weeks. Understanding the effect of his behavior on others gave him empathy for them, and this was a great deterrent against his continuing to make the calls.

The empathy he received and felt for others was of paramount importance in Bruce's subsequent overcoming of his problem. His acting-out dramatically decreased to about one instance every three months. When he felt the need to make an obscene call, he would usually call a group member for help. The honest caring and support he received were far more rewarding than the primitive thrill he had received from his acting-out, and left him feeling connected and proud, rather than ashamed and lonely.

Some group members are naturally empathic, but others have to learn empathy as an interpersonal skill. Hearing people's stories in group frequently causes one to tap into similar experiences in one's own life, and this is the beginning of empathy. The behavior and responses of highly empathic people can be noticed and imitated to some extent by the group member who is a novice in this regard.

I sometimes teach empathy to group members via the psychodramatic technique of *doubling*. In psychodrama, a double is one who plays the alter-

---

*The Family Study Center of Connecticut, Inc., Hartford, CT, January 22, 1982.

ego of the subject ("protagonist") of the drama. The double assumes a posture similar to his "subject" and, listening intently to him, tries to determine what is *not* being said. The double listens particularly for the underlying feelings, doubts, or inconsistencies. For example, Joe notices Karen casting dirty looks at the therapist and also smiling nervously. He asks Karen if he can "double" for her. He says, as Karen, to the therapist, "I'm really angry at you right now, but I'm afraid you won't like me if I tell you." He then checks with Karen to see if his hunch is correct. Karen assents, feeling more confident about expressing her anger now that she knows someone understands her ambivalence about speaking up.

Doubling is a function of *tele* and, in turn, increases *tele*. It is a skill which enhances relationships both in group and in clients' lives outside.

Compassion

Compassion is a cousin of empathy, but different in its quality and expression. Defined as "pity, or inclining to be helpful, merciful" (Oxford Dictionary, 1978), it implies a concern on the part of one person for another as opposed to empathy (understanding or "doubling"). May (1969, p. 289) says compassion is the opposite of apathy. It is the state in which something, or someone, does *matter*.

Compassion in a group is more often expressed through silence than through words, sometimes accompanied by some sort of physical gesture of caring, such as a reaching out or an embrace. Moustakas recognizes the power of the compassionate response of the group to inspire the individual to rise above his despair:

(They) . . . will fall silent . . . and the strange thing is that this silence is not felt by the other person as indifference. . . . It is as if this silence had more meaning than a thousand words could ever have. It is as if he were being drawn into a field of force from which fresh strength flows into him. He feels suffused with a strange confidence. . . . And it may be that in this hour, the resolve will be born to set out on the path that turns a wretched existence into a life of happiness (1972, p. 120).

I gratefully experienced a group's compassion in a session held a few hours after I had attended the funeral of a dear friend who had committed suicide. Overcome with feelings of loss, confusion, anger, and awe, I chose to tell the group of the sad event, rather than pretend everything was "normal." As I told them, tears welled up and I cried freely in front of the group. Along with some of the other feelings, I stated my deep sense of gratitude toward them for allowing me to help them, as my friend had not allowed his friends and his therapist to help him. I felt the group's caring in the silence that followed. When members spoke up, they spoke of their appreciation of me and how much impact I had had on them. Their words had an incredibly soothing effect on me. I did not need for them to "understand" exactly what I was going through; that would have required that they become the therapist and I the client, which would not have been appropriate or necessary. I simply needed to express my sorrow and feel their compassion for a few minutes. For some of the members, the experience of being able to help me in my time of pain was as valuable and validating as it was comforting for me.

In a good group, compassion should never be too far in the background. The most excruciating encounters, if laced with compassion, will turn out therapeutically, while the mildest confrontation in a group where the bedrock of trust and caring does not exist can be devastating for someone. Again we quote Moustakas, who, after many years as a group therapist in the days of the "total honesty" encounter and sensitivity groups, has concluded that honesty, in the sense of saying exactly what is on your mind at all times, is not necessarily the best policy in groups or in life. He says:

> the compassionate approach does not use honesty as a weapon, but as an attitude or perspective that recognizes the importance of responding uniquely to the compelling nature of each situation (1972, p. 123).

He distinguishes between *honesty* and *truthfulness*. When we are being truthful, we respond not just from our "gut," but from the larger framework of our values and beliefs, which, he believes, includes our desire to be compassionate toward others.

Relief from Loneliness

Most people, upon entering therapy, are lonely. They feel it in at least one of the following ways:

First, they may be suffering from the lack of one significant other person in their lives, usually a sexual partner. Many clients enter group on the heels of a divorce or separation, facing what they perceive as the wasteland of single life. They have joined the ranks of those who sleep alone in the bed, sit alone in restaurants, and call AAA instead of a spouse to jumpstart their car. Sunday afternoons are particularly lonely for some; Saturday nights for others.

Secondly, they may be experiencing the kind of loneliness that is related to anonymity. When I was living alone in an apartment in New York City years ago, I was so unknown—in my building and my neighborhood—that

I found myself wondering, whether, if I died, anyone would find out about it. It sometimes seemed that, since no one seemed to notice me, I was not even there. This was a terribly lonely feeling. It alleviated my loneliness tremendously to join my first therapy group at that time. I find many of my clients are in similar situations when they enter group therapy.

The third kind of loneliness is a sense of unconnectedness — with self as well as others, and with what is *real* (Moustakas, 1972). This sense of alienation can be felt alone, in a crowd, with close friends, family, or even with a lover. It is a condition in which we are cut off from our spontaneity and energy. Other people, even when they desire to help, cannot make us feel replenished. This amorphous loneliness is often intransigent and is a large component of depression. In this state we shun the very things that we need — interdependence, closeness, and stimulation.

May attributes the loneliness of modern human beings to: 1) a loss of a sense of *community* (May et al., 1958, p. 58), and 2) a distortion of *love* to the point where it is perceived as a problem as much as a boon (May, 1969, p. 1). This section and the following one will discuss how group therapy combats loneliness by restoring the interpersonal resources of community and love, integrating them into the psychotherapy process.

Loneliness is a function of one's view of the world, a frame of reference which assumes the world to be an environment which is hostile or excluding of oneself, that must be changed for successful psychotherapy. Group therapy creates concrete experiences of connectedness that compete with the subjective "realities" of isolation and alienation. As a client begins unburdening himself of his troubles and making friends in the group, he may start to see the possibilities for doing this in other environments as well. Gradually, because *he* is less lonely, the world seems a less lonely place. As he stays in group over a period of years, he develops relationships that are as close as family. He has experiences with people that he may never have had in childhood, which afford him a sense of belonging and being cared for. The therapy group does not mean "misery loves company," although connecting through pain may be gratifying. It means people need other people, far more than they themselves realize at times, and in many different ways, most of which the therapy group can accommodate.

The Therapy Group: An Alternative to the Family in Combating Loneliness?

As a therapist I vacillate in my view of how important it is or is not for people to be involved with their families of origin. Even though many of my clients have families that are crazy and destructive, I do not encourage them to break off ties completely. Family therapists have proved that even the most disturbed families, when provided with competent treatment, can be restored to health and offer their members warmth, support, and affirmation. Individual clients who are in group or one-to-one therapy can often effect changes in their family systems. On the hope that something will happen through the treatment or via serendipity to influence the family in a healthy direction, I tell my clients to maintain some contact with their family, no matter how minimal. In the meantime, however, they may still feel lonely and rootless.

Single clients tend to be lonely whether they are connected to or cut off from their families of origin, while clients who are happily married with children usually feel much more a part of things. From the therapist's vantage point, therefore, it would seem that, for adults, having a "family" of one's own might be essential in combating loneliness. Sociologists are not so sure. They debate about the value of the family as an institution in the modern world, asking whether it is an antidote or a catalyst for loneliness.

Slater (1976) has pointed out that overcrowding and technocratic expansion have caused us to seek out privacy to a pathological degree. He credits this trend with responsibility for the prevalence of loneliness in today's society. He espouses a more collectivistic culture, such as existed before affluence allowed families to buy their own houses in the suburbs and isolate themselves from one another. The nuclear family is not nourished from the outside and cannot, therefore, provide adequate stimulation and nurturance to its members.

Parsons (1954) contradicted himself with respect to the family's effectiveness in combating loneliness. For a while he saw the family as the only institution capable of providing security and love, but later he asserted some of its limitations in this respect. He pointed out that, to function smoothly, a small group must have clear role differentiation; and that this is what the family in this day and age no longer has. The emotional pressures of family life cause rifts and tensions which muddy boundaries and destroy efficiency in role performance. The family is inherently resistant to change, Parsons maintains. He suggests (I'm not sure how seriously) that a battery of doctors might be a more effective psychotherapeutic agent than a family, because the doctors' roles would be clear; they can remain objective and unified under pressure; and they are for, rather than against, change.

Lasch (1977) feels that the family has a crucial role to play in the individual battle against loneliness. He feels that the "retreat into privatism" is not negative at all; in fact, it should be encouraged, because it will lead to a return to the family as a resource for comfort and renewal of energy. He says that the family can be a "haven" for the individual, precisely *because* it is not rigid in structure. That the family is a hotbed of emotion is one of its strengths, not a weakness. Even when feelings are hostile or conflicted, the family's emotionalism induces people to feel alive and connected with one another, and, therefore, less lonely. As for psychotherapy, Lasch expresses horror at the thought of the team of doctors that Parsons suggests! Such a contingent in their antiseptic environments have no healing capabilities. With their clinical "objectivity," they epitomize the culture that has caused the loneliness and alienation, which has contributed to the client's needing psychotherapy in the first place.

Slater's and Parsons' arguments against the family and Lasch's polemical defense of it can all be used to support the usefulness and viability of the therapy group. The therapy group meets apart from the family and is not controlled by family tensions, emotions, or history. Yet, it can function as a surrogate or experimental family, offering many of the benefits and few of the liabilities of an actual family.

The therapy group promotes a sense of collectivism and mutuality, thereby disengaging clients from the "pursuit of loneliness," which Slater says the nuclear family fosters. The therapy group answers all of Parsons' criteria for a well-functioning small group and is, therefore, able to provide the indispensable emotional services that the family, because of its inability to differentiate roles and manage tensions, frequently cannot. The therapy group does not take the life out of the process of psychotherapy, as Parsons' "team of doctors" does. The therapy group provides just the environment that Lasch says people need, where emotional ties can be built and strengthened, and strong feelings expressed, without threatening the group's structure or survival.

People Needing People

Once people are connecting with one another and feeling less lonely, what are they giving to one another that is so valuable? What specifically do people need from their association with one another? Maslow (1971, pp. 228–229) suggests they seek feelings of protection and safety, belonging, affection, respect, and self-esteem. I have added to Maslow's list: an environment for expressing themselves; cheering on and celebrating; roots and security; and comfort and renewal. I will discuss each of these, giving examples of how people have found these vital resources in the therapy group when family, work, and social groups have failed them.

Protection and safety. Francine had a spotless performance record as a secretary in a large company, when she was suddenly suspended for a week without pay and given three years' probation, based on a false accusation from another employee that she was engaging in sexual activity with a co-worker. The charges, which were later proven to be fabricated, happened to dovetail with Francine's guilt regarding an extramarital affair she had had while separated from her husband. Never one to be particularly assertive, when she found herself accused, Francine acted as if she were guilty. She hid in her house for days and did not tell a soul about the incident. She refused even to answer the phone. By the night of our group meeting she felt totally wretched, having punished herself all week for something she had not done.

Francine could not confide in her co-workers because she felt too humiliated and because she was not sure she could trust them. She did not want to tell her family because they were likely not to believe her. She did not want to tell her husband because he did not know about the affair she had had while they were separated. Her therapy group was the only place where she felt completely safe in discussing the matter.

The group's response was sympathetic, but practical. They immediately addressed her inappropriate guilt, reminding her that she had done nothing to be ashamed of and urging her to stop acting as if she had. Then they gave her important information about how to pursue a grievance under such conditions. Armed with the group's support and advice, Francine marched back into her office the next week and complained to the administrator that she had been unjustly insulted and penalized for something she had not done. The matter was investigated; she was found to be correct; her pay was refunded, and all reprobations, official and otherwise, were retracted.

Belonging. The feeling of belonging is vital to well-being. Some families provide this optimally, but many people feel more out of place in their families than anywhere else. Jason, 32, had once belonged *to* rather than *in* his family. Extremely wealthy and very authoritarian, his parents had dominated and overprotected him as a child. In the past ten years, Jason and both his siblings had, one by one, been cast out of the family by the parents, literally told "not to darken their door" again. All the expulsions had followed arguments over money.

Although he had seen it happen to the others, Jason could not believe his parents did not want to see him anymore. He made repeated fruitless attempts to be taken back in, trying everything from friendly visits to desperate pleas for money. Each time he was greeted with a slammed door or a phone hang-up. Like Francine, Jason internalized the rejection, unable to see that his parents must be disturbed people if they were willing to lop off their entire progeny, including their grandchildren, whom they had never seen. Unwilling to give up, Jason clung to the idea that, if he could just find the right way to communicate with them, his parents would accept him back.

In the group, Jason tried to reenact his struggle with his parents with my co-therapist and myself. The issue centered around whether he would be "taken back" into individual therapy with my co-therapist, even though he could not pay for it. In addition to our being unwilling to see him individually for free, we felt he needed to learn how to *belong* in the therapy group and not to rely so much on parent figures, in this case the therapists. While we remained firm on this despite his complaints, we also took a very loving and welcoming stance with Jason, so he could not misconstrue our position as an effort to eject him from the group "family."

Jason's life was in shambles when he entered group. He could not find a job, despite two master's degrees, because he was disorganized and tended to sabotage himself on interviews. He had some nice friends, with whom he was too ashamed to associate because he was so broke. He befriended ne'er-do-wells, whom he allowed to become overly dependent on him. He engaged in promiscuous homosexual activity, frequenting "baths" and parks, where the likelihood of contracting a disease or being physically abused was high. (AIDS was not yet known about at that time, or we would have been even more worried than we were.)

The group spent a good deal of time during Jason's first year worrying about his passively self-destructive, even suicidal, tendencies. As he gradually learned to trust them, Jason began to calm down in the sessions and in his life. The biggest step for him was learning to call people when he felt scared, lonely, or needed practical advice. Each time he called he expected to be cut off, but, unlike his parents, group members were happy to hear from him, and gave him support and encouragement. Finally, Jason got a job as a computer salesman, which validated what the group had been telling him all year—that he was an engaging, intelligent fellow with good communication skills. That he felt he "belonged" in the group was clear when he called the group from across the country where he was attending a sales meeting, just to let them know how he was doing and that he was thinking of them.

Affection. Affection is expressed in many ways in a warm and cohesive group. Warm handshakes and hugs are as frequent as they would be in the closest of families. The prevalence of such affection meets an important need of therapy clients in whose families people were hostile or apathetic toward one another.

Another way affection is expressed in groups is through a friendly kind of teasing. When a person feels that people really like him, he can actually enjoy being kidded, and even laugh at himself. Terrence, who was so touchy when he first came into group (see Chapter III), became adept at accepting not only feedback, but some gentle ribbing as well. He was able to do this because he knew that people in the group really liked him, and that, even when they objected to his behavior, they were not putting him down as a person.

In group people take the trouble to say they like each other when they do. So often in families positive feelings are taken for granted and not communicated. Expressing positive feelings for another is an art; it can be learned in group therapy, even when it has not been taught in other environments in the individual's life.

Respect and self-esteem. Respect and protection of self-esteem are vital ingredients in any group if an individual member's self-concept is to improve. Unfortunately, many families and work environments engender disrespect and negativity, crippling their members and employees. There are explicit policies in my groups that help insure respect and guard self-esteem: the confidentiality rule; the right not to speak; the right to say whatever one wishes; the right to make one's own decision without group pressure; the right to express oneself in one's own way. When, upon occasion, as with Erica, an individual invites abuse from another member, I try to intervene in such a way that her right to dignity and self-respect will be preserved, even when she herself is jeopardizing it.

Environment for expressiveness and spontaneity. In particularly close families, people talk openly about their feelings and opinions and are free to be smart, witty, silly, or dramatic when they are so inclined. Few therapy clients come from such families, and few went to schools where such expression was encouraged. In Chapter III we discussed ways that the group fosters spontaneity and the development of new roles.

Cheering on and celebrating. When group client Melissa got married, her mother was too drunk to attend the wedding. When Harry graduated Phi Beta Kappa, his mother and father were going through a divorce, and after arguing for months about which one of them would attend the ceremony, neither one showed up. A great many group clients have had to pass developmental milestones without the kudos and best wishes they deserved and needed. When a client graduates from school or from group, gets married, has a baby, or gets a new job, the group is on hand to cheer them on. When Lenny finally got a job, some of his fellow group members were practically as happy as he was about it. When Sandra was promoted to editor, group members jumped up from their seats to shake her hand and pat her on the back. When Neil took off for Air Force training, the group gave him a party, featuring poems and songs that he could take with him to remember the group by. Hank's graduation from college at age 40 was celebrated after group with champagne. My favorite of such occasions was group's surprise party for Jacob before he went on sabbatical to Israel. As he arrived at the meeting, he was greeted at the door with a blast of Israeli folk music, and swept into a rollicking dance.

Birthdays and Christmas can be lonely for some clients. Ned had his first birthday party when he was 35 years old — in group therapy! One group has an annual Christmas party at my co-therapist's house. Each group finds some small way to celebrate important holidays together.

Roots and security. As the weeks and years go by, each group develops its own history. According to Kellerman (1979), it even has its own generations, where every two years is comparable to 20 years of an individual lifetime, in terms of the amount of change and learning that takes place. People really begin to identify with their group after a year or so, in the way that they might relate to a group of friends from high school or college, or a family they had married into. Such membership gives some of them a feeling of rootedness in the community that they did not have before. The membership of the groups is fairly stable, with a turnover of about two out of eight members a year. We sometimes quip that the groups endure longer than most marriages. For some clients whose childhood was interrupted by frequent geographic moves or changes in family structure through divorce and remarriage, the ongoing weekly therapy group represents a security that is both new and welcome.

Comfort and renewal. The way it is supposed to be in family life, one would hope to be able to find refuge at home from the problems outside. This is another of the deficits inherent in the family life of therapy clients. In fact, for many, home life in childhood provided more stresses than it relieved.

At no time is comfort and renewal more important than at times of sickness and death. When 27-year-old Mathilda contracted cancer, her mother was also dying of cancer halfway across the country. The rest of her family was splintered, and no one was apparently interested in taking care of Mathilda. Group members did a great deal for Mathilda in her last year of life, both practically and emotionally. One or two became very involved with her, but everyone was available to listen to her fears and anger about her illness and to provide her all the kindness they could during a time of extreme suffering. When Mathilda died, it was the comfort group members offered one another that was of the greatest solace to them. This incident is discussed further in Chapter V.

Lionel had been in group two years when his 19-year-old son died in a car accident. Most of the group attended the funeral on Thanksgiving day. While he could not talk easily to his wife (they had been having problems communicating anyway), Lionel was able to share his grief with the group. While nothing could take away the pain, the group made his terrible loss easier to bear.

Love

In *Love and Will* (1969), May points out ways in which love infuses itself into the supposedly clinical process of psychotherapy. Unfortunately, May mentions nothing about group therapy, which is, in my view, where the therapeutic aspects of love and the loving aspects of psychotherapy are most clearly demonstrated.

May suggests four different kinds of love: *sexual love, eros, philia,* and *agape.* All the forms are compatible; a relationship might be characterized by just one or all four types of love. With the exception of sexual love, the expression of which is limited to a verbal level by the therapeutic circumstances, all forms of love are both demonstrated and discussed in group therapy.

Eros is perhaps the most complex form of love. It is the energy between two people that propels them to create together, to "procreate," to bind together, to make a pattern out of chaos. In a marriage it culminates in the urge to have children, or perhaps, alternatively, to build something important or permanent together. An "erotic" partnership in this sense is not sexual, or, rather, it is not strictly sexual. It is an extension of *tele.* It leads to a creative product of the union between the two people. The phenomenon of *eros* seeks stimulation, whereas anxiety or apathy seeks a reduction of stimulation. The most familiar ramification of *eros* is known through love songs and poems as being "in love," but this is only one of its many forms. The healing function of *eros* far surpasses that of the physician, vitamins, or a vacation. As Socrates said, "Human nature will not find a better helper than Eros" (May, 1969, p. 81).

May complains of Freud's view of love, which holds that it is predetermined—not all spontaneous or creative.

Freud defined it as a push from behind, a force coming out of "chaotic, undifferentiated, instinctive energy sources" along predictable and prescribable paths toward mature life and only partially, painfully civilized love (Morgan, 1964, p. 35).

May prefers the Platonic concept:

> Whereas for Plato, *eros* is entirely bound up with the possibilities ahead which "pull" one; it is the yearning for union, the capacity to relate to new forms of human experience. It is wholly telic, goal directed, and moves toward the "more-than-nature" (May, 1969, p. 88).

May believes a synthesis of the Freudian and Platonic views of love is the most useful. He underlines the different presuppositions about the nature of feelings that are implicit in each view. The "Freudian" view conceives of feelings operating like "glandular hydraulics," forces which push us, predetermined by past experiences (1969, p. 90). May objects to this mechanistic view. He cites the alternative, Platonic, theory:

> . . . emotions are not just a push from the rear, but a pointing toward something, an impetus for forming something, a call to mold the situation. Feelings are not just a chance state of the moment, but a pointing toward the future, a way I *want* something to be. . . . Feelings are rightfully a way of communicating with significant people in our world, a reaching out to mold the relationship with them; they are a language by which we interpersonally construct and build. That is to say, feelings are *intentional* (1969, p. 91).

In therapy, though it is sound to ask, as Freud would, "the reason why," it is just as relevant to ask the "purpose for" an emotion, as Plato would be wont to do. Knowing feelings in this way opens up new possibilities. If we let our feelings show us what we want, or where we are impelled to go next, they will lead us to imagine goals and take more risks. *Eros* is the strongest example of the "progressive" as opposed to "regressive" impetus of a feeling.

If spontaneity and *tele* are operating over time in a therapy group, *eros* is sure to develop, and its healing magic to begin to operate on the members. *Eros* in group is marked by an increase in the amount of passion with which participants discuss their feelings about one another, their relationships outside, their work, their lives in general. Not only are their right brains activated, as we discussed earlier, but their hearts are involved as well. As this occurs, their speech becomes more alive, metaphorical, and rhythmic. The union between the creative imaginations of individuals produces dialogue which is fresh, insightful, humorous, and often very powerful.

In group, *eros* and *tele* are almost synonymous. May captures the sense of high telic energy in the group when he says,

Our feelings not only take into consideration the other person but are in a real sense partially *formed by the feelings of the other persons present*. We *feel* in a magnetic field (1969, p. 91).

The incredible fullness and exhilaration that I feel when people are really connecting in a group are *eros*. Fascinating ideas and rich imagery are left swirling in my imagination after the session. I have strong feelings about each person and am aware of their feelings for one another and for me. It makes me want to create something—a poem or a picture, or, perhaps, another session. *Eros* must have been the impetus for this book. Eros makes you feel as if you were burgeoning with creativity, or as George Bach said to me, as if you were "perpetually nine months pregnant."

Agape is a love that is concerned for the welfare of the other without hope of gain. Zinker, a Gestalt therapist, declares the kind of love he feels for clients is agapeic.

. . . more a feeling of good will toward humanity than a romantic, sentimental, or possessive love. I seek my client's good, whether I like him or not. Agape love for me is thoughtful, prudent, just, benevolent, gracious. The term "brotherly love" has been used in this sense. My own image is of "grandparently love" (Zinker, 1977, p. 6).

A client who receives such a love from his therapist is almost certain to benefit from its healing effects. In a therapy group one can receive such a love from more than one person and learn how to give it as well.

Ben, an embittered, depressed 40-year-old man, rarely seemed interested in other people's problems for the first year of group. His particular group had a remarkable capacity for unconditional caring. Although group members told him that his cold looks and lack of responsiveness were keeping them at a distance, they remained very friendly toward him. They never got angry at his aloofness, understanding that he was, after all, in pain, and would probably retreat further if pressured. Although he tried not to show it, Ben was astonished and pleased at the group's benevolence toward him, and from time to time he gingerly stepped out of his shell enough to laugh at someone's funny remark or to share from his own experience. The person in the group who sparked a bit of feeling in Ben was Lenny, the young man discussed in Chapter II who was struggling so hard to get work. Often, when Lenny was talking, Ben would listen attentively and offer support and advice. One could see that Ben really wanted Lenny to succeed. Such an unselfish concern for another was a real change for Ben and it had a liberating effect on him. He began to be able to express himself a bit more to women he wanted to date, as well as to his children The terrible wounds that Ben had suffered in childhood were beginning to be healed by the quiet and soothing strength of *agape,* as it was shown him by the group and as it was tapped from deep inside himself.

Philia "is friendship in the simplest, most direct terms" (May, 1969, p. 317). It is seen most clearly in the "chum period" as described by Harry Stack Sullivan (1940), the period between the ages of eight and 12, before the heterosexual functioning of the individuals has matured. This period is free of sexual tensions and constraints. With adults, it can exist with or without a sexual relationship. The essence of it is the simple liking of one another and the liking to be with one another in a relaxed and comfortable way. May says *philia* is a necessary companion to *eros,* suggesting that people "short circuit" on passion if they do not experience some *philia* to balance it out (1969, p. 319).

Philia seems to be a missing ingredient in many people's lives. Although the women's movement has encouraged the pursuit of same gender friendships among men and women, these relationships tend not to be valued as highly as sexual partnerships. There is often some hesitancy on the part of marrieds to fraternize with members of the opposite sex, because of issues of jealousy; so nonsexual male-female relationships are still rather unusual. All in all, philial relationships are rarer than they should be, given the fact that they provide such important satisfactions.

Group therapy is an environment where strong philial attachments are made and maintained. Group members form close bonds through their mutual group experience as well as other common interests. Over the ten years that I have been leading groups, ten of my group clients have become roommates, and two have shared a sculpture studio. Two have traveled together. I myself still have close friends from a therapy group I was in ten years ago. In every group some members seek one another out for friendship and companionship. They meet for coffee or dinner; go jogging or play racketball; attend a concert, a movie or a party; or go to an AA or Alanon meeting together. If two friends in a group develop a problem or a misunderstanding, they usually are able to work it out between themselves on the strength of the communication and honesty built up in the relationship through group. They also know the group can help them if severe difficulties arise between them.

Intimacy

Many people who crave intimacy have difficulties in managing it. The deep-seated feelings of dependency and fears of abandonment that generally accompany an intimate relationship may cause them either to cling frantically to their loved ones or to unwittingly push them away.

Group therapy is a suitable training ground on which to learn to recognize, tolerate, and enhance intimacy. The "no-sex" contract in the group makes it less threatening to make one's fears, longings, and other tender feelings known to others, and to feel a closeness with others.

Frank, who, like his family of origin, was neither spontaneous nor affectionate, frequently whined to the group about his inability to find a girlfriend. When people sympathized or in other ways extended themselves to him, he shrugged them off and resumed complaining. He invited advice which he would reject out of hand, insisting that the group did not understand his problem. He managed to make the group feel as frustrated as he was. His group behavior, unbeknownst to him, was absolutely parallel to his social behavior outside. The women he was meeting were responding to nonverbal signs of hostility that he did not even know he was exhibiting.

One night Frank's fellow group member, Sandra, told Frank that she "knew he didn't like" her, and proceeded to enumerate all the ways he had pushed her away. Since Frank did like Sandra a great deal, he was stunned to hear how cold and rejecting he had been to her. This was the beginning of Frank's realization that he had strongly ambivalent feelings about the intimacy he said he wanted. Frank was inadvertently turning people off because the highly charged feelings associated with intimacy scared him. Group became for him a process of experiencing closeness in small, manageable doses and becoming aware of his anxiety so that he did not unwittingly turn it into hostility. Sandra was the first person with whom he practiced. A warm and accepting woman, who found Frank attractive despite his reserve with her, she consistently showed Frank appreciation and acceptance. At first he responded to her with gruffness and embarrassment, but as he got used to her wanting to be close, he began letting himself feel and express positive feelings for her in return.

As he began loosening up with Sandra, Frank became aware of how he had shut off closeness with the rest of the group. Frank had a strong need for physical contact, but had not allowed himself to ask for backrubs and hugs in the group. In fact, if someone approached him to embrace him after the session, he would stiffen up or dart out of the room.

Awareness of his fear and how assiduously he had avoided closeness with people came as quite a shock to Frank, but was very therapeutic. His real problem, fear of intimacy, having been identified, Frank no longer wasted his time and the group's with depressing analyses of why he was such a social failure. Instead, he began to take risks in the group—expressing sexual attraction when he felt it, offering to hug people, asking to be held, and so on. As he developed more skill in intimacy in the group, he began having more success with women outside. When he found one he liked, he was able to relax and enjoy her rather than set her up to reject him.

Commitment

Rollo May says we live in a "schizoid world" (1969, p. 16), characterized by an inability to feel and a fear of close relationships. Love, he says, requires *enduringness*. Our society ascribes more value to sexual attractiveness and performance than to loyalty and commitment. There is an emphasis on short-term ephemeral sexual or romantic pleasures. Desire for material acquisition and instant gratification is robbing relationships of their meaning and strength.

The lack of emphasis on commitment is related by some writers to a general lack of confidence in the future of the human species (May, 1969; Frank, 1978) and our lack of willingness to insure it. As Maslow says, "We have come to a point in biological history where we are now responsible for our own evolution" (1971, p. 11); yet, most people worry relatively little about such things as the nuclear threat, devastating affronts to ecology, and severe environmental hazards to physical and mental health. May and Frank would relate this apathy to society's shared expectation of inevitable and impending doom.

The "tomorrow we die" approach to life carries with it a "tomorrow we diet" attitude toward love. Most people want to gobble love up rather than tend to and nurture it. As a result, love, like many of our natural resources, seems to be dwindling. Many people's frames of reference do not even include the possibility of satisfying short-term involvements with other people, much less a goal of a long-term, committed relationship.

In group we hope to accomplish what May says is so desperately needed, "a new consciousness in which depth and meaning of personal relationships will occupy a central place" (1969, p. 279).

One of the ways the group teaches commitment is through attendance. The very act of agreeing to attend one night a week over an indeterminate period of time is a substantial commitment, which is severely tested when, in order to attend a meeting, tempting invitations must be turned down; bad weather braved; or sizeable internal resistances overcome. One year one of my groups had four male members, each of whom traveled from 30 to 50 miles each way to attend group. One of the men was a medical student intern who worked 100 hours a week and still found time to attend group. Another was the president of a large company who adjusted his travel schedule around group meetings. Experienced members are aware that the group functions much better when everyone attends. New members see how important the group seems to be to the old members and get the message that there is something valuable for them and others about coming consistently, that just one absence affects the cohesiveness of the group and can diminish its therapeutic value for everybody.

Clients who come from alcoholic homes and other disruptive environments often have problems with commitment. In the childhoods of these clients, so many promises were made and broken, so many goals relinquished and forgotten, that the whole business of making commitments and having them made to them brings up anxiety, anger, and conflict. The group helps such an individual deal with these past experiences and separate them from the realities of the present. Group helps him set appropriate expectations of himself and others in relationships, by pointing out where he is being unrealistic or needlessly pessimistic. For clients who have trouble with commitment, the group provides a reassuring steadiness; it is always there, a reliable source of support and feedback. The client who has been undependable as a partner in marriage, as a parent, team member or employee, receives an opportunity to deal with his guilt about disappointing people and to restore his confidence in his ability to live up to his commitments, emotionally, financially and professionally. In group one can experience what it is like to be a valuable and valued member of a team. Hopefully, this will translate into a healthier attitude about commitment in marriage, family, and professional life.

For some members experiencing the group's commitment to them is a much-needed therapeutic experience. When Jason had a party and everyone in the group came, he was totally amazed. Since Jason's family had thrown him and his brothers out of their lives, he had little faith in people meaning what they said about his value to them. While it was never discussed, the group knew that Jason, in inviting them to the party, was offering a timid hope that the group would not disappoint him as his family had. Sensing this, we could not *not* come; so, even though the minimum distance for anyone was 50 miles, we all made it. It turned out to be well worth it; not only was Jason pleased, but the party was delightful.

The commitment my co-therapists and I show to our groups is very strong. We are virtually never absent. We are consistent in our supportiveness and enthusiasm. We read, attend workshops and training, and seek consultation to become the best therapists we can be for our clients. The clients model themselves after us and develop toward one another and the group as a whole an almost passionate loyalty.

Humility, Objectivity, Reason, Flexibility, Acceptance of Change

Continued love for another "requires the development of humility, objectivity, and reason" (Fromm, 1956, p. 101), as well as flexibility and acceptance of change.

The intensity of the group process causes enough anxiety to eventually elicit each person's unreasonableness, irrationality, and rigidity — at least upon occasion. Being "caught in the act" is in itself a humbling experience. Grandiose assumptions about oneself rarely survive the scrutiny of the group for very long. An inflated ego is usually quite quickly deflated by confrontation and feedback in the group. If a person survives the pain of this and attends to the negative feedback, he may cultivate a kind of humility and modesty which will command far more respect both in the group and out than did his former conceited attitude.

Extreme dependency demands that nothing change in relationships. Mother, the breast, the love partner, the therapist, must be *right there* always, no matter what. With all that goes on in group therapy, it is guaranteed that a person harboring this kind of fantasy will soon find it frustrated. Such an occurrence can be beneficial, as it was for Terrence, when the threat of change mobilized his grandiosity and rigidity:

The day before my vacation Terrence called me at home to ask for an "emergency" individual session to deal with some current employment problems. I said these particular problems were not of an emergency nature and refused. When I came back, Terrence stormed into his regularly scheduled individual session and, without greeting or social amenities about my vacation, announced he was going to quit individual therapy and just be in group. He not very subtly implied that this was because I had not helped him "recently." His anger in presenting this was incongruous, in that I also thought he was ready to terminate individual therapy and just be in group. I suggested he might be angry at me for taking a vacation. He said, no, that he was angry at me for "not being concerned about him" enough to schedule an extra appointment before my vacation.

In group that week Terrence made oblique references to losing people — his girlfriend of two years ago, friends in other cities. I asked him if he was afraid he was losing me because he was not going to be seeing me individually. He denied it, again questioning my competence and concern. I asked him if he could accept a change in our relationship without having to "make me wrong" in some way.

The question put Terrence in touch with a fear that any shifts in the structure of our relationship meant for him the possibility of its ending completely. My vacation had been a change, a mini-abandonment. He did not thoroughly trust himself or me when it came to changing our routine with one another in any way. One of us might not meet our responsibilities and precipitate a total loss of the relationship. As he worked this through he realized,

Something very special, the exclusivity of my relationship with Mary, may be coming to an end. It's my choice to make this change, and I don't have to denegrate her to be independent, the way we all had to do in my family. My relationships with you all [group members] have also changed. You people are a part of me now. You are all my therapists now. It's different for me to have more than one important person to rely on. I guess sometimes change does not always have to be worse. Sometimes change is better.

Managing Jealousy

Most people agree in theory with Maslow that if you "love you leave it alone" (1971, p. 17). Self-help books and groups talk incessantly about the need for space and flexibility in relationships. Plants need air in order to breathe and so do people, we are told, and strangling our mates is a poor way to hold on to them. We must develop autonomy, independence, self-worth. Sounds good—but how?

The feelings underlying jealousy are very deep and very painful, having to do with fear and rage. They are not easily put aside. Many of my group members have managed to do so, but sometimes it has taken years of painful work.

Many people entering group have a tremendous problem with sexual jealousy. Some have lost marriages because of it. These are often the group members who, even though the group precludes "dating," form attachments to other members based on sexual attraction. When the object of their attraction in the group seems interested in any other member, their easily ignited jealousy flares.

At first they will handle these feelings as they might outside the group. They may deny them, obsess about them, avoid the object of them, or try to turn them into other feelings. In group jealous individuals are encouraged to speak openly about what they are feeling, no matter how embarrassed, fearful, or angry they may be. In this way their jealousy can be traced back to its origins in childhood. Often sibling rivalry has been a major issue for such clients, or perhaps an intense Oedipal conflict is resurfacing that needs to be resolved. Both of these situations are replicated symbolically in the group "family," where struggles ensue among members for the attention of the therapist, or between a member and co-therapist or some other parent figure for the affections of the (other) therapist.

Jealousy issues are among the most difficult to resolve in group, but are also among the most important, as the story of Joan and Erica illustrated. For jealousies to be resolved, both parties must be shown that there is enough caring and attention to go around in the group. In many cases, in their families, caring, nurturance, affection, and approval were scarce and had to be fought over; in contrast, the supply of these resources in group is ample. The therapist, particularly, must try to be fully available to everyone, while maintaining some limits so as not to become emotionally depleted by the demands of any one member.

When jealousy is extremely severe and pathological, it may not be possible to deal with it constructively in group. The pathologically jealous person has extreme feelings of love and hate toward the therapist. He sees other members one minute as his rivals for the therapist's attention and the next as his allies in his attempts to hurt the therapist. At any given time, the therapist, the other clients, or both may be seen as having betrayed him. He is constantly bitter and paranoid, causing great fear and tension in those around him.

A pathologically jealous individual in a group is like a wounded tiger in a cage with healthier animals. The other members are afraid of the tiger and figure out strategies to avoid his wrath. Yet, when he is not attacking them directly, they can see how much pain and terror he is experiencing, and they believe him when he says that somehow they have caused it. Thus, when the jealous person finally leaves the group, they feel both relieved and guilty. They are angry at the therapist for subjecting them to this person, but they also doubt the therapist's competence, since the jealous person clearly was not helped by the experience. Secretly at first, then more openly, they wonder if they, too, will be "kicked out" of the group if they allow themselves to be jealous or angry. Their most dreadful fantasy is that they have killed the "tiger" member off, meaning that they too could be killed off. This guilty fear is revealed in their frequent questions to the therapists after the "wounded tiger's" departure. "Have you seen 'so-and-so'?" They are never interested in details; they just want to make sure the "tiger" is still alive.

Four or five people in my groups over the years were not able to manage their jealousy, despite all my efforts at providing them with reassurance and security. Eventually, they had to be removed from the group and seen in individual therapy. While the individuals in all cases did very well in one-to-one therapy, these clients' group participation had caused unnecessary pain and hardship for everyone, and I rued the day I had put them in the group. Good screening can uncover pathological jealousy, which should be brought to manageable levels in individual treatment before group therapy is attempted. Unfortunately, a severe jealousy problem does not always appear until the person has been in the group for a while and starts to develop strong feelings for people. By that time, he is already embroiled in one traumatic episode after another.

BOUNDARIES IN INTERPERSONAL FUNCTIONING

"That's what group therapy is all about," said client Joan, "Boundaries — flexible ones with doors in them."

Helen Durkin, from four decades of experience as a group psychoanalyst and writer about group therapy, says almost the same thing: "The goal of therapy, to help group members restore or enhance their own autonomy, is concretized into the more practical goal of helping group members open and close their boundaries" (1981, p. 6).

In the section on "Contact Operations," we discussed the "boundarying" process of group therapy as put forth by Durkin. Here we will briefly enumerate some specific boundary problems people bring to therapy and how they are addressed in group therapy.

Some people are never satisfied. No matter how much love, stimulation, advice, or positive reinforcement they receive, they seem to want more. They are perpetually hungry and seek satisfaction of their needs at others' expense. They do not perceive, much less respect, the "boundaries" of others. It is rare that a group will not harbor at least one such individual. These are clients who are hard to treat in individual therapy because the therapist feels she is being eaten alive. A well-functioning group, having collectively more tolerance, strength, and choices than a therapist alone, can effectively set limits on such intrusive people. For example, if a person monopolizes the conversation, the group gives him feedback which may or may not persuade him to change his habits, but which does set a clear boundary with him. If he does not understand why people are irritated with him, he will feel hurt and angry and start to withdraw, closing his boundaries very tight. Hopefully, before he retreats completely, however, he will look around and find that there are one or two people who have offered no criticism of him. He then has the option of psychologically embracing them as allies, thereby drawing a new boundary by which he includes himself in a subgroup with these members. His identification with these less verbal individuals may help him set his own limits on his monopolizing of the group.

The victims of the person who violates others' boundaries are people who cannot set boundaries. These people are constantly beset with demands on their time, energy, affection, and patience. How often in group therapy we find ourselves telling someone that she has to learn to say "no!" A mother is besieged with demands for her time and attention, and her children ignore all her rules. The wife of an alcoholic, addict, or compulsive gambler keeps giving in, abetting the spouse's illness by providing money and forgiveness until she is depleted and feels she has no "self." Erica cannot tell Jake to get out; she not only allows but encourages his sadistic behavior toward her.

Harry, when yelled at by his wife, his boss, or a fellow group member, just sits there. The "good guy" who is always helping everybody out ends up feeling "ripped off." The motherly lady is so free with her nurturing that she winds up feeling empty and depressed.

The group helps such people learn to set boundaries in several ways. First, clients with similar difficulties who have made strides in the area of assertiveness provide excellent models and inspiration for the new client who has let himself get pushed around most of his life. They share their experiences and the tricks they have learned since they have been in group.

Secondly, the group provides a place to practice setting boundaries. Clients learn to interrupt when someone is monopolizing the time. They learn to disagree with other members and the therapist openly. They learn to speak up when there is something going on they don't like. They learn to say "no" if they are asked to do something they do not want to do in the group, such as talk about a particular subject or participate in a group exercise or a psychodrama. Sam, mentioned in the Introduction, could not say no directly to Margaret when she asked him to come over in the middle of the night and change her locks; he weasled out of it by telling her he could not come over because his wife would be jealous. Later, in his participation in the group, Sam was better able to be firm with Margaret when she made unreasonable demands on him. Similarly, when Erica finally told the group that she felt betrayed and refused to take it anymore, she was setting some very important boundaries.

Finally, the group provides positive reinforcement for setting boundaries. So often, people's first attempts at setting boundaries are not immediately rewarding. "I told my girlfriend I did not want to have sex with her that night, and she got furious and walked out on me," said Tim, "So much for being assertive!" The group praised Tim for finally being clear with his girlfriend about where he stood on something. Their view was that he had taken a positive step for himself and in the relationship; they told him it was likely his girlfriend would respect him more after this, but if she did not, he might be better off without her. The session bolstered Tim's resolve to set boundaries with his girlfriend and others in his life.

Many people, including most teenagers, have a tendency to push for more freedom and less responsibility. They need rules set for them, lest they get carried away and cause emotional or physical injury to themselves or others in their exuberance or rebellion. Devising, articulating, and enforcing limits are difficult tasks faced by parents, teachers, employers, and others in positions of authority over them. We saw earlier how Jason's parents had been overprotective and then totally abandoned him. Jason kept trying to jockey group members into a parental position, so that they might set limits on his self-destructive behavior. Group members and therapists were challenged to keep their boundaries and not fall into the controlling parent role, while still providing Jason with the support and clear-minded advice he needed.

Some people do not know where they leave off and others begin. We saw earlier how Hannah's boundaries were so flimsy that she could not avoid feeling other people's feelings, and how the group helped her develop some self-protective mechanisms. To give another example, a woman with frustrated ambitions may project her high expectations for herself onto her husband or children. Such a boundary blur can cause intense frustration and anxiety in all concerned, especially when the people she has designated to accomplish her dreams are unwilling or unable to do so. The bleeding of her unconscious needs into theirs can only cause confusion. Healthy communication in this woman's family can only be restored if each person becomes clear about his or her own boundaries, desires, and needs. The woman's therapy group contributes to this being accomplished by assisting the woman in clarifying her own ambitions for herself, and helping her build enough confidence to attain them, leaving her husband and children free to do likewise.

One of the crucial boundary-changing mechanisms in group therapy is confrontation. The minute someone "encounters" or "squares off with" someone else a boundary is drawn between them. Perls (1969) and the Polsters (1973) emphasized that contact can only occur at the contact boundary; therefore, the boundary-drawing function of confrontation is crucial for maintaining contact in the group. It will be remembered that the new group, in its "parallel play" phase, can seem very undifferentiated. Sarah's group was stuck in sameness until she brought in the "strawberries" and people finally put forth their own unique responses to the set-up. After that, the group seemed like a collection of individuals rather than an amorphous blob of humanity.

When people's boundaries are too rigid, they are depressed, resentful, or paranoid; they are not available for feedback or caring, so they fail to get their emotional needs met. Couples and families also can build rigid boundaries around themselves as a system, which eventually leads to impoverishment of the system as it feeds off of itself instead of its environment. Spontaneity is the remedy here and, as we saw in Chapter III, group is the perfect place to learn it.

In many clients' families rules were imposed thoughtlessly, cruelly, or not at all; they were not age-appropriate or not enforced. Having clear rules with respect to confidentiality, payment, and attendance is of fundamental importance in many therapy group clients' treatment. Only if the therapist sets clear boundaries in every way with clients, can they in turn establish healthy boundaries in their relationships within the group. In group, unlike many families, boundaries are also respected with regard to privacy—physical as well as emotional. If someone does not wish to talk about something or to talk at all, he does not have to. If someone is adverse to being touched, no one will pressure him. In group, hopefully, no one's space is invaded.

Any dysfunctional system will be characterized by weaknesses in its hierarchical structure. In a family this takes the form of role confusion across intergenerational boundaries; for example, mother or father may be infantilized while a son or daughter plays a parent role, or grandmother may be treated as the baby in the family. Minuchin (1974) and subsequent family therapists of his "structural" school, have made these intergenerational boundary problems the target of family therapy intervention. The therapy group attempts to model the functional family, where intergenerational and other boundaries are firm, but not rigid. The skillful group therapist is constantly mindful of his own boundaries with respect to clients, not letting them insinuate themselves consciously or unconsciously into his role by trying to take care of him, be his pal, or seduce him.

Since parent-child incest is the ultimate in the deterioration of intergenerational boundaries, and since many clients have been victims of sexual molestation by family members or other adults in childhood, the group therapist must be particularly vigilant with respect to possible abrogations of boundaries in the area of sex. He must be very clear with clients that, although he might have sexual feelings toward members and they toward him, and although there is nothing wrong with this, he will not participate in any sexual activity with them. In a nonjudgmental way he will verbally recognize sexual overtures toward him (some of which can be rather blatant!), and help the client see and deal with the transferential aspects of these faulty "contact operations."

A well-functioning family maintains horizontal boundaries (boundaries between the males and the females for example), as well as vertical boundaries, and again these seem most crucial in the area of sex. In my groups, the rule of "no sex" among members is an artificial device which exists in part as a barrier to symbolic sibling-sibling incest. Even in groups where intra-group sex is not so explicitly ruled out, the incestual implications of it generally do not go unrecognized. Most members feel it is easier to talk about incestuous experiences and other sexual traumas if no sexual "acting-out" is occurring within the group. The group, unlike the family, makes everything talkable. People are encouraged to speak openly about incestuous experiences and unburden themselves of the feelings of anger, fear, and guilt associated with them. Having some of their most "shameful" secrets about incest accepted uncritically, detoxifies the memories, corrects distortions, and opens up group members to a more positive experience of their sexuality.

Within the session caring is sometimes expressed physically through hugs and holding. For most people the guidelines against acting out sexual feelings provide the necessary boundary for them to feel secure, but some clients are excessively anxious that physical closeness will result in sexual arousal. Such clients are helped to see that, even if this should happen, they would have no cause to feel humiliated or frightened. In addition, physical "boundaries" can be set up for added security, such as inserting a pillow between someone's lap and the head of someone getting a head massage.

The story of Joan and her family in Chapter III illustrates all of these boundary problems. Joan's father was hungry and intrusive, disrespectful of the boundaries of others. Her mother could not set boundaries and neither could Joan, so they were both taken advantage of by the father. The teenage brother was a classic boundary tester. Joan's mother had projected her own needs to be an accomplished career woman onto Joan. The family as a whole was never able to establish and maintain intergenerational boundaries, as evidenced by the multiple roles Joan was called upon to play (star, wife, housekeeper, and sex queen), none of which was appropriate for a daughter within the context of her family. It is not surprising that Joan had a lot to learn in group about setting and respecting boundaries. We saw her accomplishing this in the encounter with Erica and the group earlier in this chapter.

CHAPTER V

Change on the Level of Beliefs and Values

BELIEF SYSTEMS

Belief systems are frames of reference that have to do with how we order our experience *so as to know how to act*. According to Frank (1974, p. 263), belief systems have the following functions:

1) They provide a cognitive and moral map.
2) They help us construct a mental picture of an orderly and consistent universe, which enables us to predict and control physical events and evaluate the behavior of others and ourselves.
3) They bind people together.
4) They counteract "ontological anxiety," the primary anxiety, fear of annihilation or of non-being.

Freud stressed the role of instinctual and biological drives in human behavior; the drives are tempered by the anxiety and defense mechanisms attendant to them. Freud himself and almost every subsequent theorist in the field have departed in some measure from the emphasis on drive theory, to allow for the influence of operant belief systems on people's actions.

There is a wide range among cognitively-oriented clinicians as to *which* beliefs should be addressed in the therapy, and how they can be reworked most effectively. Albert Ellis (Ellis and Harper, 1976), for example, in his Rational Emotive Therapy, takes the practical approach, identifying which

138

of the patient's particular beliefs are dysfunctional for her, disabusing her of them, and replacing them with notions that are more serviceable. Taking a broader view, existentialists such as Rollo May (1969) and Becker (1975) consider one's beliefs to be the key to one's identity; therefore, they cannot and should not be so casually modified. They single out a few key beliefs as being crucial determinants of psychopathology and therapeutic change. These ideas, called "meta beliefs," out of which all other beliefs, values, and their attendant emotions and behaviors emerge, address such issues as our place in the universe, the meaning of life and death, responsibility vs. freedom, and isolation vs. connectedness.

Most interactionalists—Sullivan, Moreno and all the group and family therapists—have little quarrel with cognitive therapy's emphasis on the necessity of changing belief systems for therapeutic success. They simply add and stress the importance of interpersonal influences in the formation of these beliefs and views of the world. In this book I try to encompass as wide a range of the cognitive view as possible, infusing it with a strongly interpersonal emphasis.

Mullan, an existentialist group therapist, asserts that "a patient upon leaving (therapy) is to have a different philosophy of life, or perhaps, while in treatment is to discover a theme of living to make his life worthwhile" (in Mullan and Rosenbaum, 1978, p. 378). In group therapy, belief systems are challenged, modified, and often permanently changed, usually in ways that abet the client's effort to "make his life worthwhile." Pessimistic or naive beliefs about the way life is, ideas which may have crippled clients' efforts to act constructively or appropriately, are replaced with notions that are more positive and/or realistic. In addition, group therapy provides the individual with tools to recognize what his beliefs are and how they are affecting him.

In this section we will examine some of the belief systems most affected in group therapy, and how they are changed through the process of the group.

Values

A "value" is a classification of belief systems, "a conception, explicit or implicit, distinctive of an individual or characteristic of a group, of the 'desirable' which influences the selection from available modes, means and ends of action" (Kluckhohn, 1951, p. 396). Values determine how it is desirable to act both personally and interpersonally.

The values of psychotherapy are related to the values of the culture out of which they have emerged. Culture itself is, in part, an amalgam of the values of the people within it. To the extent that psychotherapy diverges drastically from its cultural context, it ceases to be psychotherapy and becomes something else, perhaps a counterculture. The therapies that survive the test of time seem to be those that espouse and operate according to belief systems compatible with those of the current social and political environment. For example, the therapies in the Eastern tradition, derived from yoga, meditation and the healing arts, address the body as well as the mind in treatment. These therapies have not caught on particularly well in the U.S., not because they are ineffective, but because the value of "body-mind" integration is not strongly espoused in Western culture. The Western therapeutic tradition is represented by psychoanalysis on the one hand, emphasizing intellectual insight and verbal communication, and behaviorism on the other, stressing task orientation and efficiency. When Western psychotherapy does accept techniques from the Eastern realm, they tend to relabel them as inventions of Western psychology and psychiatry. They call meditation "guided fantasy," and yoga "progressive relaxation" or "stress management." The practice of hypnosis, considered by some psychologists to be the brainchild of behaviorism, is a masterful composite of methods used both spontaneously and systematically by religious groups and healing artists throughout history. Reinventing the wheel seems to be a particularly favored activity in the psychotherapy field.

One of the greatest challengers of traditional Western values was Sigmund Freud. Freud's drive theory had our instincts for sex and aggression "running the show," controlled, not by any altruistic motives, but by our anxieties and defense mechanisms. This nihilistic view, a violent theoretical reaction to the repression of the Victorian era, needed to be tempered by the post-Freudians to allow for the possibility of some relevance in human interaction that was neither bellicose nor sexual, such as friendship and charity, and to make a place for values such as spirituality and fairness espoused by religious, educational, and judicial institutions.

Frank (1978, p. 262) has pointed out that cross-culturally belief systems differ much less in their ethical than in their metaphysical content and in their tolerance of other belief systems. He notes that cultures tend to perceive the "good" in much the same way, and try to pursue it, even though their ways of going about this may differ (p. 272). Peace, friendship, non-domination, truthfulness, and justice are usually at least *talked about* as being positive, even by malevolent leaders such as Hitler.

Each therapy carries with it its own value system. A client cannot benefit from, or even subscribe to, a therapy which is based on values he does not himself accept. The relative popularity of a given therapy depends a good deal on how much a part of the culture that therapy's inherent values are at the time. For example, when psychoanalysis was first practiced, it represented a welcome alternative to the sexually repressive views of nineteenth century society. It caught on partly because there was a readiness for such a change in values. The sexual permission afforded by early psychoanalysis is less relevant today, when people tend more often to be floundering with too much sexual freedom than struggling for more. In addition, the elitist and authoritarian structure of European-bred psychoanalysis, which focuses so strenuously on the exclusive doctor-patient dyad, is somewhat inimical to the American ideals of democracy.

Behaviorist therapies offer brief and efficient alternatives to psychoanalysis. Behaviorist models reflect the technocratic values of today's modern world, which would suggest that psychiatric treatment be as speedy, inexpensive, and documentably effective as possible. As Naisbitt (1982) has pointed out, however, the explosion of technocracy in our world makes it crucial for the world's survival that society balance its efforts at industrial expansion and advancement with a greater concern for people's individual and collective well-being — physical, emotional and spiritual. Hence, along with the demand for practical and quick approaches to psychotherapy, there is a concomitant need for the more subjective and long-term approaches, which address the total person, mind and body, including his beliefs and values, in the treatment.

While many newer therapies, such as Gestalt, Transactional Analysis, bioenergetics, psychosynthesis, and hypnotherapy, have — like their older relatives psychoanalysis and the behavior therapies — faded in and out of popularity in the past 30 years, group therapy has endured and grown slowly, but steadily. My contention is that group therapy has lasted in large measure because it is consonant with the values of the culture in which it exists.

Whitaker and Malone (1981, pp. 43–44) say that the values of culture and psychotherapy

> . . . need not be identical, but both sets of values should be interdependent and based on the recognition of the more fundamental qualities of man as a biological and social animal. Such values include the opportunity for the expression and gratification of his deep biological needs, as well as the need for independent, integral functioning along with the opportunity for dependence on other individuals as he requires this to achieve both physical and emotional maturity. These imply acceptance of a sense of interpersonal and group responsibility. Such a value system, therefore, would need to present a nice balance between the individual in his independent uniqueness and the individual as a member of a group.

Group therapy seems to offer precisely this kind of value system. It represents in its structure and its functioning the values of democracy, cooperation, and freedom of speech, which are endemic to the Anglo-American tradition. Further, it stresses "honesty, interpersonal relatedness, work, perspective, knowledge and the bearing of healthy tension" (Kaplan and Sadock, 1972, p. 79), always held in high esteem in our social and educational frames of reference.

These higher social values are being seriously threatened today by such factors as declining educational standards, faltering cultural advancement (punk rock?), prejudice, materialism, technology, arms races, poverty, and unemployment. The therapy group is one institution of a handful where such values are discussed and appreciated. By and large, the therapy group tries to encourage free speech, a peaceful working through of problems, a respect for differences, mutual understanding, and a desire to share. While governments show little respect for the human resources in our environment, the therapy group is committed to nurturing what is special and beautiful in each person. The therapy group finds itself continually grappling with such dilemmas as liberty vs. license and individual rights vs. the needs of the group — subjects that are talked about quite infrequently in other sectors. In some cases, the group even helps people acquire the thinking and communication skills that they failed to develop in their education, and which are vital to the process of forming an intelligent and consistent personal value system.

Moral Implications of Therapeutic Change
on the Level of Beliefs and Values

The issue of therapeutic change on the level of values brings up serious moral and ethical questions for psychotherapists. Helping professionals have a great deal of power to influence clients. At the same time most of them have moral compunctions, bolstered by their professional education, against "monkeying around" with such things as the clients' freedom to worship and believe in whatever god they choose or to adopt the lifestyle they want. My own field of clinical social work perpetuates a particularly contradictory approach to the subject of values. While clients' values are considered to be crucial variables in their personalities and functioning, values are off limits as targets for change in social work intervention. Social workers are taught to look at each client, her current situation, and her "personality" in the light of the client's own religious, social, and political beliefs. In social work, perhaps more than in the other therapeutic professions — psychiatry, psychology and counseling — the client's values are taken into account in the assessment of her presenting problem. The social work course of study includes learning about different cultural and ethnic belief systems, so as to allow for a greater empathy with the myriad perspectives presented by clients in therapy. It is admitted that, in some way, the client's beliefs and values may be contributing to her current difficulties, such as when a poverty-stricken mother keeps having more children because her Catholicism prohibits the use of birth control. When it comes to addressing the possible fallacies in a client's beliefs or pointing out ways in which their belief systems are dysfunctional, therapists are often taught that people's beliefs are their private property, a human entitlement, and not appropriate targets for therapeutic change.

I believe that since therapists are constantly and unavoidably influencing clients' beliefs and values in therapy, it is incumbent upon them to do two things: first, teach clients to think for themselves and to take responsibility for their thoughts and feelings; and second, be very clear as to what their own values are, so that they know what they are likely to be communicating consciously or unconsciously to clients.

A Case of Values Clarification in the Therapy Group

Judie, a 45-year-old widow, had tended without complaint to her alcoholic husband for 25 years until he died. When she entered a therapy group, it was to obtain support while attempting to reenter the community—a process which involved dating, making friends, working, and going to school. With the group's help and a lot of effort, Judie made her comeback, acquiring a boyfriend, a job, and plenty of friends, all in a very short time. Then the real issue for Judie emerged. She had no beliefs and values of her own. Hiding behind her sick husband and her sick family before that, Judie was on shaky ground when it came to having an opinion about right and wrong, or more specifically about her rights and the rights of others. Her neglect of this area of her life had, not surprisingly, affected her children, all three of whom, at the time of Judie's entering group were, as young adults, active members of the Ku Klux Klan.

When Judie first mentioned her relationship to the Klan in group, people really did not know how to respond. They were repelled, but they really did not know whether or not to say anything, since Judie was not herself a Klan member. They were also unclear as to whether this was an appropriate issue for confrontation in group therapy. Breaking into the rather polite conversation, a slightly psychopathic group member launched into a speech praising racists for "at least knowing their own minds." This elicited a shocked and negative reaction from several individuals, including Judie. The discrepancy between her espoused anti-racist view and her behavior in abetting the

Klan was pointed out to Judie by the group, and she began to take a hard look at her values for the first time in her life.

In subsequent weeks it emerged that, not only was Judie supporting her adult children financially by housing them under her own roof, but she was even driving them long distances for Klan meetings. Group members became more vocal in their feelings against her association with the Klan, some saying they had lost trust in her as a person because of it. Even the psychopathic character confessed that he was really scared when she talked about the Klan, and that his bravado had been a defensive reaction.

Judie cared very deeply for the people in the group and respected their opinions highly. Their values were more in line with what she wanted hers to be than were those of her own family. Gradually Judie realized that she could no longer take the path of least resistance on this issue. She told her children to move somewhere else and refused to do any more driving for them. What is more, she told them she heartily disapproved of their activities.

MECHANISMS FOR CHANGE OF BELIEFS AND VALUES

In previous chapters we pointed out mechanisms within the therapy group for the facilitation of changes of frame of reference on the psychological, behavioral, and interpersonal levels. Now we will look at mechanisms that influence therapeutic change on the level of beliefs and values.

The Influence of Group-as-a-Whole Phenomena

Members of a therapy group are influenced not just by other members but by properties of the group-as-a-whole, such as size, composition, purpose, and history. The therapy group, like any other group, is a "social field," with intersecting matrixes of influence. As such, each therapy group develops standards, beliefs, and values which exist apart from, and sometimes supersede those of individual members.

Yalom's (1975) studies cite "attractiveness of the group to its members" and "cohesiveness of the group" to be highly correlated with each other and with the therapeutic success of the group. Attractiveness and cohesiveness are not only linked, but virtually synonymous, because the group cannot achieve any "togetherness" unless most individual members find the group appealing enough to stay in it. In this section, however, attractiveness and cohesiveness will each be examined in terms of their influence on members' beliefs and values.

Attractiveness of the Group to Its Members

"Attractiveness of the group to its members" means that the group carries sufficient prestige for clients so that they will be willing to attend. When a person is participating in a group that she finds attractive, she will make more effort to conform to that group's standards than she would to the norms of a group that she finds unattractive (Yalom, 1975).

If she finds the group attractive, the member will try to engage in behaviors that the group finds acceptable. In a therapy group, this would involve an effort to be self-disclosing, honest, confrontative, and concerned for others. These may or may not have been behaviors she considered desirable before participation. Soon after becoming involved in the group, however, and long before she is accomplished in engaging in these behaviors, she has begun to *value* and aspire to them.

For a group to be attractive to someone does not mean she has to like everybody in it. She may have any number of different positive feelings toward various people—curiosity, respect, sexual interest, admiration, or warmth. These feelings are the beginning of her *tele* with the group, and they keep her coming and involved, despite occasional feelings of anxiety, resistance, or dissatisfaction with the group.

Groucho Marx said, "Any club that would accept me, I wouldn't want to join." Upon entering group therapy, many clients feel exactly this way. "You think I'm a sickie," one woman said when I suggested she join group therapy. Almost everybody, when I bring up being in a group, says, "I don't know if I'm going to be able to relate to *those* people." At their first meeting clients usually discard the idea that the group members are "sick." They quickly identify with others' problems and are gratified (sometimes intimidated) to find that the group members can be dealing with serious life issues and still be able to laugh and sound intelligent most of the time. Some group members are very impressive in their perceptiveness and honesty with one another, as well as in their compassion. Far from feeling superior, the new member may actually feel like a neophyte, which serves to motivate her to be forthright and take risks in hopes of fitting into the group as quickly and fully as possible.

Attraction to the group must exist not just in the beginning of participation but for the duration. The best insurance that a group will continue to be interesting to its members is its structure. Errors in group composition increase chances for early dropouts (Kellerman, 1979; Levine, 1979; Yalom, 1975), whereas well-structured groups can continue with little turnover for years. Groups that are diversified with respect to gender, age, personality type, and problem have a more lasting appeal and significantly greater therapeutic results than groups that are homogeneous. The reason for this is thought to be that, optimally, in a heterogeneous group, members' liabilities cancel each other out, preventing one type of member from dominating the group and driving others away. The depressives may calm down the hyper members, and the intellectualisms of obsessional people with dulled affect may be constructively balanced by the labile emotionality of the hysterics. The guilt-ridden may be shocked by the irresponsible sociopathic types, who may, in turn, actually find value in the more considered approach of some of their less aggressive fellow group members. Kellerman's work on creating a balance of personality types in the therapy group spells out eloquently what for me was always a purely intuitive process (Kellerman, 1979).

Unfortunately, too many group therapists ignore the factor of attractiveness of the group for members, partly out of ignorance as to its importance and partly because they have a shortage of clients to choose from when putting together or adding new members to a group. The group therapist, no matter how skilled or popular with the group she may be, cannot compensate for the lack of interpersonal attractiveness of members. If she does manage to keep a group together in which people do not like or feel interested in one another, she is simply fostering the clients' dependency on herself.

Attraction in the group is correlated with self-esteem. Feeling one belongs to a group worth belonging to makes one feel good; it increases confidence and relaxation, both necessary factors for spontaneous interaction and creative thinking, which are prerequisites for change in frames of reference. A group that is heterogeneous and appealing provides its members with many potential role models and gives them many choices of what to change *to* as well as *away from*. When old beliefs are challenged and rejected, the new ideas offered by a group one respects are likely to fall rather quickly into the places of the old ones.

Cohesiveness and Trust

"The more cohesive the group, the more its standards influence its members," says Frank (1974, p. 282), "and the more successful it is in combatting demoralization." In other words, cohesive groups teach people more and help them feel better at the same time. A stable and cohesive group lends its members the sense of security necessary to explore new ideas and the support needed to develop the courage to think differently. It provides exposure to new ways of thinking and reinforcement of positive changes in attitude and behavior.

If a group is cohesive, the trust will be high, and vice versa. Trust occurs as people begin to have experiences in group that prove to them that they will be treated with honesty, respect, and warmth. Cohesiveness binds the trust that exists in the group and generates higher trust. Such a nurturing and safe environment insures the protection of self-esteem necessary for people to take risks.

Cohesiveness, trust, and attractiveness of the group to its members in a group are linked in a circular way. An increase or decrease in any of them creates a concomitant change in the other two. Moreno's work on sociometry has contributed valuable information for group therapists on how to build group cohesiveness and use it for therapeutic advantage.

What happens in a cohesive group, which does not happen in one that is not cohesive, that would account for the therapeutic changes that occur in members' beliefs and values?

1) *People become more spontaneous, better able to express their ideas, feelings, and opinions freely.* Cohesiveness is a necessary condition for spontaneity, the "life force" of the group, through which new material and creative solutions are generated. In a group that is highly spontaneous, group members receive more input, as well as expressing more, thereby enhancing frame of reference changes.

2) *They become more questioning.* In a group that is not cohesive, to question another person may be considered nosy, to question authority dangerous, to question an idea "trying to be too smart." In a cohesive group, people feel safe and energized enough to question their own beliefs and premises, as well as those of others. Within the group they begin to pin each other down a bit more, to question statements that do not make sense, to ask for feedback and really listen to it. They even begin to question the "almighty wisdom" of the group leader.

3) Contrary to what one might expect, *members in a cohesive group are less conforming*, more independent in their thinking (Frank, 1978, p. 106). The standard of the therapy group is diversity, so the more cohesive the group, the more differentiated will be the roles and opinions of group members.

4) *They become freer to engage in conflict*, the process by which presuppositions and assumptions are most emphatically challenged. Conflict is necessary for the disequilibrium which is necessary for change; within a cohesive therapy group, conflicts are brewing, bubbling, and bursting all the time, creating new frames of reference at a rapid rate, without damaging the interpersonal trust and self-esteem of the members.

A cohesive group provides *consistent positive reinforcement* of achievements in the areas it most values: autonomy, intimacy, responsibility, and maturity. A fragmented group, like the clients' families of origin, may hold these values but are not able to positively reinforce them because the individuation necessary to effect such growth threatens the structure of the system in its already weakened condition. The cohesive group is elastic enough to accommodate the growth of individual members.

Conflict

Conflict in a cohesive group with a high level of trust fosters individuation. As Buber describes it:

> When two [people] inform one another of their basically different views about an object, each aiming to convince the other of the rightness of his own way of looking at the matter, everything depends so far as human life is concerned, on whether each thinks of the other as the one he is, whether each, that is, with all his desire to influence the other, nevertheless unreservedly accepts and confirms him in his being this man and in his being made in this particular way. . . . The desire to influence the other then does not mean the effort to change the other, to inject one's own "rightness" into him, but it means the effort to let that which is recognized as right, as just, as true (and for that very reason must also be established there, in the substance of the other) through one's influence take seed and grow in the form suited to individuation (1967, p. 69).

Lack of assertiveness is a big problem for many therapy clients. A constructively managed group conflict may lead to one's learning to strengthen one's own position in the face of opposition. Conflict tends to increase the level of self-disclosure in the group, as opponents reveal more of themselves in an effort to back up their points. When disputes occur openly within a group, they often expose important misconceptions and clarify distorted perceptions participants have had of one another, as occurred with Joan and Erica (in Chapter IV). "Battles" in group therapy should ultimately be no-lose ventures, in that the self-esteem of all the combatants is protected by the therapist and the other members. Within this framework much learning occurs about "winning" and about "losing." Timid people, when involved in a struggle with another member, may learn what it feels like to hold firm and be victorious, rather than giving in to the will of another at the first sign of resistance. Overly aggressive people, for whom "losing" has always represented the threat of terrible humiliation, learn that it can be a beneficial, even rewarding, experience to admit defeat and modify oneself in response to a "worthy opponent's" demands.

Frank (1978, p. 95) notes four major sources of conflict in a group: the patients' contempt for each other, rivalry for the therapist, real differences of outlook, and neurotic perceptions of the other. Regardless of the cause, an episode of conflict and hostility can almost always be turned into a therapeutic experience for members by a skilled therapist and a cohesive group.

In a group where people are intensely involved, conflict can reach near-violent proportions, and a leader may have to intervene with reminders that the physical expression of anger toward another is not permitted in the group. Once in a while, a member who has become extremely enraged may have to be physically restrained, although this is rare in outpatient settings, unless the group therapist is incompetent at setting boundaries, or unwittingly encourages incendiary behavior in members. Usually people who are about to lose control during a conflict in the session can be calmed down by the group. The following is an example.

Ted was talking about something and Erica noticed Terrence falling asleep. She picked up a pillow and playfully threw it at him, hitting him in the face. Terrence jumped out of his seat, absolutely furious. "CUT THAT OUT, BITCH!" he yelled at the top of his lungs. He was standing over her menacingly. Erica cowered in fear.

"Sit down, Terrence," I said quietly but firmly. He obliged.

Erica recovered quickly. (Incidentally, this was about a year after the Joan-Erica conflict.) "I'm sorry Terrence," she said. "I didn't mean to hit you in the face." Then she added, *"But you have no right to threaten me!"*

The group let the two of them argue back and forth, each one saying that the other one overreacted. The other members praised Erica for defending herself, well aware of what a new and important skill this was for her. They expressed sympathy for Terrence for having been so unpleasantly jolted by Erica's pillow, but wondered why it had made him as intensely angry as it did. He retrieved a memory of frequent occasions at the family dinner table when his mother, not liking something he was saying, reached sideways and slapped Terrence hard across the mouth, without warning or explanation. This memory brought tears from Terrence, and understanding and empathy from all, especially Erica, who had experienced similar abuses in her family.

I would not want to give the impression that conflict in a group always works out well, even if the leader is skillful and the group is cohesive. I can think of several instances in which an individual has found himself in unresolvable conflicts with one person after another in the group and eventually has left. The group has received little but frustration and aggravation from his experience. Paranoid clients are extremely sensitive to hostilities that may be latent in the group, and are often compelled to ferret out and ignite these tensions, usually becoming embroiled in struggles from which they find it difficult to withdraw without a great deal of reassurance from the leader and other members. When a group is not cohesive, and/or when the paranoid is feeling particularly mistrustful, he can tear the group apart with conflict. If he feels safe, however, and the group is strong, his trouble-shooting skills can be employed usefully into the group process, and he will be appreciated by the other members for his perceptiveness. Paranoids should not be placed in groups with other paranoids, or the leader will soon feel like a firefighter trying to put out a never-ending series of brushfires.

Psychopaths, distinguished from sociopaths by Eliasoph (1963), cannot function in a group because they have no control over their violent and sexual impulses and are incapable of empathy. Incipient psychopaths show themselves to be so in a therapy group; they are enormously seductive and manipulative and are in conflict with people all the time, and they tend to make the women in the group feel like they are being "raped." The conflicts they generate are almost impossible to resolve, because there is no good will on their part. For these reasons, psychopaths should definitely be screened out of group therapy.

Rituals

Rituals are an important vehicle for any group in conveying and reinforcing its values to its members. Group therapy has rituals ranging from the mundane to the dramatic. Gathering for coffee before group or standing in the parking lot talking afterward are rituals for some groups, while others have regular post-group meetings at a restaurant or coffee shop. Within the session, occasionally the therapist will create a ritual to heighten the effect of something important taking place. For example, when 23-year-old Tammy, continually overworked and underpaid, came into the group feverish and exhausted, I dramatized a sickbed scene with the group by her side, because I felt that she needed to learn the value of letting others care for her. We piled pillows on the floor for her to lie on, turned the lights down low. Then we recalled and enacted with Tammy our own favorite bedtime and sicktime childhood rituals. We sang her lullabies, told her bedtime stories, massaged her feet, and gave her ginger ale to drink.

A ritual for another group was a group hug. At the end of each session the group would gather in a circle at the center of the room, with arms around one another's shoulders, and just stand there for a while. The ritual was varied spontaneously from time to time. Once the circle became a dance; on another occasion it became a "huddle" as in a football game, complete with cheer.

One of my co-therapists goes around hugging everybody at the end of every session. He makes a ritual of it, which some members really appreciate and others find uncomfortable. He spells out in the session that if people do not want to be hugged, they can just tell him and he will respect their wishes, no questions asked. Tony comments in the transcript later in the chapter how much he appreciates that hug from CT. Others have said how nice it is to know that the hug will be there, without having to ask for it, like a goodnight kiss or a bedtime story from a parent — rituals a child treasures into adulthood, if he is fortunate enough to have experienced them.

Clients who did not have love expressed through these cozy routines when they were children deeply appreciate the experiences as they are reconstructed in group by means of rituals such as Tammy's sickbed scene or CT's hugs.

BELIEFS AND VALUES ABOUT SEX

The topic of sex in the therapy group is, not surprisingly, one that generates great interest and many mixed feelings. Group clients, like most people today, are confused with respect to their beliefs and values about sex. As a society we have moved from an attitude of repression about sex to one that provides a plethora of choices with regard to sexual behavior. This is reflected in media concentration on such issues as alternatives to marriage, sex in and out of marriage, homosexual sex, teenage sex, herpes, artificial insemination, sexual surrogates, prostitution, and so on. On the other hand, the Catholic church and some other religious organizations, their feet firmly planted in an earlier era, still proclaim that sex is evil except for purposes of reproduction. The Vatican refuses to relent its stand against birth control, and religious fundamentalists are intent upon keeping sex education out of the schools.

Conflicts on the social scene about sex mirror those of individuals. Most of today's adults were brought up with stricter prohibitions against sex than exist today. Old tapes of parents and parochial school teachers still play in their heads, engendering guilt and fear of humiliation and interfering with their enjoyment of sex. To make matters worse, there exists today a counter-repressive repression about sex. The emphasis on free love and sex among singles has caused many to try to mask their inhibitions and confusion. Some feel more pressured to "do it" than to "not do it," afraid of being considered "square" or sexually "hung-up" if they refrain. Many try to ignore ingrained moral compunctions, only to find their unconscious minds sending them loud

and painful reminders, through neurotic and psychosomatic symptomatology, that to dismiss the beliefs and values of childhood about sex is not so
easy.

For example, quite a few of my single clients who consider themselves sexually liberated are almost phobic about intercourse. They will go to bed with
someone, have oral sex, sleep naked with the person all night, and then virtu-
ously report that they do not believe in "going all the way" with someone until
there is a commitment of marriage! While this seems ludicrous to me, it makes
logical sense to some of my clients who were raised as Catholics. As one
former altar boy explained to the group, "Fornication is explicitly stated in
the Bible to be a sin. None of those other things are!"

One way to correct the deceptions, confusion, and insecurities people harbor about sex is to let them talk about them. The therapy group provides a
forum for clients to air their feelings, receive information, and explore and
reevaluate their values about sex, not so they will then "have the answers,"
but so that they can make congruent personal decisions about how they wish
to behave in the sexual world.

Group therapy accomplishes the following with respect to helping the individual deal with conflicts about sexuality.

1) It helps clarify current feelings and attitudes about sex.
2) It elicits and refutes negative messages about sex harbored by the client
   from childhood.
3) It assists the client in disclosing, understanding, and thereby detoxifying
   sexual traumas and other negative sexual experiences.
4) It encourages the positive expression of sexuality.

The transcript on "Attractiveness" at the end of this section, as well as previous anecdotes, amply illustrate each of these processes. I will expand just
briefly here on number 4) "encouraging the positive expression of sexuality."

The group is a culture in which the individual is accepted for sho she is.
This includes her sexual self, a part of her that may have been discounted,
or worse, downgraded, by her family. The group encourages the client to take
pride in her body and the way she looks. Members compliment each other,
reinforcing efforts to be attractive, respecting differences in personal style
and taste. They encourage each other to date, socialize, be close—to connect
with others emotionally and physically, but within the framework of one's
own moral and spiritual values. The group gives permission to be "present"
in a sexual way, to flirt, express attraction to one another, and have fun doing this. In group the client can speak about her sexual fantasies, feelings,
attractions, and values. In doing so she is revealing her uniqueness to the

group. She gets in touch with what is special about herself, a sense she must have if she is to relate congruently in a sexual way. Sharing her highly personal and sexual self, and feeling both to be accepted and appreciated by the group, is comparable to the intimate experience she might enjoy with a sensitive lover. The positive reflection of herself that she sees in the eyes of the group will encourage her to take risks and express herself more fully in loving sexual relationships in her life.

The mechanisms through which the treatment of sexual problems occurs are the same as the treatment of other disturbances in group therapy. Self-disclosure, empathy, support, and sharing start the process rolling. As the group gains in cohesiveness and trust, individual differences emerge more clearly and a rich dialogue develops, sometimes generating conflict. Such interaction and the synthesis of different points of view create changes in frames of reference in substantive ways for all persons, including the therapists. The "set-ups" and transferences that inevitably occur in a cohesive and ongoing group are enormously useful in eliciting core therapeutic issues, many of which are sexual in nature. As seen in the case of Erica, Terrence, and Joan, analysis and resolution of set-up operations in group therapy can effectively liberate clients from the bonds of sexual conflict, eliminate regressive behavior, and reactivate healthy growth processes.

Though group members love to talk about sex once they get started, getting underway is usually difficult. Verbalizing about sex is difficult for most people under any conditions, and some group members have severe internal prohibitions against discussing it, which can serve to inhibit fellow group members as well, especially in a group that is new or, for some other reason, not cohesive. If the group is in a difficult stage of development, such as "fight-flight" or dependency, no one will talk about anything risky, least of all sex.

Sometimes the most pertinent discussions of sex relate to interpersonal attractions within the group. Some group members are quite afraid of their sexual feelings for other members and need encouragement and reassurance to bring them out in the open. One group which was comparatively mature and cohesive in most respects was very blocked in dealing with sex. They were an exceptionally attractive group, most of them married or with regular partners. Superficially, they seemed sophisticated enough to realize that talking about their sexual feelings for one another did not mean they had to act on them; however, when the leaders would hint that there were such attractions among them, they would assiduously avoid the subject. The group was becoming dry and lifeless, and there did not seem to be much I could do about it.

Then, as often happens when I am feeling stymied about what to do in a group, I had a dream that gave me some direction: In the dream I am on a train sitting with a male member of this group. He and I are kissing in a rather casual, but definitely sexual, way. Another man, one who is not in the group in real life, but is a group member in the dream, gets on the train and walks up to us. He upbraids us vehemently for what he calls "having sex," which is "against the group rule." The client I was kissing gets up and walks forward to another seat on the train. I argue with the hostile man that "kissing is not the same as intercourse." Throughout the conversation I am very defensive and strongly wishing that the rest of the group would hurry up and get here. I tell the man that, when the group arrives, we can talk about it. He sneeringly replies that "talking won't make any difference." I feel very frustrated.

The dream helped me realize my own and the group's anxiety about talking about our sexual feelings for one another, our fears about being judged and humiliated. The hostile man, symbolizing our collective resistance to talking about sex, was not a group member in real life, just in the dream. He represented all the intrusive, humiliating, and cynical voices we were carrying in our heads to the group. The dream also made me aware that I was getting frustrated trying to take responsibility for the group's sexual feelings and their resistance, when they were not doing their part. The client, who was kissing me as much as I was kissing him, walked away and left me to deal with the critical intruder alone, while the rest of the group was not even on the train!

After considerable deliberation I decided to tell the dream to the group. As I had hoped, the group accepted the dream as an invitation to talk about sex, and soon confirmed that attraction within the group was high, and anxiety about these feelings even higher. One woman had even had a dream the same week as I did, in which she was standing outside of her house talking with a male member about a time, long ago in group, when he had told her she was attractive. The group was able to take my disclosure of a potentially embarrassing dream as permission for them to open up in similar ways. Hardly anything besides sex was discussed for weeks thereafter in this group.

Specific Values Concerns About Sex

Certain values issues surrounding sex emerge frequently in group therapy. Some of them are dealt with by the group in unique and helpful ways.

The difference between having sexual feelings and acting on them. As my dream suggests, confusion often exists, for me included, on what, exactly, is "sexual." Many Catholic-educated clients are explicitly taught that "the thought is as bad as the deed." Others have concerns about fidelity, even with respect to fantasies and feelings, not to mention actions. Group members find themselves struggling with "Where do you draw the line?" "Should I feel guilty for being turned on to someone, when I love and am attracted to my wife (husband, partner)?" Many people are afraid to feel sexual feelings because they do not believe that they will be able to control themselves enough to not act on these feelings. As mentioned, the "no-sex rule" provides space for individuals to have sexual feelings and not act on them. People learn that it is human, acceptable, and possible to have a friendship with a man or woman, *even when* there are sexual feelings on both sides that remain unconsummated.

Sexual jealousy. Jealousy and the way it is dealt with in group were touched on in Chapter IV. The "value" of honest, nonpossessive relationships is stressed in group therapy, gradually counteracting the tremendous fear some people have of losing their sexual partners. All aspects of group therapy that foster individuation, independence, and taking responsibility for one's own behavior and feelings help people with the terrible problem of jealousy and reinforce the value of autonomy in relationships. Also, in group, the individual is influenced to view sex as a resource, rather than a weapon or an instrument of power. This awareness diffuses the temptation to induce jealousy in another for purposes of having control over him.

Monogamy. One of the most hotly debated subjects in my therapy groups is the pros and cons of monogamy in relationships. Opinions cover the range from monogamy being neither desirable nor necessary to its being decidedly both. I find that clients in their thirties who were late teens and young adults during the sixties tend to be more accepting of marriages and partnerships in which sexual fidelity is not a top priority. The younger clients are often far more conservative in their view, believing that sex outside of marriage or a living together arrangement constitutes a betrayal of great magnitude. The older members — in their forties and fifties — are mixed in their opinions, depending on their own personal circumstances and experiences. In facilitating discussions on these topics I convey my respect for all points of view.

Promiscuity. The first dictionary definition of promiscuous is "of mixed or indiscriminate composition or kinds" (Oxford Dictionary, 1978, p. 711). Sexual promiscuity is the indiscriminate engagement in sexual activity. I have found that people who are promiscuous are usually trying to communicate to others a tremendous need for nurturing. Their sexual activity is an attempt to get closeness in the only way they know how or in a way that feels safe to them. Sometimes it is also an unconscious plea to friends, parents, therapists, or, in the case of group clients, fellow group members, to show they care by setting limits on their behavior.

Client Nancy told her group that, at age 13, she had invited all the boys over to her house to "play around" with her in the basement. She had secretly prayed her mother would come home and find her, send all the boys home, and give her the attention she so desperately needed. Eight years later, when she entered group, Nancy was prone to the same kind of behavior, inviting men whom she hardly knew to her apartment for a drink and finding herself having sex with them, wishing she wasn't doing it.

In group we enacted a psychodrama that helped Nancy with the pain and guilt of these early experiences, and clarified some of the mixed messages about sex she had introjected from her mother. First we played the scene with the boys in the basement the way it happened, as described by Nancy, with Nancy in her own role, feeling hopeless and humiliated. Then we played it again with Nancy in the role of mother. Nancy as the mother comes home and finds 13-year-old Nancy (played by another member) fooling around with the boys. Mother-Nancy promptly throws all the boys out of the house and calls up all their mothers, while young Nancy watches, in awe of her mother's power. Then Mother-Nancy sits down with 13-year-old Nancy and explains to her the responsibilities involved in sex, expresses concern for how Nancy will feel about herself if she continues to act like this, and answers Nancy's questions about sex, her body, relationships, and the like. Reversing roles again, we did the scene a third time, with Nancy playing herself and the other member playing Mother, doing the same things and using as much as possible the same words as Nancy had when she was playing "good" mother. When she heard her (psychodramatic) mother's reassurance and concern, Nancy burst into sobs. The psychodrama gave Nancy a big piece of what she needed in order to realize that she was important and loveable enough to give her body selectivity in sex, without having to degrade herself.

If a group client has a problem with promiscuity, she may let the group know about it indirectly, by boasting in a silly or provocative way about her exploits, either in the session or to a member outside. In my experience, any kind of self-report on promiscuity, no matter how casually couched, reflects a conflicted, often desperate, attitude, and should be attended to seriously by the therapist, with a view toward the possible suicidal ideation behind it.

When he first entered group, Jason was in the habit of frequenting parks, baths and bars, for the purposes of picking up homosexual partners. He only dimly hinted of this activity to the group. I pressed him to talk, not about the details of *what* he was doing, but what he *felt* like when doing it. Sure enough, feelings of fear, worthlessness, loneliness, and shame poured out. Jason was not sure he found life worth living anymore. The group, of course, responded with kindness and concern, not disgust or criticism the way he had anticipated. They were very worried about his physical safety, the likelihood of his being the victim of violence in the settings he was frequenting, not to mention his vulnerability to AIDS and other diseases. They expressed vigorously their affection for him and pleaded with him to take care of himself. They made themselves available by phone should he need help during the week. They assisted him in understanding his behavior as a desperate way of attracting the attention of his parents, who had expelled him from the family.

The group's support was well-received by Jason. With it he experienced some of the security he needed from a family. He soon lost interest in casual sex and began looking for a meaningful relationship.

Masturbation. Masturbation is a very private and individual matter. Group members benefit from discussing masturbation because it helps them recognize that masturbation is acceptable, contrary to what they may have been told as children. The group plays the role of good parent in contradicting some of the erroneous and repressive ideas perpetrated on clients in their childhood.

Josephine, a 32-year-old divorcee, was told by her Baptist father that people who masturbated "burned in Hell." Her complaint to the group was that she could not masturbate to orgasm unless she looked at a picture of her father, hit herself, and called herself a "whore." She had a second concern as well: She was gaining weight because she could not stop eating chocolate. "How are the two related?" the group wondered, amused. Suddenly, a group member facetiously associated giving up chocolate with atoning for her sexual "sins." I picked up on this and framed a paradox, saying it was my serious opinion that she would not have a pleasurable, guilt-free (meaning no voices and no slaps) orgasm until she gave up chocolate. This suggestion threw her into confusion, and she was quiet for the rest of the evening. She came back in the next week and reported that, strangely, she was enjoying orgasms all week and had lost all desire for chocolate! Evidently, Josephine needed a harsh superego instruction in order *to* have an orgasm. My directive fell right into her frame of reference, taking the place of her father's, and she was able to follow it with no problem.

This incident was interesting also from the point of view of the group's instinctive use of paradox. They, not I, picked up on the resource inherent in Josephine's unconscious association between the orgasm problem and the chocolate addiction. I simply formulated their idea in a way that Josephine's unconscious as well as conscious mind could put it to use. (For more on framing paradoxes, see Lankton and Lankton, 1983).

Abortion. Back in the beginning of her participation, Joan had been promiscuous and had seduced, among other men, her best friend's boyfriend. When her friend found out, she dropped Joan, and Joan, devastated and ashamed, decided to give up sex. This lasted a few months, until she ran into an old lover and decided to have a fling with him. She was using no birth control and got pregnant.

With all that led up to it, Joan experienced her pregnancy as the ultimate punishment for her years of sexual misconduct. She had no question that she must get an abortion, and this all strengthened her resolve to "control herself." As the time for the abortion grew near, however, the deeper ramifications of what it meant dawned on her. She revealed to the group her deep misgivings and feelings of guilt. The group was confronted with and began to sort through the many complex ideas involved in abortion. We discussed the legal versus the moral rights and values involved in the decision, the role and responsibility of the male, and the emotional implications for Joan if she went through with it. CT (co-therapist) pointed out that the decision about whether or not to have an abortion is a "grownup's" decision. We all felt soberingly "adult" in accompanying Joan through this unpleasant journey. Each one of us had to grapple with what we would do in her place, and each of us learned from her experience.

Joan did have the abortion and felt the support of the group throughout the ordeal. I wish I could say she adjusted quickly. She suffered with guilt, remaining celibate for almost two years, during which time the group was practically her only social contact. It was as if the abortion symbolized the death of a Joan who had lived in an earlier era, with two alcoholic parents, a Joan who abused her own sexuality out of neediness and desperation. To start a new life, to "carry it to term," she had to provide a healthy living environment for herself. She did, in her therapy group, and, by extension, in her living and employment situations. When she resumed sexual activity it was with a man who appreciated and loved her.

Birth control. Taking responsibility for one's sexuality means that, if one is going to engage in sexual relations, one better be ready to either have a baby or use birth control. This is equally true of men and women. Some of the problems that come up around birth control which I hear frequently discussed in group are: lack of correct information; religious compunctions about using it; fears about its effectiveness contributing to a lack of spontaneity in sex, often with sexual dysfunction as a result; one-sided or unclear allocation within a couple of responsibility for birth control. Naturally, discussions of birth control relate to the subject of family planning, a process some couples and individuals need help with. Group clients benefit greatly from the objective feedback and shared experiences they obtain from one another when deliberating about matters related to birth control and having children.

Confession and sex. Frank (1974) says that most religions include some kind of confessional activity as part of their ritual obligation. He points out that part of the value of psychotherapy may be that it serves this human need to confess. Some children feel very strongly the need to tell their parents when they have done something they feel might be wrong. If their anxieties are not allayed, their alleged misdeeds reframed into a positive or normal context, self-doubts persist strongly into adulthood. This was the case with Fred, whose poignant story, as he tells it here, brought forth in other group members memories of their own painful and vulnerable feelings during adolescence. In "confessing" to the group, Fred finally got the warmth and empathy he had needed from his parents and had not received.

This one incident really pops into my head now. I was probably about 11 or 12. It was right around the period of time when I was first starting to become aware of things going on in my body that were sexual and that I wasn't aware of before. I had my little sister who is seven years behind me, which probably made her about five at the time. . . . I had this sort of excitement going on and I wanted her to see me naked, and I remember this one day, our rooms were next to each other, and I told her that I was going to my room to change and I told her *not* to look through the keyhole.

(Laughter from Fred and group)

Surprise of surprises, she did. . . . The thing is I got incredibly guilty about it as I used to get with anything sexual and I used to confess everything to my parents. I couldn't live with myself anymore. I couldn't sleep. I had a knot in my stomach all the time. It was something in my head that said, "You must confess." I told my mother finally because I couldn't stand it anymore. I had to get it out, which is the thing I went through for a while. She was not real upset about it. I can't remember if I told my father or if my mother told him. I think my mother told him. But I just remember this one encounter and my father was so mad, which he rarely ever was. What he said to me was "I don't want you ever to lay a hand on her!"

That was so . . . it had such an effect on me because I hadn't done anything to her. I can see it now that it was an innocent sort of thing that someone that age might do, but the impression that I got from him, someone who tended not to be that vocal or that strong, was that I had done something really bad.

It just really affected me a lot. I remember years later when I was going out with Sally, I went through a stage in the first couple of years of our relationship where I'd start going through the same sort of need to confess some sort of thing and one day I got it into my head that I had done something absolutely horrid and that she had to know about it because she had to know how awful I was. It took me weeks, it was weeks of torture, of trying to figure out how I was going to bring this subject up and what the reaction was going to be and how awful she was going to think I was. It wasn't that big a deal for her. It was like "Why did you have to tell me?"

I guess it was my father that really affected me. When I discovered masturbation, it was like I didn't know what was going on. No one had told me and I would start telling him that I had masturbated and it was like, you know, it was like this torture thing inside me where I could not sleep. I would come home from school sometimes because I felt so torn apart and sick. When I finally told him he said, "It's normal, but don't do it anymore."

Fred was in group for almost four years. During that time he reframed his need to confess into a healthy tendency to talk openly and articulately about his personal feelings in group and outside. He also learned to make accurate appraisals of who was likely to be sympathetic and who wasn't, thereby saving himself embarrassment and humiliation.

Acceptance of one's body. When people discuss their mental pictures of what they themselves think they look like, many surprises are likely to result. Once the women in a group were talking about wanting to lose weight. Each of the four seemed to feel equally strongly that she needed to lose at least 10 or 15 pounds, which seemed odd to me, considering they ranged from 30 or 40 pounds overweight to about five pounds underweight for their size. I asked them to line themselves up from fattest to thinnest, relative to height. They could not agree at all on the order of fatness, even though it was patently obvious to those of us observing! The one who was by far the fattest saw herself as second to fattest. The thinnest thought she was fattest. The two middle ones at first placed themselves accurately, but then began to think they had been underestimating their fatness, and began pushing each other out of the way for the position of fattest. This illuminating exercise proved that these women had little idea what they really looked like. (The transcript later in this chapter again deals with the issue of the distortion of body image based on the "scripting" of childhood and adolesence.)

Joan was the heaviest in the "lineup," but saw herself as thinner than the other women. Joan's body image also included distortions that were not in her favor. She saw her breasts as too big, though they were firm and shapely. She was obsessed with what she referred to as the "disgusting" scars on her back. One night the group, tired of hearing about the scars, asked that she show them. With great fanfare, she lifted her shirt. They were hardly even visible!

Joan, despite her weight, was a very attractive woman, but in ways different from anyone else and different from what she thought she should look like. Like many other group members, she needed a great deal of feedback before she began to see herself accurately and accept this image. Gradually she has learned to dress and wear her hair in becoming ways. She also cultivated a "look" that is distinctly and flatteringly her own.

Sex information. The therapy group is a safe place to ask questions without fear of ridicule or loss of confidentiality. Among any eight to ten people there is bound to be a good bit of available information about sex. The group becomes a natural clearinghouse for members' combined knowledge on the subject. Of course, for every bit of valuable information, one is also exposed to considerable misinformation, and it is part of the leaders' responsibility to be well-informed on the subject so as to straighten out at least some of the misconceptions that may be floating around the group during any discussion of sex. Clients share books, journal articles, and community resources dealing with the subjects of birth control, pregnancy, fertility, abortion, herpes and other venereal diseases, sexual dysfunction, menstrual problems and premenstrual tension, breast and uterine cancer. They refer each other to competent gynecologists, obstetricians, urologists, women's health services, and family planning facilities in the area.

One instance where the information about sex given by the group really made a difference was in the case of Demont. Twenty-eight years old and a virgin, Demont said he was ready to have sex with his girlfriend and she wanted to also, but he was afraid she would get pregnant, since he would be too anxious to manage a condom. The group described for Demont some birth control méthods that the woman could use, and reassured him that his girlfriend probably would not think him crass for suggesting such a thing. Demont decided the diaphragm would be best. He went home and asked his girlfriend to please go purchase this item called a "diaphragm." She replied that she had had one for years and was ready to use it whenever he was! That night marked the happy end of Demont's virginity. The group always took credit for launching Demont's sexual career by telling him what a diaphragm was.

Sex instead of. . . . Through their discussions, group members realize that sex is used in many contexts to disguise other issues. For instance, Jason's promiscuity was only symptomatically sexual; on a much deeper level, the behavior stemmed from his neediness and depression. Sometimes intense sexual activity follows a loss by death or separation, and is part of the denial which seems to be an inevitable first step in the grieving process. Within a relationship a couple might use sex instead of nurturing, listening to each other, or showing vulnerability.

Many highly destructive sadomasochistic sexual relationships, we learn upon investigation, are only very superficially sexual, even though a fair amount of sexual activity may go on. In Erica's case, the group gradually realized that Erica's obsession with Jake had little to do with his sex appeal. What she needed from him was the very thing that she protested, his sadistic treatment of her. His consistent willingness to take the "bad guy" position made her look good by comparison. He could represent the bad part of her, and in this way she could keep herself blameless and free from criticism. As long as she was with him she could maintain her precarious narcissistic illusions, and did not have to deal with the part of her that felt worthless and weak. When she gave up Jake, Erica cried like a baby at almost every group session. She would curl up in a little bundle in the arms of one of the therapists or members, as the session continued without her participation. It was as if the grownups were talking and it was all way over the head of such a little child. After Jake, Erica dressed and carried herself like an eight-year-old for some time. Her sexy disguise was relinquished for a more accurate representation of the way she felt, like a cute but very vulnerable little girl.

Performance and potency. In my group practice there is an incredible range in expectations among clients regarding what constitutes potency and adequate sexual functioning. Some couples and individuals would consider themselves sexual cripples if they had sex less than four times a week, while others don't seem to feel it is at all peculiar not to have sex with their spouses for months at a time. Group therapy seems to be the great equalizer. In sharing facts, fantasies and beliefs, clients begin to see the limitations of their own frames of reference about sex.

When he entered group, Carl was absolutely convinced he had a severe sexual dysfunction because the first time he had sex with a new woman he would usually have some trouble achieving an erection. In individual therapy I had told him repeatedly that this was not a severe problem, but he would not believe me. He swore off sex for two years. Finally, Carl entered group therapy where he was told by the women in the group that such hesitancy was perfectly natural when having sex with someone for the first time. They assured him that, when it had happened to a man they were having sex with, it had not bothered them in the slightest. Carl was able to believe them since, he said, "They weren't being paid to make him feel better." He resumed his sex life with a new confidence.

Sol, 38, had suffered all his life from feelings of self-hatred and humiliation because of what he considered to be terrible deformity, an undescended testicle, a not uncommon birth defect. While it had never caused him any actual problem in his sexual functioning, Sol considered himself less of a man because of it, and he had more difficulty telling the group about his undescended testicle than about anything else in his three years in group. When he finally spoke up, he was amazed at how casually the group members took the news. In fact, one or two women had had sex with men who had it, and had found it to be no problem. Sol said it had never seemed to bother his ex-wife or his few subsequent sex partners, but nonetheless he had harbored deep doubts about his sexuality and had gone through long periods of not even dating because of this one small difference in his genital structure. Men in Sol's group shared their insecurities about the size of their penises, while the women discussed their likes and dislikes about their breasts and genitals.

When it comes to sex, most people think there is a "normal" and that they and/or their sex partner are not it. Some couples continually complain about one another's sexual appetites. One claims the spouse "never wants sex," while the other says the partner is "a sex maniac"; both secretly worry that there is something wrong with them. A passionate woman may feel she is undesirable if her husband is less sexually interested than she, or he may worry about impotence. Usually lack of communication and a failure to respect individual differences, more than sexual dysfunction, are the problem.

When some slight dysfunction does exist, bad feelings and misunderstandings often proliferate. Noreen, 40, was convinced that her husband was not sexually interested in her, because he rarely made advances and, when he did, "it was over so fast." The men in the group pointed out to her that her husband's quick ejaculation was probably far from voluntary. They suggested that maybe he knew that well enough, and rather than deal with his insecurities about his dysfunction, it was easier for him to let Noreen think there was something wrong with *her*. Noreen promptly brought her husband into couples therapy, where they were able to resolve their sexual difficulties.

In group it is frequently demonstrated that "potency" as a male or female has a lot more to do with people's behavior outside the bedroom than inside. Joseph was a middle-aged divorced man who was determined to be impotent. He was so positive he was impotent that he didn't have sex with anyone for two years to prove it. He dressed the part, with baggy jeans and tight shirts stretched across a pot belly. Joseph, as will be remembered from Chapter II, was equivocal about everything except his relentless efforts to put himself down. In an effort to convince the group what a loser he was, he would compare himself unfavorably to people he thought were blowhards and ingrates. The group's reaction to Joseph's unfathomable passivity was a good deal of frustration, which barely caused a ripple in his intransigent front. Someone commented that, if Joseph put nearly the energy into asserting his positive qualities that he used in arguing in defense of his position as failure, he would be an extremely *potent* group member and *man*. After months of hammering, the group began to get through to him. Joseph began to let the more powerful side of him show, and with it a marvelous sense of humor, sensitivity, and intelligence began to seep through. Not coincidentally, a few weeks later, he became involved in an exciting and rewarding sexual relationship.

Attractiveness, Sexism, Sex and Power:
Transcript of Group Discussion

In the following transcript, Erica's group, composed mainly of single men and women in their twenties and thirties, deals with the meaning and ramifications of being sexually attractive. The session took place almost exactly a year after the events described with Erica, Terrence, and Joan and this group in Chapter IV. The population of the group was exactly the same as it was the year before.

Erica: I feel like I get brushed off in here, like my problems aren't really problems. People are saying "What else is new, Erica? Your type of problems don't seem like problems to us." I guess I feel it when I talk about work and when I talk about men. I feel like a few people in here look at me and say, "Well, we think you're attractive, so we don't understand why you have problems with men or why you don't think you're attractive. Let's go on to something else." And it is a very real problem to me — one of the biggest problems I have.

CT (co-therapist): Do you feel that equally from everyone in here?

Erica (quickly): No. (*silence*)

Jason: After everything you went through with Jake, it would be hard for me *not* to know you have problems with men.

Erica: Do you believe I have a problem believing that I'm attractive — that when a man asks me out I go home and ask myself, "Gee, why did he ask me out?"

Jason: I know it can happen that way, that it really doesn't matter what the person looks like, that they can think they look like shit. I feel like that sometimes, even though people may be telling me exactly the opposite.

Erica: Does it really solve your problem?

Jason: Well, sometimes it gets through and it helps and I believe it.

Lilly: I guess even as you said that to Erica, Jason, I didn't feel like you were really connecting with her. I felt you were just kind of distancing her by saying, "Oh yeah, I have that problem too," and not really looking at Erica and really. . . .

Erica (interrupting): I guess I'm feeling . . . I'm feeling like the answer for me is not, "Well, Erica you are attractive." Telling me what I'm feeling is not true is not helping me. What I need is, "Well, Erica, why do you feel that way?" I need to know how to stop feeling that way.

Ted: Why do you feel that way?

Erica: I don't know.

Joan: When do you feel that way?

Erica: When someone shows me attention. (*Begins to cry.*)

Joan: How were you showed attention (this is good for me) when you were growing up?

Erica: I wasn't. Till I got older. By my father.

[The reader will remember that Erica's father tried to rape her when she was a teenager.]

MN: By giving you messages that you were attractive.

Erica: Not attractive. Uhhh. It was more of a physical thing.

MN: Seductive?

Erica: Yeah. Not pretty.

MN: So when you hear someone say you are attractive, you hear it as you're trying to seduce somebody?

Erica (crying): I don't know. (*long pause*) I have a real problem on my job.

Everyone in the company is really young and the men are real attractive. I love my job and I've been working lots of hours. And there's one of the owners I work really closely with. We had to go to the supply store to get some things that I needed and we stopped for lunch on the way back, and he started telling me how great I was doing on my job, how I should take the company seriously because they really saw a future for me there. I really felt good, and then later in the conversation he said, "You know it's going to be really hard to work with you." I said, "Why?" He said, "It's going to be really hard because you're so attractive and it's going to be really hard not to lean over and kiss you when I'm working with you." And the hardest part is that I'm attracted to him, *but*, I guess I reacted like, "What did I do to make him do that?"

CT: What do you answer to that?

Erica: I didn't know what to say to him.

MN: You didn't know what you said to make him feel it, or you didn't know what you said to make him say it?

Erica: I thought it wasn't appropriate, since I'd only been working there two weeks and he went on about being so attracted to me.

MN: You said he was married.

Erica: Yeah, but I guess I feel safer that he's married.

Jason: How did you feel about your boss saying that right after he said your work was so good?

Erica: I had felt good, but then when he said all that other stuff it discredited everything he had said prior.

MN: This seems like a prototypical situation for you. This has happened many times before, and you want to get a handle on it.

Erica: Yeah.

CT: I guess what would bother me the most would be feeling like I couldn't trust that my work really was competent.

Erica: Yeah, and he knew about what happened with Mr. K., too.

[Erica's former employer had consistently harassed her to have sex with him, and frequently offered her bribes if she would. He finally had fired her on false pretenses, because she wouldn't oblige, and then tried to protest her unemployment benefits. On the group's advice, she hired an attorney, fought the complaint, and won.]

CT: Really?

Erica: Yeah. I told him and he said, "Well that won't happen here. You're really attractive, but your stuff is so good, I wouldn't want to blow having you work here for such a silly reason."

MN: When Erica was telling this story, what were other people feeling? You, Joan, seemed really angry, but others didn't seem to be reacting very strongly. What were you feeling?

Erica: Before you answer. I guess what I want to know is did I do something to make him think that it was OK?

MN: Before we get into what you did or didn't do to provoke him, I think we need to know if everybody agrees he was out of line. I'm not sure that everybody thinks what he did was that negative. Was it along the lines of your father or a Mr. K. or was it different? What do people think?

Jason: It could have been him trying to lay his cards on the table, to get the stuff out of the way.

Erica: I have to say, he really is a very nice guy. He, in fact they *all*, have been very respectful to me, asking me what I think about everything, really making me feel a part of things, even after only two weeks.

MN: I think it is open to interpretation.

Terrence: I think it was really unprofessional. Saying you are attractive is one thing, although I'm not sure about that, but wanting to kiss you. . . .

Lilly: Erica told me about this last night and when you first told me about it, my reaction was that it isn't so terrible. It might be just a kind of natural thing to have happen, and it didn't seem so obnoxious or engulfing. The thing you didn't tell them, Erica, that did bother me, is about him reaching over and giving you a kiss later.

(Eyebrows start to rise.)

Erica: Oh well. (Starts to laugh.) Wait a minute, I gotta clarify that. That sounds terrible.

(group laughter)

Lilly: Oh, you mean, like when you were both lying down together in the back seat. . . .

(long laughter, group and Erica)

Erica: Yeah after he took off his clothes. I want to know if he was out of line with his clothes off. *(more laughter)* No, really—after we were leaving the restaurant, even though he was saying these things, it wasn't the main topic of conversation, and after we left, I was really quiet, and he asked me if I was upset. I said I didn't feel comfortable, but I wasn't mad, and I didn't want him to feel as if he couldn't talk to me, but I wanted him to try to be fair to me. We stopped and he kissed me, and I turned my cheek and he kissed me on the cheek. I don't know what would have happened if I hadn't turned my cheek though.

CT: It feels to me like professional and personal boundaries were just blown. My reaction when you first said it was to look at it from this totally "male position," which is something that I tend to do with you. I said, "Oh my, that's really nice." And then suddenly I put myself in your position, and I said, "Jesus, did you really think that?" I couldn't believe my first reaction was so sexist! What winds up bothering me the most, putting myself in your shoes, is winding up having no way to measure my own competence.

Erica: That's it. I like the boss-employee relationship. That allows me to say I've worked enough hours. I want more money for my work.

CT: Well, I'm wondering if you can say this to him.

Erica: Something came up today, and I had to tell him something I couldn't finish. It was hard, but I told him.

Ted: For me, that just changes the whole thing. That he actually approached you physically.

Erica: I was worried about how he got his information.

Ted: You mean from the previous job?

Erica: Yeah.

Ted: Well, I can see why that worries you given the experience you had before, but I think the issue is your own feelings about your own attractiveness and how it affects yourself and other people. I can see that if I were your boss and I were attracted to you, I would have a responsibility to deal with that so that it wouldn't interfere with our working relationship.

Erica: That's what he seemed to be telling me.

Ted: But he was telling you something very different by kissing you though.

CT: Yes.

Terrence: He really abused you. I hope you watch out for him. There are ways to tell somebody something. . . . Like if I'm attracted to women at the office and I flippantly say to them, "Are there any more like you at home?" and they laugh and they know I'm attracted to them. . . . But *he* took advantage of you.

MN: Terrence, how would you feel if a woman in your office said that to you?

Terrence: Said, "Are there any more like you at home?" I'd feel good. I'd be flattered.

Joan: I wouldn't want to hear that. I don't like these kinds of remarks. They're not respectful. It's subversive — it's not up front.

Jason: It's *really* up front.

CT: Yeah, it's really up front, but it's up front like . . . "Do you have any more hamburger?" (*much laughter*)

Terrence (laughing): Yeah, okay, I get it.

Joan: Erica, I'm curious why you didn't say something to him when he did that. I understand you were dumbfounded, but . . . why didn't you react?

Erica: That's not the way I ever react.

MN: What did you say?

Erica: That I wanted him to feel that he was free to talk to me but I didn't want him to be unfair. That I wasn't sure he was being fair.

MN: I think Erica made it clear before that what stopped her from speaking up was the issue from the past, "What did I do to cause this? What did I do to make him do this?"

Erica: My problem is that I can't see a boss making a pass at a girl in the office that he thinks is attractive unless she has done something to make him think that it is OK.

Ted: No. I can't relate to that at all.

MN (to Erica): Does every guy that you come across make a pass at you?

Erica: No.

MN: Has any guy in this room ever made a pass at you?

Erica: No.

MN: And a lot of them have said they were attracted to you, right?

Erica: Yeah.

MN: I think there is a big difference between someone putting out that he is attracted to you. . .

Jason: Someone in authority . . .

MN: Right. Someone who has nothing to lose by doing that, and someone making a pass at you. A person makes a pass at you in another circumstance, maybe you might have provoked it, but I don't think it's unusual at all for a person in authority to come on verbally or even physically when he knows the woman is not going to be able to get him into any trouble for it.

CT: That's what I was thinking. This is a very sexist society and men get away with an awful lot. There's no respect for your boundaries or even taking you seriously. Even though you're hired in a management position, you are viewed like, "Oh, well, you're just going to get married and leave, so. . . ."

(discussion of the situation with Erica's previous boss)

Stu: I'm really feeling kind of overwhelmed by this. Putting myself in your shoes, I can see how scary it would be—like CT said—no boundaries.

Lilly: Especially since he even *knew* she had been harassed before. God!

(statements of agreement from several people)

Erica: So what should I do now?

Jason: I was going to suggest glasses and a mustache.

Erica: That's not fair to me.

Jason: I know. Seriously, I feel that if I were in your place or any attractive woman's place, I would want to hide the way I look, because to run into this problem everywhere, over and over. . . .

Joan: I have attractive men on my job too. One of them came over to kiss me. And I'm attracted to this man. He's 50 years old and he's married, and I'm attracted to him. I was really flattered by it. But the point is that I know when to say no.

CT: I think it gets back to what you said before. That you tell him "Look for me to do my best work, I need for you to be in the role of employer and me in the role of employee."

Erica: But I think maybe since the subject is dropped, I shouldn't bring it up again.

Lilly: I disagree with that!

(Others disagree also.)

Lilly: I think you left it that you are confused, and I think you have to get back and let him know that you're not confused, and not wait until he makes a pass at you to tell him.

(Similar points are made by other members.)

MN: He has seen your vulnerability. You are still vulnerable with him. It may be your vulnerability in part that attracts him. I don't think you realize how vulnerable you appear sometimes. That *is* an *attractive* quality. It may also be what allows some people to take too many liberties with you. It's not that you are being seductive and you're not being unprofessional. You are being you in a kind of dreamy moment. You probably don't come across as hard-nosed as some of your colleagues.

Erica: He said one of the things that he liked about me was that I was really quiet and into my work.

MN: So he goes marching right in.

Ted: Those are qualities that you have that may be very attractive. I've heard a lot of guys say that the tender parts of a woman — not with me so much — but they say that the vulnerability is what they find so attractive.

Erica (protesting): But you don't see me at work!

Ted: But you were in a personal situation with him when all this occurred. I'm sure if you were across a negotiating table, you wouldn't be quiet. I've seen it in here. You can be very aggressive and forceful, but quite honestly, there are other times when you are not that way. He managed to turn the situation around to go his way, to make it more personal, and therefore you were in the vulnerable position.

Joan: Which made you even more vulnerable and therefore even more attractive! It's a vicious cycle.

(Advice from group to Erica to take a clear stand now.)

MN: I'm concerned that you would be attracted to this guy. One that would take advantage of you.

Erica: But I was really surprised. I was surprised when he did that.

MN: I know. That's the problem. You were always surprised when Jake took advantage of you. Even when he would announce it ahead of time that he was going to do something rotten, you were always surprised. You are far too trusting and that is something you have made some progress on, but you have a way to go.

Ted: A person can be naive in certain situations and not in others.

Erica: I wasn't naive that there was an attraction.

MN: You were naive in not understanding that he has more power than you.

Jason: He has the money and the power.

Terrence: I can understand why you worried about what it was you did because, when he asked the question initially, it seemed to be rhetorical but actually he was presenting it as if it was *your* problem. "I don't understand how I can work around you because *you're* so attractive." It's like he planted the seed in your head. It was his problem.

Erica: You know what I wanted to say? "Gee, I don't know why that should be a problem for you. I don't have any trouble working around attractive men."

MN: That would have been terrific! You know, I think that's a really good point about him making you think it was your problem. . . . Once I was a member of a therapy group in which the co-therapist in training, a psychiatric resident, told the therapist and the group that he was not going to talk to me because he found me attractive and he couldn't deal with that. Needless to say, I was quite upset. I was paying for the group, and felt this wasn't fair to me so I left. The group got pretty angry at this point. Finally, I couldn't resist coming back in. I really didn't want to let this turkey deprive me of the group, just when it was getting really interesting, so I returned and he just kind of ignored me and limped through the rest of the semester.

(*Some discussion of this*)

Ted: One thing I want to get back to — the part I really relate to — your initial problem. That you don't feel attractive.

Erica: Well, if I thought I was attractive, then obviously I could justify the whole thing!

Lilly: Now that's pretty bizarre, Erica!

Jason: That's *real* bizarre. Then what he did would be OK?

MN: It seems that "It's not OK to be attractive" is the issue. I don't believe that you don't think you're attractive. You won't admit you are.

Erica: What's the difference?

MN: Well, there is a difference. You said before that if you admit that you're attractive, that would mean that you would be saying that you were trying to turn people on, to seduce them.

Ted: When you are standing in front of the mirror ready to go out, do you think you are attractive?

Erica: I think I've told you before, when I'm going out, I look at myself and say, "Why would anyone want to go out with me?"

Ted: I have trouble accepting that.

MN: What isn't attractive? What part of your looks don't you like?

Erica: I don't think anything about me is attractive.

MN: Then I don't buy it. That invalidates it for me.

CT: I was wondering — How do you know if a woman is attractive?

Erica: She looks perfect.

CT: Who looks perfect?

Erica: Lots of women.

CT: Who?

Erica (giggling): Farah Fawcett.

CT: So for you to look attractive you couldn't have a flaw.

MN: This is all a big game. You're laughing about it, Erica. I don't buy it. I believe you have a problem being attractive, to the point where you won't admit it.

Jason: A person who doesn't think she is attractive doesn't go out of her way to make herself attractive and you do. You use makeup well and you dress very nicely. . . .

Erica: Then what is it?

Ted: Sometimes I think that you know how attractive it is to do what you're doing right now.

MN (to group): Do you believe she doesn't think she is attractive?

Terrence: It took me months to believe that she didn't think she was.

Lilly: I think she thinks she is but sometimes doesn't feel it.

Joan: I think she won't admit it. I'm going through that too. When I admit that I'm attractive, that carries a heavy burden, a tag with responsibility for maintaining that attractiveness, a responsibility for how men relate to me and how I relate to men, who I choose as a partner and who I don't.

Erica: I feel like I am being misunderstood. When I am with a group of women I wish I looked like this one or that one, not like myself.

CT: I could see how all by yourself in your room looking in the mirror, you could say, "Euch, who would want this," but when you get outside and the whole world is saying, "this woman is attractive." how could you not believe they are telling the truth? The reality-testing seems a little out of whack.

MN: Well, CT, think of it this way. You had been told all your life that you were unacceptable if you weren't almost perfectly attractive, but if you got to be *too* attractive, say, like Paul Newman, you would be shot. You would have to work very hard to look really attractive, just to get by, but if you got feedback that you were getting close to being as attractive as Paul Newman, you would want to deny it, for fear of being shot.

(Erica is crying.)

Ted: What set you off?

Erica: I can't relate to what anybody is saying.

MN: You are upset about hearing that you are attractive because it feels dangerous and it makes you feel guilty. You have to grow up and accept responsibility for something that is simply a fact. All you are taking responsibility for is that you are a nice-looking woman. You have done nothing wrong. You've been very responsible about the way you've handled yourself with men. Admitting you are attractive is not being a tease or coming on to people; it's owning that's part of who you are. Going around saying you're not attractive is irresponsible, and it sounds, frankly, rather psychotic, which is not very becoming at all.

(Erica continues to cry.)

MN: Nothing bad is going to happen to you if you take responsibility for being attractive.

Erica: If that's true, then why am I not *feeling* like that's it — that's the answer.

CT: Because it's scary given your background.

Lilly: It's something you've been scared of for years.

MN: And because people *do* take advantage of people who are attractive. Like Joan was saying, being attractive carries some serious issues. Being attractive you have a lot of fun and you also have some complicated things to deal with.

Erica: One of the things I've thought many times since Jake and I stopped seeing each other was, if I was really attractive, he wouldn't have stopped seeing me.

CT: You know, what you do is you give too much power to the attractiveness. It's like — if you were attractive then no man could possibly be pried away from you. It's powerful, but it's not *that* powerful.

Jason: There is sort of an analogy with drugs. When people are just responding to that attractiveness, it's real superficial; it's not real, it's surface bullshit.

CT: I could also see how the attractiveness could be that powerful in an environment where people don't have boundaries. If you are just walking around and somebody just whhhptttt — sticks on you, you know — you could imagine that your attractiveness was just so powerful that you're just the most powerful magnet on the planet.

Ted and Terrence (laughing): We're holding on over here, Erica.

(laughter)

MN: You guys. Your restraint over the last year has been phenomenal.

(more laughter)

MN: So your sexual attractiveness is powerful, but it's not that powerful.

Erica (with relief): That's what I've been afraid of. . . . You know, I can remember my father telling me how powerful sex was.

Joan: That's what my parents were telling me! I had my parents throwing me that when I was 13 when I was modeling. And it was like all I heard, and what do you expect . . . ?

Erica: My father told me you can control people that way.

Lilly: Yeah, anybody but his wife.

Terrence: Maybe the answer is to believe that not every man in the world thinks the way your father does.

Jason: And a lot of them do.

MN: A lot of them do, right.

Ted: I think part of the trick is acknowledging that, yes, it does go on. There are people that control other people by sexuality. There are also people that hate blacks.

Erica: I feel more comfortable with a man knowing that I am attracted to him rather than the other way around.

Terrence: It's the power.

Ted: If he comes on and says, "I'm attracted to you," he's defining the game. He's defining the rules of the game; he's usurping the power from you.

Erica: He's giving me power.

Ted: I could extrapolate from it and say, yes, he's giving you power.

MN: Just as much as *he* wants to.

Lilly: That's a trick. That reminds me of how powerful I used to feel that Ronnie [old boyfriend] was attracted to me and I was the student and he was the teacher and out of those hundreds of students I was the one he had picked. I felt very powerful. That was illusion. It's complete illusion.

MN: It's like the Pygmalion thing. When Henry Higgins turns Eliza Doolittle into the lovely lady . . . and then he has this control over her. He's taken her from the gutter but not any further than he wants to take her.

Ted: I remember when I was working for the M company and I was attracted to this woman, one of our accounts. I figured I could handle it so I asked her out and everything went downhill. She said she couldn't feel free to complain about our company when she needed to. I finally turned over the account to someone else, and shortly after that she dumped me (*sympathetic groans*). . . . Well, that's par for the course I guess.

(*Discussion moves to a different topic.*)

EXISTENTIAL CONCERNS

There is, loosely speaking, a "field" of existential psychotherapy which engages clients in struggling both intellectually and emotionally with issues related to the meaning of life, death, freedom, and isolation. Existential psychology stresses the concept and experience of identity. It values experiential knowledge rather than abstract categories (Maslow, 1968, p. 9).

Existential psychotherapy and group therapy are highly compatible. It is assumed by existentialists that all humans, regardless of ethnicity, status, age, or educational level, are embroiled in the same struggles. Group is, therefore, an appropriate setting for people from various walks of life to share the pains and joys of their respective journeys into confusion and enlightenment. The existentialist commitment to experiential learning supports the concept of a group environment for education and therapy, where "instruction" and "talking about" are replaced by interpersonal learning in the moment.

In this section we are dealing with the widest lenses by which people view the world. Changes of frame of reference on the level of existential beliefs and values occur slowly, but they exert influence in every nook and cranny of the person's life. It is no wonder, then, that in Yalom's research on the mechanisms of therapeutic change in group therapy, clients considered items related to "Existential Factors" sixth in importance in the therapy, a rating considered surprisingly high by the researchers at the time (Yalom, 1975, p. 11). The factors were:

1) Recognizing that life is at times unfair and unjust.
2) Recognizing that ultimately there is no escape from some of life's pain and death.
3) Recognizing that no matter how close I get to other people, I must still face life alone.
4) Facing the basic issues of my life and death, and thus living my life more honestly and being less caught up in trivialities.
5) Learning that I must take ultimate responsibility for the way I live my life no matter how much guidance and support I get from others. (Yalom, 1980, p. 265).

Maslow's (1968) concept of a "hierarchy of needs" suggests that existential concerns are usually consciously addressed by people only when basic physical and emotional security needs are met. Some group clients engage more fully on the existential level than others, depending on what other problems might be more immediate or pressing for them. Their degree of interest in existential questions is also contingent on their particular life experiences, depth of personal awareness, philosophical orientation, and intellectual capacity. Regardless of how much awareness is applied, however, group clients are consistently battling fears and confusion with regard to who they are and how they fit. The process of untangling these issues is both humbling and empowering for them.

The existential approach cares more about the *manner* in which existential questions are grappled with than about the answers obtained. A finely tuned awareness of the world around us, combined with an ability to see from the telescopic to the microscopic, is what is strived for. In my therapy groups I try to foster in clients the facility to change frames of reference quickly in ways pertinent to the understanding, if not the resolution, of life's dilemmas. This section suggests some ways my clients acquire this capacity in the course of facing existential issues in the context of group therapy.

The Search for Meaning and What is "Real"

When Nate entered group therapy, he was, like many clients, deeply troubled by what he perceived to be a lack of meaning in his life. He was in group for three years. When interviewed about his group experience one year after his termination, he had this to say about how the group helped him make some kind of order and sense out of it all:

> We live in a messed up situation, cast by God. Life is a collection of problems. In group you focused right in on the absurdity. People gave each other support while each person was reaching deep into the absurdity for himself. Somehow you found ways to disentangle, to sort out elements of this amorphous mass of problems. Seeing other people do it was very important.

The therapy group provides a setting in which meaning and "real-ness" is searched for and found in the context of lives that have been characterized by confusion and inauthenticity. Often the group itself may seem chaotic and meaningless, particularly when struggles related to individuation and control ensue, and group members are faced with making sense out of what is happening in the group "life." By extension and analogy, members apply the learnings derived from the vicissitudes of the group "life" to their individual lives outside. The very act of being involved in the group's struggle is therapeutic for those whose lives seem to have little meaning, for, as Yalom says, "engagement is the major therapeutic answer to meaninglessness" (1980, p. 478).

There is a validation of one's existence that occurs in a therapy group. John said he experienced it through having people remember what he said. For Martha it involved having her feelings recognized.

All her life, 40-year-old Martha's parents had insisted that emotions, even physical feelings, were unreal. When she was a girl, they taught her that she did not feel sick unless she had a temperature, and that her migraine headaches and menstrual cramps were "all in her imagination." She was instructed never to be emotional under any circumstances, for to do so was considered "making a scene" and "feeling sorry for oneself." Martha obediently stopped feeling as well as expressing pain, and got fat, something that was "real" even by her parents' concrete standards.

In group therapy Martha tentatively resumed efforts to notice and communicate her feelings. When these feelings were treated as real and understandable by the group, she tried revealing herself more and more. With each self-disclosure and accompanying validation from the group, Martha gained more confidence about the realness of her feelings and of herself. She lost weight, no longer needing pure bulk to communicate her presence to others.

Group members in time begin to monitor the authenticity of what is taking place in the here-and-now, and to question interactions that do not feel "real." Some become particularly adept at discerning what is genuine and what is artificial, frequently commenting on this during the course of a session. When the group interaction is honest and clear, members carry the sense of real-ness of what happens in group into their lives, and may be less willing to settle for muddiness or manipulation in relationships as a result.

There is real-ness in the group's struggle for identity as it moves often clumsily and painfully through the stages of formation, dependency, flight and rebellion, and struggles for closeness and autonomy. There is real-ness in the sorrow and despair of some of the tragic lives one hears about, and there is real-ness in the joy and hope that can be found through human contact. There is real-ness in the *tele* that attracts and repels persons to and from one another on a moment-by-moment basis. There is real-ness in the bond of true empathy, the heat of the encounter, the relief of the catharsis, the magic of the "peak experience."

There is also a sense of real-ness mixed with wonder in group when something someone does or says puts everyone in the room in touch with the fact that he has reached a new level of self-actualization or, as Mullan put it, has become "more of who he is" (Mullan and Rosenbaum, 1978, p. 379.)

Order in the chaos of life is found for some people in the process of learning how to doubt. Many have to learn that "current doubting does not vitiate the reality of past mattering" (Yalom, 1980, p. 480). People who always have to sound definite about everything run into problems in group therapy, where the group is aware of how few things can really be "known" for sure. Such people are encouraged to let themselves feel ambivalent or confused when they are, which will allow them to feel all their feelings and make better decisions and judgments.

Group is helpful in illuminating that the only permanence in life is change. In an ongoing therapy group, each person's process of therapeutic change is made visible to and valued by others. Over and over again members see others changing through the group experience, from year to year, week to week, even minute to minute. They witness changes in behavior, roles, attitudes, relationships, belief systems, values and assumptions. They also notice how quickly the group as a whole can change from splintered to cohesive, boring to exciting, superficial to deep, confused to clear, as well as the reverse of all of these, and more. They see how one person's absence or change in behavior creates changes in the whole group system. The observation of change in process gives group members who have a tendency to feel "stuck" in their lives the much-needed perspective that "nothing is forever." It gives group members who fear change the experience and understanding they need of the change process to help them better cope with change in their lives.

Death Anxiety and Acceptance

The paradox that acceptance of death frequently brings new life is one on which philosophers, poets, and healers of all kinds love to contemplate and expound. *Death anxiety*, frequently encountered in therapy disguised as many other forms of mental illness, is a condition in which the person is so afraid of dying that he cannot bring himself to live fully. The therapy group treats this "dis-ease" in profound and interesting ways that are rarely possible in individual therapy. The upshot of the "treatment" of death anxiety is the realization that the specter of death need not be an albatross; rather, it can be reframed as a helpful spur to live each day and moment the best one can.

Yalom, in *Existential Psychotherapy*, describes "death as a boundary situation" (1980, p. 159). He points out as an example how "cancer cures psychoneurosis," citing instances where a person's neurotic concerns vanish when cancer is diagnosed. He suggests that, frequently, all that is needed in order to "get to" the process of living in an energetic and purposeful way is to be confronted with a limitation on the time one has to live. Existence cannot be postponed. The sense of the death being really the *end*, with no guarantee of a "hereafter," leads one to make full use of the here-and-now.

The impetus to live now, generated by an awareness of the inevitability of death, is fundamental in being able to "choose paths" or make important life decisions. Group client Lew had stalled for years about marrying his girlfriend, Rebecca, whom he loved dearly. On his thirtieth birthday he unexpectedly proposed and they married very soon thereafter. When asked what caused him to decide, he said, "I suddenly realized I was going to die some day, and I did not want to live my life without Rebecca."

An awareness of death somehow brings into focus what is truly important in life, as well as a dissociation from all that is peripheral or spurious. People who report "near-death" experiences almost always live differently subsequent to these events. Much of their materialistic and power-seeking endeavors are dropped in favor of engagement with people on a more relaxed and satisfying basis. There is also an intensification of altruistic and spiritual interests.

Persons skirt the fear of death by skirting life. Yalom refers to this as "life anxiety" (Yalom, 1980). Tillich said that "neurosis is the way of avoiding non-being by avoiding being" (1952, p. 66). If there is little investment in life, death will not seem so catastrophic. Yalom frames psychopathology as having to do with fear of death and concomitant fear of life. By avoiding stimulation, strong emotions, commitment, creative expression, involvement in groups and causes, an individual makes himself a little dead during his life, which dulls the terrifying prospect of deprivation, aloneness, and abandonment represented by the prospect of dying.

Yalom (1980) talks of two modes of defending against death anxiety: the narcissistic mode, where one is too special to die; and the "ultimate rescuer" fantasy, which holds that some magic will occur to keep death from occurring. Both are illustrated in the transcript at the end of this section: the first by Melissa who prattles on about her father's death, valiantly pretending the rest of her decrepid family is somehow immune from what seems like inevitable destruction; and the second by Trudie and Noah, whose faith in chiropractors, magic, group therapy, and allergy doctors somehow pushes them past the terror brought up for them by Melissa's death-filled monologues, during which both of them suffered such anxiety that they were compelled to leave the room.

In my experience, often the persons most nervous about death and dying are those who have never experienced the death of someone close to them. A group I was leading with a co-therapist seemed preoccupied with the subject of death and cancer, despite the fact that nothing currently going on accounted for these discussions. All the active participants in the discussion, including the co-therapist, had had no experience with death, but spent considerable group time imagining "what if. . . ." The less interested members had been through the loss of someone by death, and while illness and death were a concern, they were not a source of tremendous anxiety for them. In group therapy, over a period of two years or more, it is likely that at least one member will lose a loved one through illness or accident. In some ways, group therapy provides a useful practice ground for the uninitiated in dealing with issues of death and disease, which serves to decrease the level of death anxiety of these individuals thereafter.

The group is an excellent support during a time of dying and bereavement. It helps the member deal with the stress and the feelings associated with caring for and saying good-bye to a dying person; in addition, the group comforts and listens to the bereaved member after the death of his loved one.

In three instances in my practice group members themselves have died; and members and therapists alike had to cope with the loss and fears these deaths generated. These were terrible experiences from which we all learned a great deal.

The death that had the most impact on a group was that of 27-year-old Mathilda, mentioned in Chapter IV, who died of cancer with no family in town to support her during her illness. When Mathilda received her diagnosis, she told her group before anyone else. Shocked and frightened, the group members held her and told her that, whatever happened, they were her friends and wanted to help. When it came time for her to be sent to New Orleans for a special operation and she had no money to get there, the group participated in fund-raising efforts organized by one of her friends. When she returned to New Haven, much too ill to attend group, Marge, a fellow group member her age, visited Mathilda regularly in the hospital. I visited a few times, and brought back to the group her best wishes and greetings for them, her appreciation for their cards and gifts. I told them of my last visit with her, two days before she died.

She was emaciated and exhausted, her lips bright pink from red juice, which is all she would eat or drink. I guess because of the intimacy we all experienced with her in the group, I felt perfectly comfortable asking her if she would like a backrub. She said yes. As I ran my hands gently over her incredibly frail and bony back, she asked faintly, "Mary, how was your sister's wedding?"

"Just lovely, Mathilda," I replied, weeping.

"Oh good," she said, and fell asleep.

I talked to the group about how I had been surprised that I felt no revulsion in touching Mathilda. I really wanted to communicate my caring for her in this way. (This experience served me well later in enabling me to really be with a friend during his last days as he was dying of cancer. As with Mathilda, it was terribly sad, but not frightening. I knew it was *he* and not *I* who was dying.) Marge, in being with Mathilda, had a similar experience. She was not at all traumatized or disgusted by the illness she saw, and was able to accept Mathilda's death without undue trauma. It was clear that Marge's and my learnings were helping the rest of the group understand a little more about death and dying.

One night, a few weeks after Mathilda's death, many people in the group were in touch with feelings of sadness, loss, and fear of death. We put out an empty chair and people talked to "Mathilda." When Marge had difficulty imagining Mathilda, Greg courageously offered to play the part. In a scene of great tenderness, Marge got a chance to say good-by to Mathilda, as played by Greg, and they cried in each other's arms. Painful though it was, mourning together was a great comfort. Also during that session, some members expressed what had heretofore been unthinkable thoughts about their own mortality, which helped them start to deal with these anxieties in their lives more directly.

Frequently, clients have unfinished business with people who have died. Sometimes a client's depression revolves, unbeknownst to him, around his unresolved grief over the death of a loved one months, even years, earlier. Clients often enter group to receive help with accepting the "death of a marriage" or the terminal separation from a loved one in a relationship. These endings require the same process of grieving and adjustment as literal deaths, and involve the four stages of mourning: denial, anger, depression, and acceptance (Kübler-Ross, 1969). In helping the client deal with separation or death, the group supports the person in cutting ties with the deceased and moving on to connecting with the living.

As a group member faces the inevitability and reality of deaths, past and future, powerful feelings emerge. Surges of previously forbidden guilt and anger toward the deceased and departed are expressed and accepted by the group, freeing clients to complete the mourning process. One person's struggle may well touch off painful and buried memories for others, leading to important grief work for them as well.

Within the group life there are many symbolic deaths, both sudden and prolonged. Some of these endings are abrupt and jagged, such as when a person terminates prematurely and without warning. When Helen, after six months of intense though conflictual participation, announced laughingly on the way out the door that this was her last meeting, we felt as if she had dropped a bomb on us. There was no dissuading her, and she evidently felt no obligation to consider the feelings of others in her leave-taking. On the other hand, when long-term and valued group clients successfully complete therapy, their departure is cause for celebration in the group. When Elizabeth left, worlds happier than she had been when she entered group three years before, Tony wrote her a beautiful song, and Jeanette, who had only been in the group a few weeks, but had already developed deep feelings for Elizabeth, burst into tears.

Even though the group is ongoing, people know that someday they will leave. The time boundary on their stay, if they pay attention to it, can make them work a little harder. In the same way, the hour-and-a-half time limit on each session, shared with seven other people, leaves very few minutes to waste. The "mini-deaths" or endings associated with group sessions and group life help clients to recognize the urgency of living for today and capitalizing on each moment.

"Although the physicality of death destroys man, the idea of death saves him" (Yalom, 1980, p. 30). Death issues in group therapy, whether real or symbolic, propel members into a more active consideration of the priorities of living and stronger connections with other human beings.

Responsibility

"Responsibility avoidance may be bad for mental health" (Yalom, 1980, p. 262). Yalom also says that the therapy group provides "especially optimum conditions for therapeutic work on responsibility awareness. . . . All group members are born simultaneously: each are in the group on an equal footing . . ." (p. 239). (Actually, in my groups, this is not quite accurate. Members come in at different times chronologically, but they are equal at their respective starting points.)

> . . . Each, in a way that is visible to the other members and — if the thera-
> pist does his job — apparent to himself, gradually scoops out and shapes
> a particular life space in the group. Thus, one is responsible for the inter-
> personal position one scoops out for himself in the group (and by anal-
> ogy, in life as well) and for the sequence of events that will occur to one.
> The group has many eyes. . . . Members do not need to accept another's
> description of how he or she is victimized by external persons or events.
> If the group functions at a here-and-now level (that is, the primary focus
> is upon experiencing and analyzing intermember relationships), then the
> members will observe how each creates his own self-victimization — and
> they will eventually feed these observations back to each member in turn.
> (Yalom, 1980, p. 239).

The interactional group format is more directly conducive to the individual's learning to take responsibility than is one-to-one therapy, provided the leadership is not too directive, and members give and accept honest feedback freely. In group the client is much more likely to *demonstrate* his particular problem with assuming responsibility, making pertinent confrontation possible, than he is in individual therapy, where he can hide behind "talking about," relegating the therapist to having to guess what contribution the client himself might be making to his own difficulties.

Members enter the group with conscious or unconscious expectations of being rescued, particularly by the therapist. Helen (the woman mentioned earlier who left so precipitously), when she first came into group, had only had a single initial interview with me. She entered group the first night, sat down and said, "Mary, you look just like my cousin who was older than me. When I was little I fell in a bees' nest and she lay down over the bees to keep me from getting bitten."

I knew right then what she expected from me and that I was not going to be able to give it. Helen's core issues all had to do with being "stung" by all the important people in her life, beginning with her vituperative alcoholic mother, and she was desperately looking for a protector in me. She had been ejected from her family of origin with the words, "All our problems are on account of you and we think you had better leave." From the beginning Helen set the group up for a repeat performance, but with the fantasy ending that I would rescue her. She interrupted people and subtly "put them down" whenever she spoke to them. She constantly indicated that I was the only person in the group she trusted or respected. It seemed she wanted to "sting" the way she had been "stung."

Unlike most clients, Helen was impervious to the therapists' and the group's efforts to make her feel included or to get her to take responsibility for her own situation in life or in the group. If we were patient with her, she monopolized the group with complaints about people abusing her. If we confronted her with her own part in it, she became very defensive. Finally, I tried seeing her individually to see if she and I could establish a more trusting relationship than the phony hero-worshipping one she had set up. Nothing seemed to make any difference. If there was something we missed, I still do not know what it was. It seemed Helen was hell-bent on leaving the group feeling unwanted and blaming us, and that is exactly what happened.

Helen's termination was the most irresponsible I have ever experienced in group; it was worse than all the people who just disappeared and never contacted us, or even the few who left furious and upset and never came back. As she was walking out the door after a session during which she had participated enthusiastically and rather pleasantly, she turned to the group and smiled. "Well," she said, "this is my last session. Now you don't have to deal with me anymore." There was only one word to describe what everyone felt at that point: rage. (Not surprisingly, I suppose, Helen still has not settled her bill with me, almost two years later.)

Anecdotes in this book have illustrated instances where clients have learned to take responsibility. The stories of Joan, Erica, and Terrence (sadomasochism), Elizabeth (prejudice against men), Walt (Nebbish), and Frank (intimacy-avoidance) are a few examples of group clients who, through changing their frames of reference, were able to stop blaming other people, the past, even themselves, and begin to put their lives in gear.

In my groups a big emphasis is placed on taking responsibility for oneself on the physical as well as emotional level. People are positively reinforced for taking care of themselves by diet, exercise, giving up smoking, controlling their intake of alcohol and drugs, and being on the alert for toxic substances in food, the environment, and so on. Some clients, like Jason and Erica, need to be taught to take responsibility for their own physical safety, since experiences in childhood have taught them a careless disregard for human life. The money problems of someone like Jason or Terrence are also addressed as indications of the client's unwillingness to grow up.

While empathy can be shown to such clients regarding the childhood conditions that engendered their immature posture in life, it is important that group members and leaders not collude with one another to avoid responsibility. When Terrence spent his insurance reimbursement that was supposed to be signed over to me, I got very angry with him about it, right in front of the group. I refused to accept his excuses or pleas for sympathy, and told him I did not trust him. I held firm with Joan when she broke the group confidentiality in her dealings with Erica. By the same token, I myself expect to be confronted if I am shirking responsibility or abrogating an agreement of obligations. Recently I was unduly sarcastic with a group member regarding her lack of assertiveness. She appropriately (and assertively!) upbraided me for it in the next meeting, and I expressed my sincere apologies to her.

As a therapist, I have to take responsibility when I believe I am right, even though what I am saying may seem unduly harsh. The following is an example of my assuming the initiative for shifting the responsibility for a member's problems back to where it belonged—on her shoulders.

Frances, a very quiet and intelligent woman in her thirties, had been unhappy in her job for six years. She almost never spoke up in sessions. When asked for her comments she had a delayed reaction of about 45 seconds before answering, and when she spoke, it was to complain that she did not know how to participate in group. I had seen Frances for some time in couples therapy and, coincidentally, socially on several occasions; in these contexts, she was far more verbal and assertive. One night the group was getting very frustrated with Frances, her lack of commitment to anything, her helpless attitude. I said,

> Frances, I think you'd rather have someone else do it. I don't think you have any intention of changing, because you figure if you just hold on long enough someone will take care of it, whatever "it" happens to be. Someone else should bring you the new job. Your husband should discipline the kids. Someone else should do your work for you in here, make it easy to speak, be assertive, whatever. I do not believe you can-

not speak in group. I've seen you in other situations, and you can when you want to. Frances, I believe it is our obligation as adults to take care of these things. People have their own problems, Frances, and they need you to pull your weight in this world.

Frances acted as if she had not understood a word I said and tried to get me to repeat the whole speech, at which point most of the group was hooting with aggravation.

The next week, it was as if a miracle had occurred. Frances came in and started right out talking! She said she had been very upset all week, mostly with wondering whether it was true that "she did not want to change." Then she had looked around her and seen that the things she hated most about her co-workers, their tendency to dump everything on everyone else and never take responsibility, was what she had been doing. She realized at that moment that she did want to change. Frances confronted other members of the group about their responsibility avoidances, pointing out how Fred, whenever he was unhappy with the group, threatened to leave it, and how Henry always blamed his wife for all his problems. Frances began looking for another job and found one, and her effectiveness with her children improved dramatically. The changes she made lasted, because she had changed her frame of reference regarding the locus of responsibility in her life, and now accepted it as resting entirely with her.

Frances' story brings up an important aspect of responsibility which I call "willing, wanting and wishing."

Willing, Wanting, and Wishing

Joke: "How many social workers does it take to change a light bulb?"
Answer: "Only one, but the light bulb's gotta really want to change."

How much do people have to "really want to change," in order for change to happen? Therapists disagree on the issue of how much motivation to expect or demand from clients. Behavior modification assumes that the client has the "willpower" to follow a well-structured program, and usually disregards the possibility of secondary gain for the client in *not* making a change. Existentialists object to the controlling, infantilizing role of the therapist in most therapies. They wish to divest themselves of "responsibility" for the client's changes, emphasizing the client's autonomy in deciding what he will change and how. Behavior modification and existential therapies both try to activate the conscious will of the client in his own behalf. Meanwhile, both virtually ignore the role played by the unconscious in therapeutic change and in resistance to change.

Milton Erickson, master hypnotherapist and strategic therapist, proved through his work that change occurs much more elegantly, quickly, and lastingly when one addresses the unconscious frame of reference responsible for the problem. Strategic therapists, many of whom are family therapists, assume that the individual or family does, consciously and sincerely, "really want to change" or they would not be coming for therapy. They also presuppose a good deal of unconscious resistance on the part of the client and/or the client's system(s). Strategic therapists address the not so obvious "parts" of the client, which are secretly harboring objections to the supposedly desired changes. For example, in the case of a passive person who wants to be more assertive, the part of him that is afraid of losing approval, or the part that knows how to use passivity to get control in relationships, might creep in and sabotage his conscious efforts to speak up. Internal psychological obstacles must be reckoned with for change to be allowed to happen. The strategic model of psychotherapy assumes that there usually is a good deal of secondary gain in the existing state surrounding the presenting problem. If this were not the case, the client, having his own best interests at heart, would have been able to make the needed changes himself already without having to go to a therapist.

Like anything else, the strategic approach can be carried to an extreme. One therapist friend of mine, when first studying Milton Erickson, irritatingly tried to trick everybody into doing things they would have been happy to do voluntarily. People do not enjoy making a change if they feel they are being manipulated. When they feel controlled or insulted by the therapist, their unconscious minds will not cooperate any better than their conscious minds. Any therapeutic gains that are made under such conditions will likely be reversed fairly soon thereafter.

Methods directed to making changes by communicating with the unconscious should only be used when communications to the conscious mind have failed, and when there is a clear contract for change between therapist and client, as well as a relationship of trust and rapport (Lankton and Lankton, 1983).

Erickson often said that the unconscious is a "vast store of resources," the key to which resides within the client himself. Ericksonian therapy helps clients obtain access to their own riches. Presupposing a positive intention for all the conscious and unconscious parts of the client, the Ericksonian approach mobilizes the "will" or "wills" of the person in an efficient and dynamic manner. When the needs and desires of different parts of a person conflict with one another, the object becomes to find out the positive purpose of each part, help the parts negotiate a solution acceptable to all parts, and liberate the energy, or "will," of all parts to the benefit of the whole client. In my groups I teach group members to recognize and validate the "wills" of the different parts of themselves and others.

While I fully subscribe to the Ericksonian model and believe that each part of a person has its own will, I think there is also one "Will," which is the "responsible mover" part (Yalom, 1980, p. 291). This part is like the contractor who agrees to take responsibility for the project and mobilizes the other parts to cooperate for the benefit of the whole. Like the contractor he has to keep everybody working and everybody happy.

Early in his participation, and periodically after that, each group member is asked to make contracts for change. What does he want to be different in his life? What behaviors is he willing to change in order that the desired state might occur? What parts of him will assist or sabotage the change? How can he practice these behavioral changes in group? What can the group do to assist him? In thinking these questions through, the client learns to take responsibility for his therapy.

Most therapy group clients are suffering some disorder of willing. The depressed person is a good example. (Most clients are, in some measure, depressed.) A depressed person is separated from his will. He has ceased to care; he doesn't dream of what could be better, so he is making no efforts in any positive direction. He may somatize his feelings, conflicts, and anxieties, unable to face and "responsibly move" into feared situations. He may use alcohol or drugs to hide from himself his will-less condition, a process which increases the incapacitation of his will.

"Recharging the batteries" of a depressed and tired individual often takes more energy than just one person can provide. The group provides several live bodies for the person to connect with, touch, talk to. The group is a setting for "engagement," the one true antidote for a disturbance of the will.

When a depressed person enters a group, sad, fearful, and lonely, the group will almost always be kind to him. They will try to include him in conversation, tell him about the value of group for them, show concern for him. They will activate his need to please by showing themselves as pleasant, nonthreatening, and supportive people.

Often the straightforward support of the group is appreciated by the individual, but it does not touch his pain or mobilize his will. He makes little effort to respond to the group, to move in any way. He blocks contact with people and resists their suggestions for change. The group begins to get frustrated with the depressed client as they notice how hard they are working and how

little he is doing in his own behalf. When someone finally expresses exaspera-
tion with the depressed client, it usually provokes a negative reaction. How
can they criticize him? Don't they see how miserable and powerless he is? How
can they assume that he has some control over his behavior, feelings, and attitude? He feels insulted, misunderstood, frightened, and angry. If he expresses
his anger, he is at that moment suddenly jarred from the passive position.
The group is happy to see him responding, and they are proved right: He does
have a will! If the client does not express his anger and gets stubborn, this
also shows he has a will, which he could choose to use in other ways besides
passive resistance. If he falls apart and leaves the group at the first confrontation, he has demonstrated that he was not ready to be in group in the first
place, since his will was not intact enough to be mobilized by the challenge.

Many clients' biggest problem is that they have spent all their energy trying
to please unpleasable people. Their will is thus extant, but misdirected. Through
feedback received from the group and by experiences in the group itself, clients learn to put themselves first when appropriate, to assert their will even
in the face of the loss of love from critical parents, spouses, or authority figures. They are able to make the decision to stop throwing away their love and
energies on people who would never appreciate them, and to devote their efforts to themselves and to persons who can give back.

Throughout group participation, each client is barraged with evidence that
he has the power to affect others. At each session he is given hundreds of
chances to assert his will, to influence his environment. He can speak up instead of holding back, reach out instead of closing up, ask instead of "doing
without," try instead of giving up, take responsibility instead of blaming
another. For every opportunity not taken there are 50 more that will soon
present themselves. Successful clients take more and more of these chances,
building a sense of effectance and mastery, which carries them through more
challenges and successes in their lives outside.

A component of "willing" is "wanting." Many clients do not know what
they want from life and, therefore, cannot focus their will on its attainment.
When someone doesn't "want," it usually means he is afraid to. The fear has
two parts. If he wants "to do" something, he will be saddling himself with
expectations, which he might not be able to meet. If he "wants" something
from his environment, from other people, he risks disappointment. In my
groups I notice that clients who are the children of alcoholic parents seem
to be particularly impaired in the area of wanting. It is not hard to understand how this came about for them in childhood. Wanting to accomplish
something in order to please parents was counterproductive, since the parents'

drinking usually precluded any recognition, much less congruent support, of their children's academic, athletic, or artistic achievements. Expecting anything good to happen, like a nice birthday party or holiday, was a foolish desire, since it would either be forgotten or, if it took place, ruined by the alcoholic behavior of mother or father.

People who have difficulty "wanting" will have the problem in the group context as much as in any other area of their lives, but in group the problem can be addressed and resolved. Group clients with a disorder of "wanting" will go out of their way to avoid asking for anything from anybody. When times are bad and they need support, rather than appear vulnerable, they might call and cancel that session or come and start an argument with someone. In this way they insure that they will not get the nurturing they need from the group, but they are safe from what they perceive as the threat of being disappointed or looking foolish.

The "wanting" disorder can be corrected if the group can show the afflicted individual that nurturing and attention are available for the asking — and even without asking. One of the quickest and easiest ways for this to be accomplished is for someone in the group to say, "What do you want from us, John?" or, "I wonder what the group might be able to do for you right now?" This suddenly opens the option to want in the here-and-now, an experience so unfamiliar to some as to throw them into confusion or even panic. Questioning them as to what they want within the group context forces clients to think about the answer in a wider, more existential way as well. It is also useful for the therapist to address with group members how they learned as children not to ask for what they wanted. What happened in their families when they did? Were their hopes continually built up and then frustrated? Were they called selfish and humiliated for wanting? This tactic uncovers extremely important historical material which encapsulates clients' long-harbored and very negative frames of reference. The frames can be changed by providing the client with the right kind of corrective experiences within the group setting. For example, if someone is afraid of being put down for wanting, the leader and/or other members can be sure to praise them when they risk stating even the smallest request from the group, and they can do their best to honor the request promptly and cheerfully.

Clients need to be shown that, in the group, it is their own suspiciousness and hostility, and not a shortage of resources, that is causing their emotional starvation. In group, clients are rewarded for asking clearly for what they want, rather than discouraged or punished for it as they probably were in childhood. It may take months of participation before these clients can ask for someone to call them during the week or request a hug during the session. Of course, group is not Utopia, and people do not always get everything they want or ask for. Some disappointment is inevitable in group as in life. At least if the wants are felt and expressed, however, they have some chance of being fulfilled, and other group members get to know the person that much better. Primarily, there should be no humiliation for the client in "wanting," for it is a core emotion that needs to be aired and not repressed.

"Wishing" has to do with dreaming. More than willing or wanting, wishing is in the area of fantasy. Reveries about what might be are the seed from which are germinated "wants" and directions to follow. With no fantasies of the future people sink into the past, which for most therapy clients is not only counterproductive but depressing. People are afraid to wish for the same reason that they are afraid to want, because they do not want to risk disappointment or looking foolish. Wishing for some is unpleasant because it quickly brings the realization of "not having." Some clients say "it is stupid" to wish for something that can never come true, so they try not to do it.

Yalom points out that we all have wishes anyway, whether we choose to pay attention to them or not. He considers neurosis to be the condition of "wishing without a wisher" (Yalom, 1980, p. 300), where we do not "own," or take responsibility for, this highly unique and powerful part of us. Depressives turn off their wishing capacity. Impulsive people avoid wishing by doing (Yalom, 1980, p. 311), and compulsives will only let themselves wish a very few things (Yalom, 1980, p. 313).

Wishes are what our unconscious feeds our conscious mind to give us clues as to which choices to take out of the thousands available to us. To stop wishing is to pretend that there are not always other choices. Wishes fuel our imagination and inspire action. To be blocked from wishing means to stifle creativity and spontaneity. Repressed wishes cause feelings of frustration, bitterness and pain, which encumber the ability to enjoy life in any way. It is therapeutic to liberate a person's wishes to consciousness, allowing him to see the possibilities they suggest. If a client's wishes are manifest, he can do something positive with them. If the wishes are unattainable in their initial form, they can, through group discussion, be modified creatively so as to be more realistic.

Freud taught us that much of dreaming is wishing. The therapy group is an excellent place to explore dreams. I am often amazed at what fresh insights clients can give one another regarding the relevance of dream metaphors in the dreamer's life. No exercises or techniques are necessary; the mere telling of the dream provides a wealth of images which other members can use to understand the dreamer or as a springboard for associations relevant to his own therapy. When it comes to getting in touch with wishes, however, revealing dreams to the group is a particularly potent mechanism. In sharing dreams, and decoding their symbols in group, clients find themselves revealing to one another their deepest and most personal wishes. Sometimes I encourage my clients to finish their dreams in ways they would like them to end, a fantasy exercise that mobilizes their conscious as well as unconscious wishes. Occasionally clients get to act out their wishes in psychodramatic sessions, a process which renders everyone involved satisfaction and the spontaneity to keep on wishing.

Like Platonic love, wishing is a creative impulse for the future. As regressive or pathological as wishes may sometimes seem, they all contain a grain of constructive possibility, which can be nurtured to reality by the processes of communication and creativity in the group. Through dialogue with others about his wishes, combined with increased skill in reality-testing, the client can learn to transform his wishes into new frames of reference that expand his current experience of the world and point toward useful changes for the future.

Autonomy

Another value on the existential plane which is realized through group therapy participation is that of autonomy. Each individual, as well as the group-as-a-whole, goes through stages of depending on the group therapist and on the group, as well as stages of pulling away from or opposing them.

Struggles to separate, however clumsy, are normal steps toward individuation, which, if all goes well, occurs throughout group participation until one is truly autonomous and ready to terminate. Almost all group members go through a period where they resent "*having to* go to group." They feel controlled by the group and/or the therapist. They say they want to leave and "try it on their own." Sometimes they do leave. If they stay on past this point, however, they realize the obvious — that no one was making them go to group in the first place, and they were and still are "on their own." In some ways they are more autonomous if they choose to stay and participate than if they "react" in an adolescent fashion to what they falsely perceive as parental-type control. It is not very independent to muster up energy to "break out and away" when the exit door has been open the whole time. This is something that the client learns not from being told, but by experience.

It is neither useful nor appropriate to try to convince someone to stay in group once he has made up his mind to leave, especially if the intent of the termination is to become more autonomous. If the therapist or group members believe that the client is leaving out of avoidance or resistance to the treatment, they have a therapeutic responsibility to put forth their opinions, but group pressure to stay is unfair, because it deprives the individual of a chance to take responsibility for his decision. If there is group pressure, he has no choice but to react to it, and this renders the decision less his own. If the person is leaving because of negative feelings about the group or the therapist, he should be urged to take responsibility for those feelings and express them before he goes.

One way autonomy is experienced in group is through the challenging of authority. Lilly, in training to be a therapist herself, was in the habit of being a "good girl." She had no memories of ever disputing or rebelling against her parents. One night my co-therapist (CT) and another member were having a discussion about the member's individual sessions being cancelled because of inability to pay. Lilly became very anxious and irritable, saying that she was "mistrustful" of all the men in the group. Realizing that she meant him, the co-therapist reversed roles with her and said, as Lilly, "I'm not sure you're doing the right thing with this client, CT." Back in her own role, Lilly expressed some cogent criticisms of CT's work with the member in question. CT listened seriously to her comments and discussed them with her. Allowing herself to have an opinion different from the leader "on his turf," and presenting it maturely and congruently, was a big change for Lilly. Before that time she would have expressed her dissatisfaction through an overidentification with the other member's feelings of being abandoned by CT, and whining to CT about it from the "Child" rather than "Adult" position.

We mentioned before that Frank's studies showed that members of a cohesive group are more likely to think autonomously and differently from one another than members of a non-cohesive group (Frank, 1978, p. 106). The new group, like an embryo, consists of the potential for differentiation, but is still a mass of parts that are glued together and dependent on one another. This stuck-together state is not genuine cohesiveness, however, but a pseudo-variety, one that pulls apart at the first sign of intragroup conflict. A group that has grown and developed into a well-functioning unit is a composite of highly unique individuals, integrated, but each autonomous in his or her own right. By differentiating himself from and within the group, a process which is often uncomfortable, even painful, the individual emerges in three dimensions, standing alone. He can then walk in the world as a more complete person.

Guilt and Anxiety: Positive and Negative

Frank (1978), extrapolating from Fromm and other existentialists, suggests there are two different kinds of conscience, negative and positive, producing two different forms of guilt. Negative guilt is the anxious and shameful feeling we experience when we transgress the code of our society. Whether conscious or unconscious, this kind of guilt is destructive and should be treated in psychotherapy, with the idea of getting rid of it as one would a disease. Positive conscience makes us feel guilty when we fail to live up to the best that is in us. It is a force for constructive growth and should be respected, even encouraged in treatment.

May says, "When the person denies his potentialities, fails to fulfill them, his condition is guilt" (May in May, Angel, and Ellenberger, 1958, p. 52). Accepting this premise, Yalom queries:

> But how is one to find one's potential? How does one recognize it when one meets it? How does one know when one has lost one's way? Heidegger, Tillich, Maslow, and May would all answer in unison: "Through Guilt! Through Anxiety! Through the call of conscience!" There is general consensus among them that existential guilt is a positive constructive force, a guide calling oneself back to oneself. When patients told her that they did not know what she wanted, Horney often replied simply, "Have you thought of asking yourself?" In the center of one's being one knows oneself. John Stuart Mill, in describing this multiplicity of selves, spoke of a fundamental, permanent self which he referred to as the "enduring I." No one has said it better than Saint Augustine: "There is one within me who is more myself than my self" (1980, p. 125).

Death anxiety, primary and existential, has crucial positive benefits for the individual when it is faced and experienced. As we discussed earlier, the fear of death and annihilation, of non-being, when recognized can become the impetus for someone to take responsibility for and begin to appreciate one's life. Like existential guilt, existential anxiety has its negative offspring, "secondary anxiety" (Yalom, 1980, p. 112). Secondary anxieties are "derivative" of primary anxiety, very real and enormously crippling. For example, the reluctance to separate from mother (stemming from a profound fear of isolation, a form of death anxiety) may interfere with attendance at school or the development of social skills, which may generate considerable self-contempt and social anxiety (Yalom, 1980, pp. 111–112). Group therapy, like most other therapies, is geared largely to the management and eventual elimination of secondary anxieties.

Everyone, to one degree or another, builds up defenses against primary anxiety. People seem to need, sometimes desperately, to believe that they, themselves, not fate and *not* other people, control their destiny. Many people need to keep proving to themselves and everyone else that they are in the driver's seat. On the pathological level this can take many forms—workaholism, compulsive risk-taking, obsession with acquisition of money and power, to name just a few. Panic ensues when one begins to realize that there is nowhere to hide, that one's mechanisms for sublimating primary anxiety are beginning not to work.

Group therapy, while helping the person divest himself of secondary anxieties, simultaneously operates to increase the client's awareness of his primary anxiety, to accept this as a fact of being human, and to stop trying to run away. The group does this by creating a "nowhere to hide" kind of situation, where each individual is cast in a sometimes brutally clear light. His foibles, his fears, his neuroticisms, his uniqueness are clearly visible, and sometimes this generates in him an awareness of his essential aloneness and vulnerability.

The therapy group as the therapeutic agent forces the client to face himself. By being continually unpredictable the group disrupts the narcissistic assumptions of the client that he controls the universe. While on one level the group is meeting his legitimate needs for nurturing and closeness, on another the group cannot do what the client most wants it to do—to make the fear go away. The group is unable to repair the dreadful aloneness. In fact, sometimes it even makes it worse! Just when he wants to forget, they make him remember. Just when he wants structure, the group gets chaotic and confusing. Just when he might want to crawl back into the womb and feel totally protected, they remind him he is a grownup. When he tries to lose himself in another person, they set boundaries and show him he is separate.

Watching a person fight to hold onto his illusions, lose his grip on them, struggle to grab them back, and finally let go, is an awesome spectacle and one that can be frightening. It is incumbent upon therapists and group members alike to keep a firm footing so as not to be swept into that client's turmoil. In his terror he may lash out at members of the group, castigate the therapist for incompetence and cruelty, threaten to leave the group, or do it. If he comes out on the other side of this, however, he has learned something fundamental about himself, "that, ultimately, he's all he's got." It is hoped that he will, by facing the pain, finally, as Carl Whitaker says, solve the "koan" (riddle) of the self (Whitaker, 1982, p. 155), find out who he really is. When this happens, the client becomes able to find his own paths. He does not need to cling to a grandiose self-image, a magical rescue fantasy, or another person. He is operating under his own power.

Existential Dilemmas in the Group Context: Transcript

In every group session the existential themes discussed in this chapter are addressed in some way. The session that is recorded here, however, is an excellent example of how clients actually live these struggles in group therapy.

The group consists of seven members, ranging in age from Noah in his fifties to Jeanette in her mid-twenties. Melissa's father has just died a month earlier after an excruciatingly long and painful illness. Her mother is alcoholic and her sister emotionally unstable. Melissa has had the responsibility for the family dumped in her lap. She is a bright, narcissistic, and courageous woman, who is involved in a sadomasochistic relationship with a depressed and angry married man. Melissa and Fred (the sensitive, articulate, overly serious young man frequently quoted in this book) have been in group about two years. The others have been in six months or less.

While it was not totally clear to me at the time, Melissa's father's death has had a tremendous impact on the group, eliciting all their deepest fears of death and dying. They are not cohesive enough as a group to express this openly, nor are most of them individually ready to struggle with this terror directly; however, it is getting pretty hard for them to avoid it — what with Melissa dragging in every little detail! Hence, we see primitive defenses in operation — somatizing, running away (literally), deflecting, seeking oral gratification and fantasizing magical cures.

The dialogue in the first half of the session seemed very superficial at the time. In the transcript, however, we see how much is going on at the unconscious level: *anxiety about death* and accompanying denial and rescue and magic cure fantasies; *ontological anxiety* with a fear of any intense feeling, especially sexual, and a need to dull anxiety with depression, and consequently, a sense of meaninglessness and unreality; a *lack of autonomy* evidenced by an unclarity of wants and needs, grudging dependency on the leaders, and a discounting of the separateness of individuals.

The leaders help the group find a middle ground between the terror they are running from and the awful kind of stuck place they have chosen for protection, but now find themselves mired in. The key to that middle ground is open expression of feelings in the here-and-now, starting with the negative ones, which will then liberate the positive. This sparks contact and engagement, remedies for their existential "angst." Suddenly and magically, in the second half of the session, they come alive, their own spontaneity empowering them in exactly the way they had thought could only occur by magical means outside of themselves.

They will not be able to eliminate death and fear, but they *can* contact each other. They may not be able to recreate or immortalize the all-giving parent (represented by Melissa's father), but they can find meaning, solace and a good deal of gratification in their relationships with one another and with us, provided they are willing to face their disappointment and rage with us as leaders for not being able to rescue them from death and from life. Being honest about negative feelings may be risky, but it brings fresh air, and shows them how they are unique one from another, which helps them choose and form attachments with one another for different kinds of satisfaction in many different kinds of relationships.

In the first half of the transcript I have included my notes and comments on the righthand side of the page, elucidating some of the underlying existential issues. In the second half, I let the group speak for themselves, as they busily connect with one another, inspiring, pushing, challenging and leading one another out of the quagmire.

(Trudie starts out by explaining why she bolted out of the room the week before while Melissa was talking about her father's funeral. Fred had had to leave early, and had announced it at the beginning of the session. When he excused himself, Trudie left with him, with no explanation.)

Trudie: I had to leave last week because I felt myself getting dizzy. I couldn't hold it. I got scared. It seems this is how my anxiety comes out now, by getting dizzy. The shakes I had when I first came into group are, by some miracle, gone. I feel more comfortable being dizzy than with the shakes. This fear I can hide from. I'm proud of myself that I don't have the shakes anymore.
    Somatization of death anxiety.

Tony: What are you afraid of?

Trudie: Of becoming more independent. Of really being separate from my husband.
    Fear of autonomy — fused with death anxiety.

MN: Wasn't it scary to hear about Melissa's father's cancer and his death?

Trudie: I don't know. I had a dear friend in school, just diagnosed with a malignant tumor and she's dying.

MN: Didn't you once have a cancer scare?

(Two years earlier Trudie had had a liver disease which was diagnosed as cancer. The diagnosis turned out to be incorrect and Trudie recovered after several months of illness.)

Trudie: My liver? Oh yeah. Not sure what got me upset last week. Bill and his discussion of autonomy from his wife. And Noah talking
    Denial of death anxiety.

about turning into a poor teacher. . . . Why can't I stand on my own two feet? It's silly.

Tony: It's not silly. You're changing your relationship to the whole world.

MN: Is your individual therapist still on vacation?

Trudie: No, she's back. In fact she said, "It's time to stop hiding and being a prisoner of yourself. Now with a year of therapy you know where you're at. Stop hiding in the house. Get out, call your friends."

> Talking "about"—but not really *feeling*—dependency.

MN: Maybe you want to let your therapist know how anxious you are by getting dizzy. Maybe you are trying to get her to lower her expectations.

Trudie: You see, my mother has always lived her life through me and me through her. There is no going back to being the little girl. My therapist isn't going to be my mother. She's going to be a guide, a mentor, so go out and live. I see that now.

MN: You have strong feelings for her. You're trying to negotiate some kind of relationship with her that allows you to grow. You're not sure how to have a relationship with her, how to be dependent on her in a sense, without her having to be your mother. What to do with those strong feelings.

Trudie: Group has become special to me too. Kind of like something to get me through the week. . . . I don't know where the marriage is going. I need to develop and become more independent. I used to be able to run here and run there and nothing would bother me. . . . I just realized somewhere along the line that the group is for me.

> Group is a good "fix."

(Laughter—quips—recognition that group seems at times to be an unpleasant duty, not a nurturing experience.)

(Melissa enters, late, a regular occurrence since she is not able to get out of work in time to get to group promptly.)

Tony (to Melissa): Hi, Sunshine! (To Jeanette) Are you wearing Chalimar cologne? You are! You'll have to change perfumes. Too many memories. | Wow! Ooops. Watch it. No sexual attraction allowed here.

Trudie (giggling — to Melissa): I'm sorry for running out last week.

Melissa (quickly): Don't worry about it. I understand. | Sickly sweet; hostile.

Trudie: Tom (another therapist in the building) didn't know what was going on with everyone running out, first Fred, then me. | Last week was all a joke, right?

CT (Co-therapist) (joking): He suggested a double lock. (Laughter)

Tony: Last week I was talking about being independent. I'm having trouble with that. (Sounding very calm) I'm hurting, I'm dying. | Incongruent.

I feel like I'm being torn apart. It's hard for me to get through two minutes of dialogue without stuttering. I haven't had that problem | Denial through exaggeration.

in a couple of years. I can really understand Trudie. (Still sounding calm) I feel like someone's ripping off my arms. I am furious with my wife for putting me in the position of having to be independent because she isn't going to play the game anymore either. It's a very difficult time. I mean in the morning I'm not even awake and I say (getting louder), "Where's my coffee." I say, "Well Jesus I always bring you coffee in the morning and where's my coffee?" I was shitty to her tonight too. | Escaping the tension in the here-and-now, rescuing the group by taking them outside the room and trying to give them something dramatic to focus on.

MN: What did you do on Saturday morning. | Rage at having to be a grownup.

(Tony and his wife had had a couple's session the previous week specifically to deal with Tony's Saturday morning temper tantrums. Tony had been given the assignment to plan his Saturdays in advance, with activities that | Time structuring — necessary for combatting primary anxiety.

he could enjoy by himself while his wife and child were busy.)

Tony: I found a guitar that I wanted to buy. It was expensive, but it's just what I want. It felt good. But it felt AWFUL. I felt very guilty afterwards.

It's hard to take responsibility, even for getting what you want.

(Attention turns to Melissa. Greetings. Melissa starts a very long speech, about 15 minutes, uninterrupted, which is abbreviated here).

Melissa: My mother feels very abandoned, because her lawyer brother went to Florida. I told her she had to train herself to be independent. We have a real problem with Marina (Melissa's sister). She has been shaking Mother down for money, lots and lots of money over the years and she's still doing it, even since Daddy died. I want to tell her, but what's hurting me is, because of her background, I am afraid of pressuring her. (Sister is diagnosed manic-depressive, stabilized in the last few years, but with a history of severe suicide attempts.) I want to tell her, "You're 28 years old. Pay your own rent. Get a decent job." Meanwhile Mother's checks are bouncing all over the place. . . . Last Tuesday she and I had a nice Valentine's Day dinner, just the two of us. She offered me a drink and I said, "Sure," and I knew she would drink more than me, and I didn't let it bother me too much.

Melissa's mother's alcoholic and helpless condition clearly illustrates the consequences of avoiding the process of growing up.

Melissa's legacy from her father is the responsibility for caring for two ravenous and out-of-control "children" — sister and mother. She is her father's widow.

She wasn't drunk, and I thought, wow, we might have this nice mother-daughter relationship. Then I got back here and I called her on the phone and her speech was all slurred and I knew she was just smashed. . . .

Maybe some magic will happen, and mom will be a mom. Forget that.

Well, I'm open to suggestions on how to make my sister understand. (Goes right on talking.)

> No input, please. I'm teetering here as it is. My only defense is to make you feel as powerless as I do.

Oh, by the way, my mother says she's going into business with my cousin. That would be cute. He's an alcoholic, too. Selling car parts, no less. They could sell parts from the cars they total.

> Grotesque image. Meant as a joke to deflect — but aptly describes the feeling she has of being "chopped up."

(*Silence*)

MN: What do you do when everyone in your family falls apart any time any demands are made?

(*Melissa takes off again. Discussion of father's will. Everything left to mother. Mother too incompetent to employ a lawyer.*)

Melissa: (winding down): . . . Oh somebody else talk. I don't know what I'm talking about.

Fred: Here! Here!

MN: Fred, you look tired.

Fred: I'm tense, I've been partying a lot.

Group: YOU?? (Fred, a depressive artist, had made a big point in group about "choosing" to stay isolated.)

Fred: Yeah, well, I've been drawing too. I have a commitment for a show in May.

Group response: That's great. (Fred gives details.)

Tony: So did you meet someone interesting?

Fred: Someone from Pennsylvania. I enjoyed the weekend, then was depressed on Monday. As usual. (Fred had discussed in group previously that any time he has sex with a woman, he feels catastrophically depressed afterward.) Didn't surprise me. Life goes on. This is a weird time for me. Kind of overwhelming. I wish I could get into partying. It's

> Fear of closeness and of loss of self in the sexual act. Primary anxiety.

disappointing that after a *whole year* of not
being with a woman, that it wouldn't be OK.
Next morning I didn't want to see her. Funny
thing is once I was alone—she left about two
in the afternoon—I felt terrific. I talked to my
sister on the phone. Went for a walk, felt terrific. It was a BEAUTIFUL day. That crash
afterwards is so distancing. I was talking with
my friends later that night and they said I
shouldn't try to hide that depressed part of
me, that friends should be able to share their
moods. But I feel like I don't want people
there, so that I can work it through and re-
charge. That's no way to have a relationship.
Crashing every Sunday. Even when I don't
have sex but am just with a woman. But the
biggest crashes are after sex.

> Fear of intense feel-
> ings. Feels himself to
> be the object or
> victim of his power-
> ful feelings as op-
> posed to the subject
> or "feel*er*."

MN: Does it have anything to do with who
  you're with?
Fred: No.
CT: Does it happen after masturbation?
Fred: Yeah, but it's not as bad, because I don't
  feel guilty about hurting someone else with it.
(*Conversation dwindles.*)
Trudie (to Noah): Did you go to the chiroprac-
  tor?

> Did you get a fix this
> week?
> Yeah!

Noah: He was full of hot air, but I was
  impressed.
MN: You like people like that.
(*MN is recalling that Noah spent the last two
sessions "dumping on himself" by comparing
himself* unfavorably *to people whom he clearly thought were blowhards and brutes.*)
Noah: He was nice, responsive. He gave me a
  very complex analysis. He gave me some pills
  that really worked.

> I sure don't get any-
> thing here that makes
> me feel good.

Melissa: For what?
Noah: I've had heartburn for three years. I've
  been popping antacid pills for three years. He
  gave me some kind of enzyme and it really
  worked.

> Man, what a fix!

In relation to the chiropractor — I'm convinced there is showbiz in the process, but it
really worked. *It really worked*! I'm feeling
much better here (stomach) than I have felt in
three years. Otherwise I've been feeling really
lousy. I don't know whether that is because of
the pills. I think since Thursday, that session
last week I really crashed. I really went down
and even today I could feel everybody. I'm
getting more and more anxious tonight sitting
here.

Between fixes, and when somatization stops, primary anxiety resurfaces.

CT: Was that two or three weeks ago when you
talked about your date and meeting that
woman?

MN: That was when you and Fred were throwing each other off the chair. (Fred had been
testing Noah's passivity by seeing if Noah
would let him steal his chair.)

Noah: That was part of it. I almost "did a
Trudie" (got up and left) just before. And I'm
not sure why. I know that I am extremely
tense and I've been feeling very sad over these
past few weeks. Spending lots of time just
feeling sorry for myself and not doing anything about it. I think I am doing a half-ass
job at work. And I guess I was looking forward to the group, but really not looking forward to it. Not feeling very positive about being here or anywhere.

Probably desire to retreat from intense feelings related to death and illness themes in Melissa's monologue.

Depression as a defense against death anxiety

MN: Sounds to me as if you are blaming the
group since you imply your mood began two
weeks ago here.

Noah: It's possible that the group may in some
ways symbolize my life.

Fred (sarcastically): What does that mean?

Noah: I feel down when I'm in the group. I feel
down when I'm outside of the group. I find it
very hard to express myself. Maybe I look at my
participation here and my inability to find myself
here and I know that's what is going on everywhere else. I can see it very clearly here.

Paradox: In group I see how lost I really am, and feel.

Fred: So your position here symbolizes your
   position in the outside world
Trudie: That's the way you perceive it. Because I   You're not lost.
   remember the story you told about the sun al-   You're not lost. I'll
   so rises or whatever . . .   help you not feel it,
                                                          and you help me
                                                          not feel it.

CT: But that was much more than two weeks
   ago.
Trudie: . . . then a lot of times you come out
   with, a lot of things that I find myself inter-   Notices the "nega-
   ested in. I see you as an interesting person.   tion" in Noah's lin-
   Then you just get down on yourself and say,   guistic pattern. The
   "I'm not interesting and I'm not this and I'm   reader will remember
   not that." Aside from you as a person, just   that Noah's linguistic
   the story itself was good.   patterns were part
                                                          of his problem (see
                                                          Chapter II).

MN: I think it's time I put out what I'm hearing here. Actually I'm hearing one thing and
   not hearing something else. The thing I'm
   not hearing is people expressing any kind of
   feelings *to* each other or CT or me. The thing
   I am hearing is a lot of stuff about ways to
   "get fixes" outside. Both of you, Trudie and
   Noah, especially, whether it's stimulation or
   pills or allergy analysis or whatever it is, you
   know. There's all kinds of references being
   made to the more exciting fix. You said something about there was more showbiz in the
   chiropractor and before group people were
   making references to Dynasty and some other
   TV show about people with a lot of power
   and money. There are things that you are saying, I think without realizing it, that indicates
   to me a lot of disillusionment and disappointment with what you are getting here. And
   you're not *going* to get anything here unless
   you deal with those feelings first. Jeanette had

said two weeks ago that she was very unhappy
and miserable here. Noah is now unhappy and
miserable here. What about the rest of you?

Melissa: I didn't want to come here tonight.

MN: You didn't want to come here either.

Melissa: I'm here under duress.

Tony: I had a real battle myself. A real struggle
whether I should come or not. Of course I
knew I would. But I really didn't want to.

Melissa: I always feel that no matter what I say,
like when I said, "Well I really don't know
what I'm talking about anymore," and Paul
piped up, "Here, here," I took it as — "Melissa,
enough already, we're all bored." And I really
feel that no matter what I say, it's never as   I'm not important
important as the other one's problems. Or if
people think I'm so normal, what the hell am   I don't know how to
I doing here or I always feel as if I'm sitting   use my resources. I
in the back seat. I don't think I know how to   am all alone. Teach
utilize the group. I've been here for two fuck-   me, MN and CT, the
ing years and I'm still sitting here saying,   way my parents
"Why is there a group? Why do I come here?"   could not.
It's like, you know, very confusing. I also
don't know how to utilize you and CT.

MN: I sense you defending against that confusion by talking without letting anybody in. It's
almost like I can predict when you are feeling
like that because you almost . . . it feels as if
you are trying to compensate for that.

Melissa: Compensate for what?

MN: It seems that you try to compensate for
what you and everybody else are not getting
here by sharing more and more of Melissa.
It's very real stuff, and I can see how you
wind up feeling ripped off, because you don't   Melissa's narcissistic
really know whether people are really there   defenses are not hold-
with you or not. You probably kind of sus-   ing up against the
pect they aren't, so you go more. I think that   tremendous stresses
what you need to do in order to use the group   in her life.
is to learn how to live with the anxiety of peo-

ple not knowing what the hell they are doing for a while instead of . . . rescuing them. You rescue them. I noticed this last summer, too. When the group went through a slump. You take care of the group the way you take care of your family—by sharing more and more and more. And making fewer and fewer demands, until you finally get really pissed off.

"Rescuing" from the narcissistic position just results in more pain for her.

Melissa: Mmmm.

CT: There are a lot of resources in this group. Why don't we talk about what we are not using. There are men and women. There are male authority and female authority. There is changing of seating patterns. I could go on endlessly, but it's like a lot of people are not tapping in as opposed to just talking about things.

Noah: I take a back seat. I always have the feeling that my problems are not important enough. The issues are not important enough. The issues are not important enough to present when there are all those other issues. Then I leave and I feel badly. I somehow feel that I am not being or doing the right thing. I've been really very confused. Both about being here and being elsewhere.

MN: Noah, I wish you'd complain less about yourself and more about other people. It would be refreshing to hear you complain about somebody else for a change. But that would be a risk for you.

Melissa: You mean complain about us?

MN: Yes. Noah, who are you really blaming for having such a rotten time here? Me? CT? Tony? You seem to blame yourself for everything that happens everywhere in the world.

CT: Maybe people have been too nice. Maybe they haven't shared their reservations. Feelings of being slighted. Feelings of not being paid attention to.

Melissa: I'm afraid to say a word.

Fred: I think this is all very recent. For me it's very recent. It's been all like the past two weeks. Even last week I didn't feel this way. Tonight I feel it. The reason I spoke up and said "here, here" is because I wanted to know what's going on with *you*, Melissa. Sorry. I'm very sorry that you are having all these problems with your family, but I can't give you an answer about what to do about your sister. How does it affect you? IIow does it affect you—the fact that you're responsible? How does that relate to us in here?

Melissa: If I say anything I'll get accused of rescuing the group.

Fred: No, you can't use that as an excuse.

Melissa: I'm very confused about how to speak about what hurts me inside. What I want to share with these people.

MN: You see, until the group dynamics are straightened out, people will not be responding to you. Everybody is anxious and crabby, dependent and angry at one another. If you go ahead and talk about your problems when everybody is like that, you will not get a response.

Melissa: Well, I didn't *know* everybody was crabby and angry.

MN: I know. That's why I'm telling you. You're not giving yourself a chance to be heard in the way you deserve to be. I feel sad for you when you go on talking about stuff that is very meaningful for you and not realizing that everyone is somewhere else.

Melissa: Why are they somewhere else?

MN: That's what I want to know. They are all sitting on things they are not dealing with, things that may not have too much to do with you, because you have not been here for a month. One thing I notice is that no one ever

Melissa feels "wounded" by MN, who has challenged her narcissistic position. MN considers it healthier for Melissa to get her rage at her mother *out*, even though it is still displaced onto MN, than to hide behind the narcissistic mask.

talks to CT. People talk to me once in a
while, and I will talk back to them. Fred talks
to just about everybody. But nobody talks to
CT. It's really interesting. If he says something, they'll answer, but it will never be back
to him.

CT: What do I represent?

MN (to group): I'd really like an answer. Why
don't you talk to him?

Melissa: I never noticed it until you mentioned
it.

MN: How about you, Jeanette?

Jeanette: I just don't know you that well, and I
don't always feel comfortable talking with
you, and I have sometime gotten the impression that you have a hard time staying awake
in group. That's just my opinion, and I could
be 100% wrong.

CT (raised voice): Do you feel I was falling
asleep while you were pouring your heart and
soul out two weeks ago?

Jeanette: No, I don't think so. I didn't really
look at you until you told me to look at you
that week, and it took me about ten seconds
to do that. I haven't felt that the last couple
of times I've been here, but I did several times
before. I've just been feeling uncomfortable
about the whole group.

MN: If I felt that one of the group leaders was
falling asleep, I'd be angry.

Jeanette: I feel aggravated. But, I just forgot
about it. I knew Mary, and had met with her
a couple of times before I came into the group
so I feel more comfortable with her.

MN: But also, since I'm a woman, I'm more
sensitive, smarter, and more dependable.

Jeanette: I think that's how I feel about it.

Trudie: You take more control than CT, and
that's why I keep focusing on you. Also, I enjoy when you pick up the topic and it goes

At this point, contact
begins to be made
among group mem-
bers. There is no
more talk of fixes.

My commentary
stops here, because
the group's words say
it all.

around to each person so that everybody has
the feeling on something. Like at Christmas
time, you did that. Then I get a lot of insight
and each had a limited time as opposed to
when we all ramble—which may be necessary,
I don't know. Just from my own coming I
find that more important, more beneficial.

MN: So how did you feel when you thought that
CT was bored?

Trudie: I was bored too, so I thought that he
had a right to be. Sometimes when the ram-
bling starts, I'd like to go off in my own little
world and block it out. It was boring as opposed to some of the sessions when we were
all interacting.

MN: Let's stay with specific people. I can't figure out whether you are saying I do structure
things, or I do not structure things enough.

Melissa: You kick more ass.

Mary: I kick more ass. This is true.

Trudie: I feel the group moves when there is
more structure.

MN: The point is not who leads the group better. The point is, Trudie, that the structure
you expect you only expect from me. You
think CT isn't doing anything, and yet it
doesn't bother you at all. I'd be upset with
him, but you just accept that. If I were bored
would you feel that way about me? No. You'd
be mad at me.

Trudie: You're right! You're right!

CT: You can't get mad at me.

Trudie: I can get mad at you but . . . you're
very right. I can be furious at you and not say
a thing. You let her go off in this direction.
But I'll never blame CT once.

*(Tempo of the group has picked up greatly. Peo-
ple are talking directly to each other, with
hand gestures, changes in voice inflection and
facial coloring.)*

MN: How about you, Fred?

Fred: The other thing I was thinking was that I like it when CT kicks ass. He does once in a while. Although you don't do it enough for me. I would like you to do it more. At those times I feel that I could or would like to rise to that challenge. Maybe I don't have enough opportunity and I have not thought of it at all until just now. But I did notice it earlier when I was talking that I was looking around, and I would look around this way and I would get to Mary, and I would stop. I realize that I was avoiding you.

Noah: I noticed today as a matter of fact, that I did talk to CT. I was surprised. It was new. So when you said that no one talks to CT, I said, "I did, I did."

Everyone: Good boy, Noah. (Lots of laughing.)

Fred: Noah, were you aware of the fact that, when Mary asked why don't you get mad at others instead of getting mad at yourself, you looked at CT instantly?

Noah: No, I wasn't.

MN: Whew!

Fred: Wasn't I supposed to say that?

MN: That was really quick. I didn't see him look at CT. I just assumed he was looking at me, and looking all hurt and miserable, so I didn't even watch him.

Tony: CT, you are the most important person in the group to me. I feel closer to you than to anyone else here. In a way you are my father, and in a way I don't want to displease you. It's very difficult for me to talk with you. I think I come to group for the hug you give me at the end of the group. I mean that was the only reason why I came tonight. I thought that CT is going to hug me. I would have been so upset had you not been here, because that is one of the main reasons why I come.

But I don't want to displease you and I don't
want you to think of me as I often think of
me, which is as some kind of mean, ugly, disgusting, disreputable and unworthy individual,
and I see you as an important role model for
me and in many ways I would like to be like
you, or how I imagine you to be, which is
very sensitive and very supportive and very
giving and I feel very unworthy of your
friendship. That is why I very rarely direct
any conversation or anything I may be saying
to you specifically. I'll say it to Mary because
she doesn't hold that place. I can talk to Noah
like that or to Fred, Jeanette, or even you,
Melissa (slight laugh). That's OK, and I know
it. I've been aware of this for a long time and
it was a very difficult subject for me to bring
up because I have never been close to another
man. I have never felt the way I feel toward
you. I wish I had a father who would give
me a hug and say, "You're doing real good"
or "You're my boy," or just hug me the way
you do and never having had that it is really
important and I don't want to lose that.
I don't want to lose that hug at the end of the
group. I don't want to risk saying anything to
you because you may get mad at me and with-
hold that, and that would just devastate me,
so rather than do that, I won't say anything.
MN: So you really have all this affection for
    CT, but don't trust him.
Tony: I've learned not to. Not here, but I've
    learned not to trust.
MN: You don't trust him *yet*.
Tony: That's right, exactly.
MN: How would you be able to trust him?
Tony: I don't know. Maybe just by talking
    about this. Talking about feeling good about
    you helps me trust you. You haven't said a
    word since I've been talking although you've

been looking right at me. I'm wondering what
you're feeling.

CT: I'm feeling like I'm being tested too, because to trust me you will have to share something that's so black and ugly about yourself,
and my gut reaction has to be one primarily
of love and concern and not, initially, "oh
that son of a bitch." So I have to be ready.
And that will be your task, where you've done
something bad and someone can still accept
that and like you as a human being. Also I'm
feeling that I wish I could be worthy of what
you are saying. It is good hearing that I can
be that important to you and I want to be
able to use that to help you, which is what it's
all about.

Tony: I'm scared. I'm absolutely terrified.

MN: I don't blame you.

CT: I've also noticed that my relationship with
the men . . . there may be issues, but we look
at each other and we relate. But with the
women it is different. Mary and I were talking
about that. You all are relating to me as the
male, older man, which may be representing
fathers, whatever else—abusers in some cases.

MN: Tony, I think that took a lot to say that to
CT. High on the risk scale.

Melissa: Well, I like you, CT, because you always remember my name.

(*Laughter.*)

MN: That's about as much as Melissa would expect from a man. As long as you do that, as
long as you remember her name, you probably won't fall below her expectations, because to go below Melissa's expectations of
men, you would have to be about 40 feet
under.

Melissa: Are you saying I have low expectations
of CT?

MN: Very low.

Melissa: Why do you say that?

MN: Why do I say that? Because you never ask anything from him. I mean, I think that what CT said about the women's feelings towards him is correct—that he is representing men in general, especially men in a certain amount of authority. I have noticed that.

Melissa: You're the therapist. I guess you're right.

MN: Naturally. (Group laughter.) You are full of it, Melissa. Since when has that made any difference?

Melissa: Why argue? You'll prove me wrong anyway, so why bother. I know when you're not here, CT, when you're playing in a tournament or something, I am kind of . . . I say to myself, why is he off having fun when he should be here?

CT: I want to make it clear. I never missed a session for a tournament.

MN: Yes you did! Yes you did! You were in Philadelphia.

CT: What?

MN: And the one in Atlanta.

CT: Detroit.

MN: Right, Detroit!

(*Lots of laughter from everyone.*)

CT (referring to Jeanette): She's enjoying every goddamn second of this! Look at her. I haven't seen her look that good in I don't know how long. I don't believe it!

(*More laughter.*)

Jeanette (laughing and turning red): That's terrible!

CT: Well, when Mary goes on vacation, I will be here.

Trudie: Yeah, but we can't say who else is going to be here!

Everyone: Ooooohhh . . . (much laughter).

CT: Okay, well, we will see.

Tony: I'll be here.

Melissa: He'll come for five minutes, get his hug and then leave.

CT (smiling, to Melissa): She's such a bitch; she's the greatest.

MN (to Noah who is squeezing the pillow in his lap): That is very phallic what you're doing with that pillow.

Trudie: Yeah. I thought we were supposed to talk about sex and we never got to it.

(*Laughter.*)

MN: We're creeping up on it.

Noah: I'm still puzzled about Fred's observation and I'm still trying to figure it out. It's still there and I'm really bugged by it. That I look at CT . . . and the best I can do with that is that I was looking for help. I really didn't want to do that.

MN: That's a lot of bullshit. I think you are quite hostile to CT and have been since you first walked into this group. Your expectations of him seem even lower than Melissa's. It seems to me you avoid him like the plague.

CT: Well, he doesn't avoid me completely outside of here, but I agree he may be hostile and I'll throw out a reason. I had occasion to meet Noah's former wife and him to talk about an issue around his daughter. I found her to be a pretty interesting woman.

(*Lots of nervous laughter.*)

CT: That should cause you to have some reactions or feelings.

MN: Hey, maybe you'll start dating her.

Tony: Oh shit!

Melissa: You can't date the client's ex-wife!

MN: He can't?

Noah (blushing): It's interesting that I thought about that.

CT: You did think about that?

Melissa: It must have been pretty obvious then.

MN: What did you do, CT, drool?

CT: No!

Noah: I didn't think CT did anything like that. I haven't talked to Judie (ex-wife) about it, but what I perceived was Judie seeing you as a very interesting person.

CT: All right. So there was double electricity between her and me and you were witness to it.

Trudie: That would be pretty heavy.

Tony: I would be *so* hostile as if you did that to me. If I were there and that happened, that would do it. You would become human at that point.

CT: I'm not talking about his *wife*. This is an *ex-wife*.

Tony: I don't care. If I was in Noah's position I would be hostile.

Fred: It was interesting what you just said. You would consider him human. I must confess that I felt a bit uneasy when you were talking to CT and I would like to just talk about that a little bit, because first of all I felt uneasy about your observation about yourself. That the only reason you came to group was to get a hug from CT. It was the first thing that you said. I'm sure that you were generalizing.

MN: Do you feel jealous?

Fred: I felt hurt and left out that that could be the only reason that Tony would come. Even though at the same time I thought he was generalizing, it was the first thing you said and I thought it was based on something. I also thought there was some element in what you said—an element of pleasing somebody.

MN: Try to talk about your feelings about Tony without criticizing him. He took a risk.

Fred: I thought that I have tried to offer Tony things and I think that I have and I felt that I should be a reason also why you should come and I would like to be and I felt—frankly, I was hurt.

Tony: OK. You have helped me. When I was talking about how I was feeling about CT it was specifically how I was feeling about CT and not about how I was feeling about the rest of the group. It is regrettable that you took it to mean that you are not important because I've said it in group before . . .

MN: Don't clean it up, Tony. Let him have his feelings.

Tony: I'm not cleaning it up. I said it in group before. I am letting him have his feelings.

MN: No you're not. He felt hurt because you said that CT was the only reason you came to group, and now you are starting to take it back.

Tony: No, no, no. That is not what I am saying. I've said it before that everyone is very important to me. (To Fred) I've said it to you, too. I'm a little hurt that you think I was leaving you out, because I was talking with CT. I'm a little angry about that too, that you could think that you are not important.

MN: Why should you be angry at him for feeling not important at all on account of something you said?

CT: He can be angry if he wants to be angry.

MN: Yeah, but — wait, I disagree. Because I think you are discounting Fred's feelings, Tony. You said yourself that CT was more important than anyone to you, and Fred has feelings about that.

Tony: He feels that he is not important, but I am saying, "Yes, you are."

Fred: I'll tell you something that is just clicking for me now. It is that I felt left out at the expense of you pleasing CT.

(*Long silence.*)

Tony: What do we do with that? (Long silence.) I'm not sure what I'm supposed to do with that.

Fred: You're not supposed to do anything, man. You know. Just be yourself, don't do what you're supposed to do. Just sit if you don't want to say anything.

Tony: I've just been made responsible for your feelings.

Fred: I didn't make you responsible for anything.

Tony: No, you did, man. . . . You said . . .

MN: You know, sometimes it is very hard to be important to people, and that is one of the things you need to learn, Tony. That you might be just as important to him as CT is to you.

Tony: Yeah . . .

MN: And if that scares you, that's your problem, not Fred's.

Tony: No, but doesn't that make me responsible for his feelings?

MN: He never said anything about you being responsible for his feelings. He stated his feelings. He took responsibility for his feelings simply by saying them to you. If he hadn't said them, he wouldn't have been taking responsibility, but he did. He didn't say you had to change.

Fred: I don't want you to do anything.

MN: I think what is scary about group therapy is what CT said before. There are so many resources here, and each person really can get what he or she needs. . . . You know, like in life, if you spend your life trying to get from your parents what you never got, you might miss the fact that there are people right next door who can give you all the stuff that you need. . . . It is wonderful that you told how you felt about CT. It is also wonderful that Fred talked about how he felt about you.

Tony: Yeah. It's hard for me to see. I see you as criticizing me.

Fred: I wasn't. I was telling you how I felt.

Tony: Yeah. But I see it as . . .

MN: Fred must really care about you.

CT: If he didn't feel strongly, why would he be hurt?

Tony: That's what is hard for me to handle.

CT: You are in the same position that I was before. He is doing that to you now. Someone thinks you are terribly important and doesn't want you overlooking that.

Tony: Yeah, I have real problems with that.

Noah: You did that to me once. You told me that I was important to you and I was overlooking you.

Tony: That's right.

Fred: Well, how do you see me as feeling about you?

Tony: I feel like I took a nice feeling you might have had for me and made it shit by not recognizing it, by overlooking it when I was talking with him. That has just happened to me my whole life, where I've had that done to me, and that is just like one of the *worst* feelings. Having that feeling of being passed over. I guess I feel like I've hurt you deeply, and it is irrevocable. I've taken something beautiful and I've smashed it.

Fred: Why don't you ask me if it is irrevocable?

Tony: Okay. Is it irrevocable?

Fred (Pause): Of course it's not irrevocable.

(*Laughter.*)

MN: That was great. I like that little hesitation, too.

Noah: It's funny that I had exactly the same feelings. I never said it, but when I was sitting here I had exactly the same feelings.

Fred: I've been there so many times myself. I'm so glad I said what I said because that was real important. In the past I would have just sat on it, and I would have left without saying anything. And that was just real super for me.

Tony: I'm glad you told me how you were feeling. It may not have been what I wanted to hear, but I am still glad you said it.

CT: When the group gets cluttered, it is because these feelings are cluttering it up. Suspicions, jealousies, controversies, and a lot of that has gone by, and that is when it gets boring. Because you don't want to think about those things.

MN: Right. It takes a lot of energy to sit on all of that.

CT: Yeah, it uses up all of the energy.

Melissa: It takes a lot of energy to keep from blowing up.

CT: That is one of the toughest tasks for some people.

MN: Do you feel like blowing up now?

Melissa: No, I feel better. Still confused, but better. It feels good in here.

Noah: What you said about the clutter, CT. I guess I was wondering where it went, because I don't . . .

MN: You want to find it again?

Noah: I don't know if I want to find it. But I know that I don't feel it.

(Some discussion follows with Noah about his inability to complain about people other than himself, and then group session concludes.)

CHAPTER VI

The Paradoxes
of Group Therapy

A STRANGE GAME OF CROQUET

Alice thought she had never seen such a curious croquet-ground in her
life; it was all ridges and furrows; the croquet balls were live hedge-
hogs, and the mallets live flamingos, and the soldiers had to double
themselves up and stand on their hands and feet, to make the arches
(Carroll, L., *Alice's Adventures in Wonderland,* 1932).

Group therapy reminds me of the adventures of Lewis Carroll's Alice. In
Wonderland and *Through the Looking Glass,* Alice finds herself in myriads
of situations, none firmly located in time and place—each unique, colorful,
confusing; each populated by interesting characters that mercurially change
size, personality, and function at the blink of an eye. Alice herself keeps getting bigger and smaller, which radically alters her perspective and keeps her
constantly befuddled about her actual versus perceived relationships to the
other creatures and structures around her.

Being in a therapy group as a member or a leader is frequently very similar
to having fallen down the rabbit hole or wandered into the Looking Glass
House. In group therapy, as in Alice's worlds, it is often hard to know what
is happening, but one can depend on two things: Everything is alive and
nothing stays the same.

In Wonderland, every time Alice begins to understand what is going on,
the scene changes, the characters turn into beings of a different sort, or Alice

220

eats or drinks something which makes her grow or shrink. In group therapy, just as we begin to grasp what is happening in the session, another dimension becomes apparent, and we suddenly have an entirely different, equally valid view. What makes the stories of Alice and group therapy mystifying and humorous is that, in both settings, changes are always occurring with respect to the frameworks of time, space, and perspective—dimensions which we generally think of as relatively constant. In group we cannot help but look at things in many different ways over a short period of time. The following will illustrate.

Many group members and I are talking with Gertrude about the coping strategies she has been learning in the course of her divorce. I look around the room and notice that all the men are sitting on one side of the room and the women on the other. As I listen more intently to the discussion, I hear that it is beginning to turn into an argument between the men and the women. This brings my attention to the hostility that Gertrude is *not* expressing toward her husband, even though she has substantial reason to be angry. I then begin to wonder if Gertrude is unconsciously acting out her hostility toward her husband and the men in her life "out there" by getting the women in the group to ally with her against the men. Todd's tirades about "all those creeps out there," men who will take advantage of a woman alone, make sense as projections of his own unexpressed rage toward his mother. Frank, who rarely agrees with Todd about anything, is joining right in with him on this, perhaps pairing with Todd in reaction to the formation of an aggressive female subgroup. I begin to feel a certain charge in the air. People's faces are registering excitement and intensity; many are flushed; some jaws are clenched. Voices are rising in volume, and talk is rapid, with considerable interrupting. I smile inwardly at how oblivious they all seem to themselves right now. I am comfortable letting the group continue with this for a few minutes, as I formulate some interpretations of what is going on.

Let us review some of the frames that I consider in this very brief snatch of group interaction. There is the theme of divorce and separation on a manifest level. This relates directly to Gertrude's relationship with her husband and her situation as a woman alone, as well as her past relationships with men. Then we have Gertrude's relationships with men outside and with the men in the group. There is the relationship between all the men and the women in the here-and-now, and each member's current relationships outside as well as his or her personal history with the opposite sex. Todd's history with his mother is needed to understand his participation here, as well as his relationship with other women both outside and inside the group. Todd's past relationship with Frank is seen in contrast to the current interaction between them;

the interlocking transferences between them may come more clearly into focus here. I myself am paying close attention to nonverbal communications and trying to determine patterns of these as they relate to the content and group interaction. I am also attending to how I am feeling in the group right now, while formulating ideas about the process and how to intervene.

Clients are usually only peripherally aware of the simultaneous realities of group interaction. Like the queen and her cohorts in "Alice," they are very involved in the "sport," and rarely step back and look at themselves in such a way that they can appreciate how many things they are trying to deal with at one time. When they do, they are very impressed with the complexity of it all. The therapist, on the other hand, does not have the luxury of "just play-ing the game" or of simply observing. She must join right in as a thoroughly competent player, while keeping the score and interpreting the rules at the same time. She must keep track of and sometimes coach the players, as they change roles, time frames, and positions on a practically moment-to-moment basis. The willingness to go through such gyrations requires a sense of humor, considerable skill, and, above all, a great love of the game.

> The chief difficulty Alice found at first was in managing her flamingo; she succeeded in getting its body tucked away comfortably enough, under her arm, with its legs hanging down, but generally, just as she had got its neck nicely straightened out, and was going to give the hedgehog a blow with its head, it *would* twist itself around and look up in her face with such a puzzled expression that she could not help bursting out laugh-ing; and when she had got its head down, it was very provoking to find that the hedgehog had unrolled itself, and was in the act of crawling away; besides all this, there was generally a ridge or a furrow in the way whereever she wanted to send the hedgehog to, and, as the doubled-up soldiers were always getting up and walking off to other parts of the ground, Alice soon came to the conclusion that it was a very difficult game indeed *(Alice's Adventures in Wonderland).*

THE PARADOX OF THERAGNOSIS

Jerome Frank has noted that "psychotherapy is the only form of treatment which, at least to some extent, appears to create the illnesses it treats" (1974, p. 8). This even more true of group therapy than of individual. Throughout this book we have recounted anecdotes of "set-ups" and interpersonal tangles group members have engaged in with one another. Many is the time that clients have said to themselves or out loud, "What is the purpose of all this? All I'm getting out of group is more problems, not fewer!"

It is certainly the case that in group therapy the individual's particular brand of psychopathology sooner or later leaches to the surface and begins to operate in combination with that of others. Group therapists agree that these occurrences, though frequently unpleasant, are at the heart of the therapy, since they allow for the dual diagnostic and therapeutic process of "theragnosis" (Bach, 1954).

The therapy group automatically elicits the relevant symptoms of its clients without conscious effort on anyone's part. All a client has to do is come to the session. Whether he is cooperative or resistant, he cannot help displaying his symptoms, making them a target for the therapy, and allowing treatment to begin. As one of my long-term clients, Ronald, says,

> If someone new coming into the group does *not* within the first two months make a total fool out of himself doing whatever screwed up thing it is he normally does, then he isn't going to get anything out of the group and he might as well leave.

Heightening the paradox of theragnosis is the fact that, in order to elicit all the clients' worst interactive behaviors, we have to raise their anxiety. (Otherwise they won't make fools out of themselves as they are supposed to.) Ironically, anxiety usually numbers as one of the clients' major complaints in their lives, and here we are aggravating rather than relieving it! However, when people are stuck in outmoded frames of reference and/or their motivation is low, they often need to be made a bit anxious and confused in order for their inadequate frames to be broken apart.

Of course, some people are so anxiety-ridden that to make them more anxious is not therapeutic and, in fact, could be destructive. These clients are really not available for theragnosis, and should not be in groups where intensive theragnosis is taking place. They can be seen in one-to-one therapy instead, or in a group whose function is purely supportive. Clients who do need theragnosis, however, will nevertheless find growing through the group process quite an anxiety-provoking and difficult process at times.

In *Through the Looking Glass,* Alice asked the Tiger-lily why the flowers were talking.

> "Reach down and feel the ground," said the Tiger-lily. "Then you'll know why."
>
> Alice did so. "It's very hard," she said, "but I don't know what that has to do with it."
>
> "In most gardens," the Tiger-lily said, "they make the beds too soft — so that the flowers are always asleep."

In most life situations, people can avoid displaying their symptoms. Group therapy is such a context. In group therapy the "ground" is often "very hard," a fact to which Joan, Jason, Erica, Terrence and most of the other clients mentioned in this book would surely attest.

NOT A MAD TEA-PARTY

"But I don't want to go among mad people," Alice remarked.

"Oh, you can't help that," said the Cat; "we're all mad here. I'm mad. You're mad."

"How do you know I'm mad?" said Alice.

"You must be," said the Cat, "or you wouldn't have come here."

The client who enters therapy is often, and usually erroneously, considered by family and friends to be mentally or emotionally ill, while if he did not seek treatment, he would not incur any such pejorative labels. The defining is not only done by people in the client's world, but to some extent by the therapist and the client himself. If the person is seeking "medical" attention for his emotional and psychological difficulties, then, by definition, he must be "sick." Social workers', counselors', and psychologists' "clients," as well as psychiatrists' "patients" frequently are considered "crazy" by psychologically unsophisticated people, when, in fact, they are simply taking good care of themselves. It is unfair that responsible people who voluntarily seek psychotherapy are, like Alice at the tea-party, typed as "mad," simply on the basis of their presence in a therapist's office.

Therapy clients often comment that they seem to be functioning much better than people who are not in therapy and claim they do not need it. Group clients are more aware of this paradox than individual clients because they have more of an opportunity to compare notes. They also notice that the therapy environment is saner than many situations often considered to be normal.

Group is not a mad tea-party. The many levels of reality dealt with and the dream-like aspects of the group experience make it richer, not crazier. In group people can talk honestly and freely. Relationships are nonmanipulative, and closeness is encouraged.

Much of the therapy process involves helping a person to recognize his strengths, resources, and uniqueness and to see that he has no "illness." Sheldon Kopp (1972, p. 188) says, "Once a patient realizes that he has no disease, and so can never be cured, he might as well terminate his treatment." In group people can "get better" without having to be sick to begin with.

Although group clients are usually less "ill" than many people not in therapy, they are usually in acute distress of some sort or they would not be in treatment. Most of them, as we have noted, bear many scars from emotional wounds of the past. How is it, then, that people who have problems in relationships can make each other better? Why don't they infect each other, make each other worse? How does it happen that they become cohesive on the basis of healthy rather than unhealthy group standards (Frank, 1974, p. 282)? Foulkes (1948, p. 29) answers that " . . . the deepest reason why (group) patients can reinforce each other's normal reactions and wear down and correct each other's neurotic reactions is that *collectively they constitute the very Norm, from which individually they deviate.*" Given that people are troubled when they arrive, what is it that allows the potential "mad tea-party" to be transformed into such a nurturing and humane environment? Yalom chooses a well-known Hasidic story to explain these important phenomena in group therapy:

[The] Rabbi . . . had a conversation with the Lord about heaven and hell. "I will show you Hell," said the Lord and led the Rabbi into a room in the middle of which was a very big round table. The people sitting at it were famished and desperate. In the middle of the table there was a large pot of stew, enough and more for everyone. The smell of the stew was delicious and made the Rabbi's mouth water. The people round the table were holding spoons with very long handles. Each one found that it was just possible to reach the pot to take a spoonful of the stew, but because the handle of his spoon was longer than a man's arm, he could not get the food back into his mouth. The Rabbi saw that their suffering was terrible. "Now I will show you Heaven," said the Lord, and they went to another room, exactly the same as the first. There was the same big, round table with the same pot of stew. The people, as before, were equipped with the same long-handled spoons — but here they were well-nourished and plump, laughing and talking. At first the Rabbi could not understand. "It is simple, but it requires a certain skill," said the Lord. "You see, they have learned to feed each other" (Yalom, 1975, pp. 12–13).

Heaven in the story captures the essence of what we try to achieve in group therapy. A newly formed group is very dependent on the group therapist because they have not yet learned to feed themselves. The group mentioned earlier with the "strawberry set-up" has been going for over a year; however, people still tend to call me if they have a serious problem between group meetings. The people in the other four groups are much more likely to call each other for support or advice than to call me. In the new group conversation is very often directed at me, and I am asked lots of questions. In the older group, the attention of members is much more focused on one another. In any new group, the leader has to structure the time carefully, setting limits on monopolizers and making sure the shy people speak up. The therapist must be alert to the possibility of serious issues lingering with individuals, and make sure they are brought out into the open; otherwise someone is likely to go home without talking about something important. A mature group usually finds a way to cover the priority items on everyone's agenda in some way in each session. They can do this because they are sensitive to one another's needs and keep up-to-date on the developments in each other's lives. They are not afraid to interrupt each other and change the flow of the group if it is in the best interests of the group. They know each other so well that they can dip into one another's past for material that seems to relate to current interaction. ("Isn't what you said about Ted the same thing you said about your father when you were a kid?" asks Terrence of Lilly.) They begin making interpretations as finely-tuned and on the mark as any therapist possibly could.

Throughout Chapter IV, and in other places in the book as well, I depicted many wonderful ways in which group members "feed" each other through the interpersonal processes of group therapy. In most groups, members provide each other ample nourishment, but how gracefully and efficiently they do so seems to depend mainly on the length of time of their life together. The Erica-Joan group, together for two years, is virtually self-sufficient at this point, barely requiring a group therapist all, much less two of us, to make the session function well. The Tony-Fred group in the second transcript, having matured a year and a half since the time of that session, and with a low turnover in membership, is almost equally as effective in its member-member interactions. The "strawberry set-up" group still needs considerable guidance from me as they gradually learn to make therapeutic use of one another.

"HOLD ONTO YOUR FAULTS"

Milton Erickson said, "Hold onto your faults; you'll need them to understand the faults of others" (Lankton and Lankton, 1983, p. 77). Another way group members help each other is by acknowledging to one another their own particular imperfections. In doing so, they create an environment, a frame of reference, in which there is no pressure to be more or different than we are, and where understanding rather than competition is the main commodity.

Many people who join group feel inadequate and are constantly trying to compensate for something or somebody. Group is a place where one can learn to relinquish some of the outlandish demands one makes on oneself and learn, as a poet friend of mine Emily Burton put it, that

To attempt to be more than human
Is to sentence yourself to being less.

THE PARADOX OF THE PEARL

Said one oyster to a neighboring oyster, "I have a very great pain within me. It is heavy and round and I am in distress."

And the other oyster replied with haughty complacence, "Praise be to the heavens and to the sea, I have no pain within me. I am well and whole both within and without."

At that point a crab was passing by and heard the two oysters and he said to the one who was well and whole both within and without, "Yes, you are well and whole; but the pain that your neighbor bears is a pearl of exceeding beauty." (Gibran, *The Wanderer,* 1932).

Another paradox that makes group therapy work is the fact that, through the revelation of the pain and ugliness he feels inside him, a person actually reveals his uniqueness and beauty. There is spiritual and emotional redemption experienced by an entire group when one individual reveals his deepest feelings. A person may have carried around a dreadful rage, terror, or shame. He may reveal deeds so heinous that, in any other situation, he would receive horrified reactions and condemnation from others; yet, in group he receives understanding, empathy, and admiration for his courage in disclosing himself.

My husband, Gene Eliasoph, did a powerful psychodrama in an inpatient psychiatric unit with a young woman whose father had raped her. A few weeks later, just after the daughter had been discharged, the father was hospitalized on the same unit. The father asked Gene to do a psychodrama with him about the rape. Most of the other patients on the ward had been in the psychodrama with the daughter, and Gene was not sure how they would feel about participating. As negatively as they felt initially toward the man, once the drama was underway, the group was able to empathize with his incredible pain and guilt, and to find some good in him through the shambles he had made of his life. In some inexplicable way, the group was able to see some beauty at the core of him, inextricably linked with his pain.

THE "BE SPONTANEOUS" PARADOX

"Speak when you're spoken to!" the Queen sharply interrupted her.

"But if everybody obeyed that rule," said Alice, who was always ready for a little argument, "and you only spoke when you were spoken to, and the other person always waited for you to begin, you see, nobody would ever say anything, so that — "

"Ridiculous!" cried the Queen. "Why, don't you see, child — " here she broke off with a frown, and after thinking for a minute, suddenly changed the subject of the conversation (*Wonderland*).

The "be spontaneous" paradox of group therapy also works to develop clients' assertiveness. The submissive member, who, in compliance with the group's standards, forces himself to act aggressively, does so because he is basically submissive (Frank, 1978, pp. 105–106). In time the assertive behavior, first tried out of compliance, begins to generate its own rewards for the individual both inside and outside of group. Assertive behaviors become incorporated into the role repertoire of the individual, considerably increasing his choices and broadening his frame of reference.

THE PARADOX OF TERMINATION

The first step in getting *out* of the therapy group is learning *why* and *how* one is *in* it. This may take anywhere from six months to two years, sometimes even longer. There are many clients who spend most of their time in any relationship, including group therapy, looking for an exit, checking to make sure that they are free to depart at will. Nate spent the first two years in group deciding whether or not he really needed to be there. Almost every week he would complain that he was not getting anywhere. He seemed very invested in this "always-about-to-leave" position; frequently he would have a very intense session where he would work on emotionally charged issues, and then he would return the next week wondering why he was in group, having completely forgotten the previous session.

Meanwhile, during the two years, Nate made great strides in his life. His depression lifted, he found a steady girlfriend, bought a house, made new friends, enjoyed increasing success on his job, gained in assertiveness and improved his communication skills. (We joked about how great he would be doing if the group was really helping him!) Nate's group was alternately sympathetic and irritated with Nate's constant ambivalence.

One night Nate talked about his experiences in the Viet Nam war for the first time in the ten years since he had been home. He released a great deal of feeling — shame, fear and anger — and felt understood and greatly comforted by the group. This session Nate remembered, and his talk of leaving the group ceased for six months. During this time Nate participated spontaneously and openly, uncovering and resolving early conflicts and making excellent contact with other members. At the end of six months he announced a termination date a few months hence, a decision the group felt was a positive one for him. He said,

> I spent years wondering, "Why stay?" Then, somehow, I found out why, and the question became "Why leave?" Now I'm not worried about why. I simply know it is time for me to go.

A great deal of time is spent in group, as in life, trying to figure out why we are here. The irony is that just when we discover why — what our associations with other people really mean, and what we have to learn about ourselves — it may be just about time to leave.

PARADOXES IN THE ROLE OF THE GROUP THERAPIST

Not *a Member;* Is *the Group*

In discussing the theory of paradox, it was stated that a class cannot be a member of itself. Logically, therefore, the therapist cannot be a participant in his own group. Practically, this is both true and not true.

The group therapist is, in some respects, the most involved person in the group, and yet, he is not a member. Bach says, "therapy groups assume and consider the therapist to be an outsider. A therapy group will not include a therapist as part of itself" (1954, p. 293). In my first years of leading groups I attended post-group get-togethers on a regular basis. I was treated more like a parent or older sibling than a part of the group. Minuchin (1974) and other family therapists consider a clear boundary between generations to be essential for healthy family functioning. Similarly, the therapy group needs a clear leader/member boundary. Group members appreciate a friendly style on the part of the leader, but not at the expense of his professionalism. Aware of their own and other members' frequent lack of objectivity, they count on the relatively mature and unbiased viewpoint of the group therapist.

While the therapist is not a member, everything about the group reflects his/her personality, point of view, priorities, and personal interests. Whatever therapeutic issues or preoccupations the therapist has at a given time will often, through not-so-conscious pathways, insinuate themselves into group themes and processes. For example, while I have been writing this book, clients have frequently "just happened" to discuss issues closely related to the chapter I was working on at the time. While the therapist's very being, including his unconscious, influences the group at all times, he occupies a position on a different logical level from that of the members.

The Most Human Person

The therapist, while not a member of the group per se, should be, as Kopp (1972, p. 11) describes the guru, "the most *human* person" in it. Moment by moment he must be more aware of his feelings, prejudices, vulnerabilities, and resistances than anyone else. He should be the first to admit when he is wrong. He must have a higher degree of sensitivity and empathy than most of the group members and less need to be recognized for it. He must realize how much he can hurt as well as help. He must be aware of how his personal history and conflict areas might impinge on his work and accept his limitation in these areas. He must always seek therapy himself when he needs it.

The therapist's humanness may sometimes be his Achilles' heel, but, if handled properly, it is his most important therapeutic tool. The group therapist, more than the individual therapist, is able to reveal information about his personal life and express his own opinions and feelings in the sessions. This is very useful to clients as long as it is kept within the boundaries of the therapeutic role, and not used as a way for the therapist to do his own therapy in the group. Levine says, "In the long run, the therapist's progressive sharing of himself as a human being seems to help the members feel equal to the therapist, and helps to reduce anxiety and legitimize their own feelings" (1979, p. 293).

How much sharing from the therapist is appropriate or useful depends greatly on the stage of the group's development and the level of its cohesiveness (Levine, 1979). Ruth Cohn (1974), designer of the "Theme-Centered Interactional Method" of group leadership, considers "selective authenticity," the ability of the therapist to know what and when to share, to be a major group leadership skill. Yalom talks about the usefulness of "therapist transparency" (1975). Examples have been given throughout this book of ways in which I have shared my own feelings, dreams, and life experiences in the group, usually with positive therapeutic results.

Lifetime Training for Life

The group therapist is the instrument of his own craft. He commits himself to trying to be the kind of person he would like to be, modeling for clients the motivation and self-discipline they will need to follow their respective paths.

The therapist has a responsibility to try to keep physically as well as mentally, healthy. He should exercise and eat nutritionally. In my opinion, he definitely should not smoke cigarettes, for in doing so he is setting an example of suicidal behavior for his clients. As mentioned, he will be in therapy himself as needed.

The group therapist must continually be working to become more sensitive, interesting, spontaneous, nurturing, and learned. He will attend courses, workshops, conferences, and lectures to further his professional and personal growth. He will try to compensate for the limitations of his particular graduate school training; for example, psychiatrists may need training in systems or social group theory, while psychologists and social workers may need to familiarize themselves with medical factors in mental illness.

A good group therapist is eager to learn about anything that relates to his psychotherapy work. If he is referred a patient suffering from anorexia nervosa, he learns what he can about eating disorders. If a client is a survivor of suicide, the therapist studies whatever he can find concerning the problems and therapy of such cases. If he has a client in menopause, he educates himself about the physical and psychological aspects of this life stage.

Therapy groups almost always have members who are affected by alcohol. About 50% of my clients have alcoholic parents and/or spouses. It is mandatory that a group therapist understand the individual and family dynamics of alcoholism. An excellent way to gain this knowledge is to attend meetings of Alanon, the corresponding group to AA for relatives and friends of alcoholics. Alanon educates its members about the disease of alcoholism, while teaching them "detachment with love," a skill that is supremely valuable in dealing with alcoholics and other difficult people.

In order to understand his group, the therapist has to be somewhat educated in the frames of reference brought to the group by each client. This involves learning about clients' life work, their cultural and social backgrounds, and areas of interest. If a client is a musician, the therapist familiarizes himself with his music; if the client loves Japanese poetry, the therapist buys the books and reads them. A therapist with a large group practice may find himself becoming fairly well-informed about subjects he never knew or cared much about before. In the past few years, my group clients have exposed me to: building condominiums, interior decorating, newspaper editing, World War II history, computers, real estate, yoga, aerobics, Smokeenders, vitamins, kinesics, retailing, marketing, civil litigation, Kaballah (Jewish mysticism), and many other interesting fields and topics.

Becoming more aware, healthy, and educated is a commitment I make to my clients and myself. Ironically, the harder I work at it, the less like work it seems.

Power: More Shared; More Acquired

Another paradox regarding the role of the therapist is that the more of his power the therapist gives to the group, the more he gets back from them.

Group therapy is less elitist and authoritarian than individual. Except during stages of group dependency, wisdom and, therefore, power are thought to lie in the group as well as the leader. The group therapist is far more subject to criticism than the individual therapist. Many pairs of eyes see him in many different situations, making his flaws quite apparent. The peer support the client has in group will make him more likely to risk telling the therapist what he thinks of him than he would in individual therapy.

Most entering group members have an archaic frame of reference regarding power, which presupposes that if one person has more power, another must have less. This view is considerably altered for group clients by their experience with the group therapist. In group therapy, power does not reside alternately with the therapist and group members. Instead, the therapist and group members share their power and, in doing so, reproduce it many-fold.

In the life of a group there are fluctuations in the relative quantities of power held by the group and the group therapist. At the beginning of a group the leader is generally seen to have all of the power. He has professional power by virtue of knowing the background of the clients, their problems, and so on. He has political power since he is the designated authority and has met everyone in the group, while they are still unknown to one another before the group starts (Levine, 1979, p. 286). On the other hand, in the early stages, when the group is not cohesive, the members are more likely to leave the group precipitously, an occurrence which can erode confidence in the leader and diminish his power. Also in the early stages, members may vehemently and rudely challenge the leader's authority, which can sometimes make him feel powerless.

As the group progresses, stabilizes, and becomes more cohesive, the leader begins to be appreciated more than feared. His therapeutic skills are valued more, and he is trusted and looked to as a nurturing rather than destructive authority figure. He then goes about his "task of distributing his own (real) power" (Levine, 1979, p. 286).

His "real" power is his therapeutic perspicacity and skill, and his humanness. The group therapist "gives" power by giving up control. He recognizes the clients' rights to be who they are, helping them to change only what they themselves feel needs to be changed. He gives members space and acceptance to approach themselves and each other in their own way. He refrains from instructing, interpreting, criticizing, or giving advice. He makes himself available for criticism and tries to be open, sharing, and honest. Group members learn how to take the power — becoming more assertive, perceptive, analytical, confrontative, articulate, spontaneous, creative, energetic, productive. As their potency increases, that of the therapist is not reduced, but enhanced in their eyes. They value the "real" power in themselves and in him. They feel confident enough in themselves to let the therapist know the impact he has had and the help he has been to them.

The Extras

When the therapy fails, we can usually identify what the therapist did wrong. On the other hand, when the therapy succeeds, we are rarely sure what made the difference.

We know some personality traits, attitudes and behaviors on the part of group therapists that correlate with client and group success. Warmth, spontaneity, and caring are mentioned most frequently in studies (Yalom, 1975). But to determine which interventions, techniques, or insights contributed by the therapist made the difference in the successful therapy of an individual in group therapy would be extremely difficult because of the tremendous number of variables involved.

Yalom compares the successful therapist to the successful cook (1980, p. 3). The fabulous cook may have elaborate recipes, but it is actually the ingredients he throws into the pot without measuring that make whatever it is he is cooking so delicious. Yalom says that when no one is looking, the therapist throws in the "extras," and these are what make the difference. In therapy the extras can be almost anything: the way the therapist uses his sense of humor or welcomes people into the office; a particular touch or tone of voice; an accepting attitude or way of loving people; or a time he went out of his way for a client — sending a card or giving him a ride home. The "extras" are often the things the client will always remember, while the therapist does not even consider them important.

The hard-working therapist might protest:

But what about my abilities in group process, my expertise in psychodrama, my knowledge of psychoanalytic theory? What about the sensitivity training and hypnosis workshops I attended? How can it be that my hugs or the simple compliments I pay are more important than my talent and skill?

Of course, in the long run there is no substitute for good clinical training and ability, but it is amazing how far the extras will go sometimes. I once had a co-therapist in training who had very little education and no experience doing therapy. He had been in groups himself and had overcome a serious depression. To this day, I cannot say why he was so effective with clients in what was, without doubt, the most difficult group I ever led. It had something to do with his smile and a direct, simple way of speaking. Old, young, psychotic, and neurotic — without exception, all the members of the group respected and responded positively to this man as a leader.

In this same group, I also threw in my share of extras — everything I had in the cupboard, in fact, for this group needed all the help it could get! I know my characteristic determination and enthusiasm gave the group heart when two of the members died of cancer, two members became psychotic for short periods, and a third was hospitalized three times in ten months following bizarre unpremeditated suicide attempts. In the latter instance my "extras" as a group therapist probably saved a life. Although he was in individual therapy at a mental health center, I took it upon myself to find out what was wrong with the client, refusing to "buy" the facile diagnosis of schizophrenia offered by the hospitals, when he showed no psychotic symptoms between the episodes, which happened four months apart. My diagnostic hunch, temporal lobe epilepsy, was validated by the neuropsychiatrist to whom I referred the client. When properly medicated with anticonvulsants, his suicidal behavior and panic attacks ceased, and he returned to the group, where he made progress in his therapy (Nicholas, 1981).

In group therapy, the therapist's extras can be the real thing and vice versa. Rather than puzzle too much about which is which, the group therapist should just keep on learning and growing, fostering his natural creativity and spontaneity and satisfying his curiosity. In this way he will cultivate his own brand of "extras" that will make his therapy special in its own way.

THE PARADOXES OF TIME

Milton Erickson was fascinated by the paradoxes inherent in time. He mentions that Einstein posited the existence of a "subjective" or "T" time which is not measurable by a clock or by chronological events and that "subjective experience seems to be inseparably woven with time sense" (Erickson, 1980, Vol. II, p. 231). People's perceptions of time ("it flies"; "it crawls"; "never enough"; "time hangs heavy") are dependent on their attitudes and feelings at the moment of consideration. Their perception of time in general dictates their attitudes toward the way in which they use time. Some people believe time is "short" for them, and, therefore, work at being productive. Others feel they have "all the time in the world" and act accordingly.

Erickson's experiments wtih hypnosis showed that a person's perception of time can be altered in trance, and that such "time distortions" can be used constructively in therapy. It is my contention that group therapy creates its own time distortions. The following is a brief explanation of Erickson's hypnotic time distortion techniques and how they occur naturally in group therapy. The time distortions of group are among its more tantalizing and therapeutic paradoxes.

Time expansion is when a short period of "real clock time" is experienced as a long time. Such distortion is useful in enhancing the processes of learning, memory, and skill training on the cognitive and motoric levels. For example, a young musician who worked two jobs was depressed because he did not have time to practice his guitar, and was about to lose his music job. Putting him in trance, Erickson taught him to "expand time" in his mind. With practice (in trance) the man became able to practice in his head for ten minutes a day, and accomplish as much as he might in several hours of actual rehearsal (Erickson, 1980, Volume II, p. 278).

Therapy groups greatly expand the 90-minute time allotted to them. The heightened awareness created in the group can mean that learning may take place at a much faster pace than would happen in another setting. Students of biorhythms have found that 90 minutes is a natural interval for any learning session, because it corresponds with the normal cycle of bodily energies and attention span. Perhaps the use of this optimum time frame in group therapy serves to increase the illusion of time expansion.

Time expansion is a function of what Carel Germain (1976) calls "transactional time." Transactional time deals with "cycles and the spiraling accumulation of recurring patterns and processes" (Rabkin, 1970). It is to be differentiated from "linear time," the framework used in the historical perspective, which relies on the laws of cause and effect. Transactional time cuts across the boundaries of causality and space as well as chronology.

The therapy group weaves through different time frames via the phenomena of transference, corrective emotional experience, and future projection. Transactional time allows all time frames to be connected. In group, paradoxically,

. . . the straight line of linear time bends back on itself and becomes a closed loop, a temporal orbit in life space (Germain, 1976, p. 426).

The process of time expansion or transactional time is therapeutic because it allows for the resources from one time period to be made accessible in another. Resources for positive therapeutic change lie in the past, present, and future. Something one needed in the past and did not get, such as nurturing or discipline, can be experienced in the group, and the developmental deficit can be made up. Something one had in the past and needs now, such as a loving parent or a sense of security, can be remembered and reexperienced, bringing this resource into one's current life for immediate therapeutic benefit. Something one needs now that one believes one could have in the future, such as a good job, financial solvency, or a good relationship, is made palpable when discussed with the group as a dream or a fantasy. Interestingly, future projections, once shared, become part of the group's history, as real as the actual past in many respects.

The reverse of time expansion is *time condensation* — when a long period of clock time is made to feel very short. It is a particularly useful technique in hypnosis for pain control. Through hypnotic suggestion, a long, painful childbirth or dental procedure can be compressed to seem like a few minutes.

Most group sessions fly by very quickly. This is not an uncommon phenomenon in any situation where people are involved and interested. Time condensation, like time expansion, is related to "transactional time," a function of the connectedness of all time frames in the mind. Whenever we connect what is going on among members in the group session with comparable interactions in the past of individual members with "others," we are compressing two events which are widely spaced chronologically into one event in the present, making a long period of time seem like just a few minutes. The process of time condensation makes our lives comprehensible. If we had to rely on "linear time" and could not synthesize events in our mind, we would have no way of organizing our experience.

As we discussed in Chapter II, the microcosm is a very important mechanism in group therapy. Through it the past and the present of the client are fused in very interesting and often perplexing ways. For example, when Erica was struggling with Joan (Chapter IV), Erica was simultaneously reenacting situations from the past which were similar in structure (often referred to in systems terms as "isomorphic") to the present one: her sadomasochistic relationship with Jake for one; the attempted rape by her father and betrayal by her mother and the priest for another. The time condensation factor in group therapy allows events from many different time frames to play themselves out at the same time. The overlay of one event on top of its antecedent, because they are the same in form if not always precisely in content, serves to clarify both the historical and the current situation for the client.

Another paradox of time condensation in group therapy occurs at a broader level. Kellerman (1979) has suggested that a therapy group with a relatively stable population, meaning a turnover of two per year out of eight or less, matures at an exceedingly more rapid rate than is generally thought possible in human development. According to Kellerman, every two years in the life of such a group is equivalent to 20 years in an individual life cycle—in terms of people's perceptiveness, accumulated knowledge, and what he calls "wisdom." When it is six years old, therefore, the group's collective "wisdom" is that of a group of people in their sixties. Kellerman does not see this as strictly a whole-group phenomenon, but claims that the individual within the group gains maturity along with the group at the same accelerated rate.

From my experience with people in groups I would tend to agree with Kellerman's imaginative hypothesis, although it would be hard to substantiate. Certainly the Joan and Erica group, the population of which has not changed in two years, grows more astute, sophisticated, intimate, and thoughtful with each meeting, and I marvel that most of the individual members are under 30 years old.

The phenomenon of time condensation works greatly to the benefit of people who are developmentally way behind schedule. People have been known to enter my groups with practically no successful experiences with family or peers. They stay in group for what may seem a very long time, perhaps six or seven years. In group, rather than having to trust to luck and what might occur outside, clients gain the interpersonal experiences and learnings they need to help them grow into mature and healthy adults. These clients are not in individual therapy. Group is their only form of treatment. They are spending 75 hours and about a thousand dollars (considerably less if they have insurance) per year for reparenting, a surrogate family, social skills training, friend, emotional support, and complete vocational preparation and counseling. Group therapy may not be "brief treatment," but it is the least time-consuming, least expensive, and most efficient way I know of to buy what is tantamount to a whole new life.

Another interesting time distortion is the ability the mind has to shut out the past and the present and believe for some time that the only reality is the present. Learning how to "be in the *here-and-now*," without getting distracted, is necessary for making contact with other people, for concentration, for relaxation, and a number of other mental activities. Meditation techniques and experiential therapies stress learning to screen out thoughts from other time frames and focus in on the present. There are two dimensions of here-and-now awareness: internal (awareness of what one is picturing, hearing, feeling inside, for example); and external (awareness of one's immediate environment).

In group therapy a client's capacity to stay in the here-and-now is fostered and developed. Improvement of this facility through the therapy serves him well in many endeavors, particularly in the area of intimacy.

Age regression is a time distortion phenomenon that is used extensively in all therapies. It means going back in time, "reliving," or "reexperiencing." Age regression is useful for three reasons: It clarifies the past and its relationship to the present; it provides an opportunity for "redoing" parts of one's history that were unsatisfactory; and it provides access to needed resources that are lodged in the past. We saw age regression occurring throughout the book — especially in the psychodramatic incidents, such as Dorothy's excursion back in time with her stepsister Beth, and in the corrective emotional experiences of Lenny, Joan, Erica, and others.

Some group clients are blocked from the ability to regress themselves back to an earlier age. As a result, they probably have difficulty accessing memories of childhood, or, if they do, they are not be able to recapture the feelings associated with those memories. This could result in an inability to feel necessary "child-like" feelings of joy, spontaneity, playfulness, and vulnerability. In group, through role and spontaneity training, and "suggestion" from the group and therapists, clients learn to bring themselves back through time, for a variety of therapeutic purposes.

THE GROUP AS DREAM: CONCLUSION

"Sometimes I get so confused," said Fred. "I know group is an artificial situation, and yet sometimes, it's the realest thing I know."

When Alice gets back from the Looking Glass World she struggles to sort out what of her journey actually happened and what was just in her mind.

> And what did Dinah turn into, I wonder. . . . Tell me Dinah did you turn into Humpty Dumpty? I *think* you did — however, you'd better not mention it to your friends just yet, for I'm not sure.

Trying to figure out which level of group experience is "more real" is a tantalizing process, which, because of the inherent paradox, never yields a definite answer. The transference experiences in group often *seem* as "real" when they are happening as the more authentic, honest encounters between people who see each other as they really are.

Sometimes members (and leaders) block out the group's reality, because we do not want to face the all too real feelings inherent in the situation. When Henry was not picked in a sociometric exercise ("Who in the group do you trust and feel comfortable with?"), he tried to discount the significance of the rejection by saying that the group members were not his real friends, so their not choosing him didn't mean anything. On the other hand, some people get too caught up in the group reality. Jason, whose parents had cast him out of the family, found it particularly hard to keep the group in perspective. When it looked at one point as if Erica might leave the group, Jason actually missed a session, because he could not bear even to hear discussion of her leaving. Forgetting that he could see her anytime he chose, even if she did leave the group, he was giving Erica's potential departure the emotional value of the separation from his parents, while denying the seriousness of his situation with them. On another occasion Jason called to say he was not coming to group that night; in talking with him I learned that he was afraid to come because of his exaggerated fears about a minor argument that had occurred between him and another member the week before. I thought maybe Jason could use one of Alice's Wonderland cakes, the ones that make you bigger and the situation smaller. I said:

> Jason, I want to tell you something about group therapy that you don't seem to realize. That is that group therapy is absurd. Now, really, Jason, when you really think of it, it is absolutely outrageous! A bunch of people sitting around once a week for month after month, year after year, paying us leaders good money supposedly to help them, when mostly what they do is talk to each other. But that's just part of it. What are people doing here anyway? Turning people into other people, which is very weird, trying to talk about what is going on as it is happening which is impossible, and talking about the past as if it is still going on, which is psychotic. And they make it all seem so important. People pay us money to lead them in this insanity? Absurd. Totally absurd. Now Jason, don't you feel a little silly worrying so much about something that is ridiculous to the very core?

Jason relaxed and chuckled. "I see your point," he said and attended the session.

The group session is in many ways like a dream (sometimes a nightmare, but usually just a dream). It usually contains many themes and ideas interwoven in a dream-like fashion and, as we have discussed, it has many levels of reality going on simultaneously, which creates a disorientation in time and space for the participants. Early group psychoanalysts recognized the similarities of free association to one another's thoughts and ideas to the process of free association in dream interpretation. In fact, free association to one another's dreams in group therapy is a powerful tool for eliciting unconscious material. The group develops an ego through incorporating and synthesizing symbols, transferences, and more-or-less censored expressions, just the way the individual ego is strengthened through the psychoanalytic work done on dreams and their interpretations.

Group offers instances of what I will call "dream reality," where communication occurs on a much more intense level than it does in everyday life, and where even extrasensory factors come into play. Psychodrama gives structure to the many simultaneous realities of the therapy group, but even without the use of psychodramatic techniques the same phenomena occur repeatedly.

When the *tele* is very strong in a group, people will communicate not only verbally and nonverbally, but also through their fantasies and dreams. We have mentioned occasions when people in group have dreamed about each other and the material has been relevant for both the dreamer and the member in the dream, as when Joan dreamed of Jason's spotless kitchen, I dreamed about the group on the train, and Jeanette dreamed of the tulips and the elegant party that she gave for Melissa. We even have synchronicity of dreams, as when I dreamed about being in a train waiting for the group to come on board to talk about sex, and Jeanette dreamed about standing outside a building with another group member talking about a time when they talked about sex in the group.

Not infrequently, a group member will dream another's reality. The following is a particularly dramatic example. A few years ago a good friend's son, age six, was terminally ill with cancer. On the night of this particular session I was called out of the room to take a telephone call just as the session began. It was someone calling to say that the little boy had died. The news came as no surprise, and I chose not to tell the group about it, feeling I could put off dealing with my feelings about it until after the session. The session proceeded rather uneventfully. At the next meeting of this group, Frank reported a dream that he had had the night of the previous session. He dreamed that the group was assembled and I was late. I opened the door and was preceded into the room by a six-year-old boy with black curly hair (this described the boy that died). In the dream I said to the group, "This is a new member of our group."

When he told his dream, I must have turned ashen, because Frank, very frightened, asked, "What's the matter?" I told him about my telephone call and the child's death. A shudder went through the group.

Often unconscious suggestions are picked up by group members from one another in group therapy. One night my co-therapist, CT, noticed that the group did not seem to be connecting. Everyone was talking about his or her own problems, not really listening to one another or expressing any caring or concern. CT, who had been studying Ericksonian hypnosis, told them the following story:

> The kids in the math class I was teaching were all having a problem with this one lesson. There was a great deal of frustration and discouragement, and each person was feeling inadequate in his own way. I told them a story about Einstein who used to get the answers to his problems in dreams. And I told them that if they wished, they might each have a dream that would solve a particular problem most relevant to them at this time. No one in my math class knew why I was telling them such a foolish thing, and yet they all had dreams that gave them new perspectives on their math problems.

> The next week, Joan piped up right away with a dream that she had had about Lilly. Terrence told us of a dream about Jason. Lilly had had a dream about me, and CT had had one about all of us. I had one about Erica, and so it went. *Everyone* in the group had had a dream about someone else in the group without consciously associating this to CT's story. CT's suggestion to solve a problem by having a dream about it had "taken," in the sense that we had unconsciously solved our "problem" of not connecting with each other by connecting via our dreams!

Like Alice's experiences in Wonderland and Through the Looking Glass, and like the participants' dreams, group sessions are crammed with strange tales, paradoxes, metaphors, and fascinating unconscious connections between symbols, people, and ideas.

When we dream in sleep, we dream alone, whereas we experience the group dream in the company of others. At the end of *Alice in Wonderland,* Alice tells her sister about her experiences, and her sister falls asleep and dreams about Alice's adventures with herself as the main character, "and the whole place around her became alive with the strange creatures of her sister's dream." She then dreams about Alice, as a grownup, telling little children about her adventures in Wonderland. The dream pictures how Alice will "make their eyes bright and eager with many a strange tale"; and "how she would feel with all their . . . sorrows; and find a pleasure in all their joys."

In considering a session or the group experience at the time it is going on or afterward, we are like Alice at the end of the Looking Glass adventures, puzzled as to "Who dreamed It?"

"Now Kitty, let's consider who it was that dreamed it all. This is a serious question, my dear, and you should *not* go on licking your paw like that. . . . You see, Kitty, it *must* have been either me or the Red King. He was part of my dream, of course—but then I was part of his dream too!"

When we are all in each others' dreams, how do we know who is the dreamer and which is the dream? Does it matter?

Carroll, at the end of *Alice,* reflects, "Life, what is it but a dream?" For me it is the very aspects of group therapy that we consider dream-like that make it an accurate reflection of what life is. It is its unreality that makes it real—as a laboratory for the conjuring of new resources, and a stage on which we can create and recreate, frame and reframe our experiences.

Bibliography

Adler, A. *Understanding Human Nature.* New York: Chilton, 1927.

Alexander, F. & French, T. *Psychoanalytic Therapy: Principles and Applications.* New York: Ronald Press, 1946.

Allport, G. Comments on J. L. Moreno, transference, countertransference tele. *Group Psychotherapy,* 1957, 7, p. 307.

Assagioli, R. *Psychosynthesis.* New York: Viking, 1965.

Bach, G. *Intensive Group Psychotherapy.* New York: Ronald Press, 1954.

Bandler, R. & Grinder, J. *Frogs Into Princes.* Moab, Utah: Real People Press, 1979.

Bandler, R. & Grinder, J. *Reframing: Neuro-Linguistic Programming and the Transformation of Meaning.* Moab, Utah: Real People Press, 1982.

Bandler, R. & Grinder, J. *The Structure of Magic, Vol. 1.* Palo Alto, CA: Science and Behavior Books, Inc., 1975.

Bateson, G. *Mind and Nature: A Necessary Unity.* New York: Dutton, 1979.

Bateson, G. *Steps to an Ecology of Mind.* New York: Ballantine Books, 1972.

Becker, E. *The Denial of Death.* New York: Free Press, 1973.

Becker, E. *Escape from Evil.* New York: Free Press, 1975.

Berne, E. *Games People Play.* New York: Grove Press, 1964.

Berne, E. *Principles of Group Treatment.* New York: Grove Press, 1966.

Berne, E. *Transactional Analysis in Psychotherapy.* New York: Ballantine Books, 1961.

Berne, E. *What Do You Do After You Say Hello?* Beverly Hills, CA: Grove Press and Bantam, 1972.

Bion, W. *Experiences in Groups.* London: Tavistock, 1959.

Bowen, M. *Family Therapy in Clinical Practice.* New York: Jason Aronson, Inc., 1978.

Buber, M. *The Knowledge of Man.* M. Friedman (Ed.). New York: Harper & Row, 1967.

Buchsbaum, M. The mind readers. *Psychology Today,* July 1983, pp. 58–62.

Bulletin for Training in Psychoanalytic Psychotherapy, Psychoanalysis and Group Therapy of the Washington Square Institute, New York, 1982–83.

Cohn, R. The theme-centered interactional method. In J. B. Shaffer & M. D. Galinsky (Eds.). *Models of Group Therapy and Sensitivity Training.* Englewood Cliffs, NJ: Prentice Hall, 1974.

A Consumers' Guide to Group Psychotherapy. Pamphlet published by American Group Psychotherapy Association, New York.

243

de Mare, P. *Perspectives in Group Psychotherapy: A Theoretical Background*. London: George Allen & Unwin, Ltd., 1972.

Dilts, R., Grinder, J., Bandler, R., DeLozier, J., & Bandler, L. *Neuro-Linguistic Programming, Vol. I*. Cupertino, CA: Meta Publications, 1979.

Durkin, H. Change in Group Psychotherapy. *International Journal of Group Psychotherapy*, 32, 4, 1982.

Durkin, H. *The Group in Depth*. New York: International Universities Press, 1964.

Durkin, H. A systems approach to multiple family treatment. In L. R. Wolberg and M. Aronson, (Eds.). *Group and Family Therapy 1980*. New York: Brunner/Mazel, 1980.

Durkin, H. The group therapies and general systems theory as an integrative structure. In J. Durkin, (Ed.). *Living Groups: Group Psychotherapy and General System Theory*. New York: Brunner/Mazel, 1981.

Durkin, J. (Ed.) *Living Groups: Group Psychotherapy and General System Theory*. New York: Brunner/Mazel, 1981.

Erickson, M. H. *The Collected Papers on Hypnosis. Volume I: The Nature of Hypnosis and Suggestion; Volume II: Hypnotic Alteration of Sensory, Perceptual and Psychophysiological Processes*. E. Rossi (Ed.) New York: Irvington, 1980.

Eliasoph, E. Classification of delinquents. *Berkshire Farm Monographs*, I, 2, June, 1963.

Ellis, A. & Harper, R. *A New Guide to Rational Living*. Hollywood, CA: Wilshire Book Co., 1976.

Ferguson, M. *The Aquarian Conspiracy: Personal and Social Transformation in the 1980's*. Los Angeles: J. P. Tarcher, Inc., 1980.

Foulkes, S. *Introduction to Group Analytic Psychotherapy*. London: Heinemann, 1948.

Foulkes, S. *Group Psychotherapy: The Psychoanalytic Approach*. London: Penguin, 1957.

Frank, J. *Persuasion and Healing: A Comparative Study of Psychotherapy*. New York: Schocken Books, 1974.

Frank, J. *Psychotherapy and the Human Predicament: A Psychosocial Approach*. New York: Schocken Books, 1978.

Freud, S. *Group Psychology and the Analysis of the Ego*. New York: Liveright, 1951.

Freud, S. *Totem and Taboo*. London: Kegan Paul, 1950.

Fromm, E. *The Art of Loving*. New York: Harper & Row, 1956.

Germain, C. Time: An ecological variable in social work practice. *Social Casework*. July 1976, pp. 419–426.

Gibran, K. *The Wanderer*. New York: Knopf, 1932.

Goffman, I. *Frame Analysis*. New York: Harper & Row, 1974.

Grinder, J. & Bandler, R. *Transformations, Neuro-linguistic Programming and the Structure of Hypnosis*. Moab, Utah: Real People Press, 1981.

Grinder, J. & Bandler, R. *The Structure of Magic, Vol. 2*. Palo Alto, CA: Science and Behavior Books, Inc., 1976.

Hale, A. *Conducting Clinical Sociometric Explorations: A Manual for Psychodramatists and Sociometrists*. Roanoke, Va.: Ann Hale, 1981.

Haley, J. *Strategies of Psychotherapy*. New York: Grune & Stratton, 1963.

Haley, J. *Uncommon Therapy: The Psychiatric Techniques of Milton Erickson, M.D.* New York: Norton, 1973.

Haskell, M. *Socioanalysis*. Los Angeles: Role Training Associates of California, 1975.

Houston, J. *The Possible Human*. Los Angeles: J. P. Tarcher, Inc., 1982.

Huxley, A. *The Doors of Perception*. New York: Harper & Row, 1954.

Jung, C. *Man and His Symbols*. New York: Doubleday & Co., 1964.

Jung, C. *The Portable Jung*. J. Campbell (Ed.). New York: Viking Press, 1971.

Kadis, A. et al. *Practicum of Group Psychotherapy*. Philadelphia: Lippincott, 1974.

Kaplan, H. & Sadock, B. (Eds.). *Comprehensive Group Psychotherapy*. Baltimore: Williams & Wilkins, 1971.

Kaplan, H. & Sadock, B. *Group Treatment of Mental Illness*. New York: Dutton, 1972.

Kellerman, H. *Group Psychotherapy and Personality.* New York: Grune & Stratton, 1979.
Kelly, G. *A Theory of Personality: The Psychology of Personal Constructs.* New York: Norton, 1963.
Kluckhohn, C. Values and Values-Orientation. In T. Parsons and E. Shils (Eds.) *Toward a General Theory of Action.* Cambridge, MA: Harvard University Press, 1951.
Kopp, S. *If You Meet the Buddha on the Road, Kill Him!* Palo Alto: Behavior Sciences Books, 1972.
Korzybski, A. *Science and Sanity.* Lakeville, CT: The International Non-Aristotelian Library Publishing, Co., 4th ed., 1933.
Kübler-Ross, E. *On Death and Dying.* New York: Macmillan, 1969.
Lankton, S. *Practical Magic: A Translation of Basic Neuro-Linguistic Programming into Clinical Psychotherapy.* Cupertino, CA: Meta, 1979.
Lankton, S. & Lankton, C. *The Answer Within: A Clinical Framework of Ericksonian Hypnotherapy.* New York: Brunner/Mazel, 1983.
Laqueur, P. The theory and practice of multiple family therapy. In L. R. Wolberg and M. Aronson (Eds.) *Group and Family Therapy 1980.* New York: Brunner/Mazel, 1980.
Lasch, C. *Haven in a Heartless World: The Family Besieged.* New York: Basic Books, 1977.
Levine, B. *Group Psychotherapy: Practice and Development.* Englewood Cliffs, NJ: Prentice-Hall, 1979.
Lewin, K. *Field Theory in Social Science.* D. Cartwright (Ed.) London: Tavistock, 1952.
Lieberman, M., Yalom, I., & Miles, M. *Encounter Groups: First Facts.* New York: Basic Books, 1972.
Maslow, A. *The Farther Reaches of Human Nature.* New York: The Viking Press, 1971.
Maslow, A. *Toward a Psychology of Being.* New York: Van Nostrand Reinhold, 1968.
May, R., Angel, E., & Ellenberger, H. (Eds.) *Existence.* New York: Basic Books, 1958.
May, R. *Love and Will.* New York: Dell Publishing, Delta Book, 1969.
McNamara, K. Newsletter of Finger Lakes Psychodrama Center, 1982.
Minuchin, S. *Families and Family Therapy.* Cambridge, MA: Harvard University Press, 1974.
Mintz, E. *The Psychic Thread: Paranormal and Transpersonal Aspects of Psychotherapy.* New York: Human Sciences Press, 1983.
Moreno, J. Fundamental rules and techniques of psychodrama. In J. Masserman (Ed.) *Progress in Psychotherapy, Vol. III.* New York: Grune and Stratton, 1958.
Moreno, J. *International Handbook of Group Psychotherapy.* New York: Philosophical Library, 1966.
Moreno, J. *Psychodrama—First Volume.* Beacon, NY: Beacon House, 1946. Fourth Edition, 1977.
Moreno, J. Psychodrama. In H. Kaplan and B. Sadock (Eds.) *Comprehensive Group Psychotherapy.* Baltimore: Williams & Wilkins, 1971.
Moreno, J. Psychodramatic treatment of marriage problems. *Sociometry,* 3, 1, 1940.
Moreno, J. & Jennings, H. Spontaneity training. *Psychodrama Monograph,* No. 4, Beacon, NY: Beacon House, 1944.
Moreno, J. *Who Shall Survive?* Beacon, NY: Beacon House, 1953.
Morgan, D. *Love: Plato, the Bible and Freud.* Englewood Cliffs, NJ: Prentice-Hall, 1964.
Moustakas, C. *Loneliness and Love.* Englewood Cliffs, NJ: Prentice-Hall, 1972.
Mullan, H. & Rosenbaum, M. *Group Psychotherapy: Theory and Practice.* New York: Free Press, 1978.
Naisbitt, J. *Megatrends.* New York: Warner, 1982.
Nicholas, M. Diagnosis and treatment of temporal lobe epilepsy in an outpatient psychiatric setting. *Interaction, Journal of the Elmcrest Psychiatric Institute,* Spring/Summer 1981.
Nicholas, M. The narcissistic personality in group psychotherapy. *Group,* 7, 4, pp. 27–32, 1983.
Oxford Dictionary (The Pocket Oxford Dictionary). Oxford: Oxford University Press, 1978.
Palazzoli, M., Boscolo, L., Cecchin, G. & Prata, G. *Paradox and Counterparadox.* New York: Jason Aronson, 1978.

Parsons, T. Illness and the role of the physician: A sociological perspective. In C. Kluckhohn & H. Murray (Eds.) *Personality in Nature, Society and Culture,* 2nd Edition. New York: Knopf, 1954.

Perls, F. *Gestalt Therapy Verbatim.* Lafayette, CA: Real People Press, 1969.

Polster, E. & Polster, M. *Gestalt Therapy Integrated.* New York: Brunner/Mazel, 1973.

Powdermaker, F. & Frank, J. *Group Psychotherapy: Studies in Methodology of Research and Therapy.* Cambridge, MA: Harvard University Press, 1953.

Prigogine, I. & Glandsdorff, P. Thermodynamic theory of structure, stability and fluctuations. *Chemical Engineering News,* April 16, 1979.

Rabkin, R. *Inner and Outer Space.* New York: Norton, 1970.

Rogers, C. *Carl Rogers on Encounter Groups.* New York: Harper & Row, 1970.

Rogers, C. *Freedom to Learn.* Columbus, OH: Charles E. Merrill, 1969.

Rogers, C. *A Way of Being.* Boston: Houghton Mifflin, 1980.

Ruesch, J. & Bateson, G. *Communication: The Social Matrix of Psychology.* New York: Norton, 1951.

Schad-Somers, S. *Sadomasochism.* New York: Human Sciences Press, 1982.

Scheidlinger, S. *Focus on Group Psychotherapy.* New York: International Universities Press, 1982.

Scheidlinger, S. (Ed.) *Psychoanalytic Group Dynamics.* New York: International Universities Press, 1980.

Siporin, M. *Introduction to Social Work Practice.* New York: Macmillan, 1975.

Slater, P. *Microcosm.* New York: John Wiley & Sons, 1966.

Slater, P. *The Pursuit of Loneliness.* Boston: Beacon Press, 1976.

Spotnitz, H. *The Couch and the Circle.* New York: Alfred A. Knopf, 1961.

Sullivan, H. *Conceptions of Modern Psychiatry.* New York: Norton, 1940.

Sullivan, H. *The Interpersonal Theory of Psychiatry.* New York: Norton, 1953.

Tillich, P. *The Courage to Be.* New Haven and London: Yale University Press, 1952.

Totman, R. *Social Causes of Illness.* New York: Pantheon, 1979.

Von Bertalanffy, L. *General Systems Theory.* New York: Brazillier, 1968.

Watzlawick, P. *Change.* New York: Norton, 1974.

Watzlawick, P. *The Language of Change.* New York: Basic Books, 1978.

Watzlawick, P., Beavin, J., & Jackson, D. *Pragmatics of Human Communication.* New York: Norton, 1967.

Whitaker, C. *From Psyche to System.* J. R. Neill & D. Kniskern (Eds.). New York: Guilford Press, 1982.

Whitaker, C. & Malone, T. *The Roots of Psychotherapy.* New York: Brunner/Mazel, 1981.

Whitaker, D. & Lieberman, M. *Psychotherapy Through the Group Process.* New York: Atherton, 1964.

Wilbur, K. Reflections on the new age paradigm. In K. Wilbur (Ed.). *The Holographic Paradigm and Other Paradoxes.* Boulder, CO: Shambhala Publications, 1982.

Wolf, A. & Schwartz, E. K. *Psychoanalysis in Groups.* New York: Grune & Stratton, 1962.

Wolf, A. Psychoanalysis in groups. In S. deSchill (Ed.) *Challenge for Group Psychotherapy.* New York: International Universities Press, 1974.

Wolf, A. The Psychoanalysis of groups. In M. Rosenbaum and M. Berger (Eds.). *Group Psychotherapy and Group Function.* New York: Basic Books, 1963.

Yablonsky, L. *Psychodrama.* New York: Basic Books, 1976.

Yalom, I. *Existential Psychotherapy.* New York: Basic Books, 1980.

Yalom, I. *The Theory and Practice of Group Psychotherapy.* (2nd edition). New York: Basic Books, 1975.

Zinker, J. *The Creative Process in Gestalt Therapy.* New York: Brunner/Mazel, 1977.

Index